D0497511

Experiencing THEATRE

PORTER WOODS
Colorado State University

PRENTICE-HALL, INC., Englewood Cliffs, New Jersey 07632

Library of Congress Cataloging in Publication Data

Woods, Porter.
    Experiencing theatre.

    Bibliography: p.
    Includes index.
    1. Theater. 2. Drama—Collections. I. Title.
PN2037.W72 1984   792   83-3244
ISBN 0-13-294488-X

Printed in the United States of America
10 9 8 7 6 5 4 3 2 1

Editorial/production supervision and interior design by Paul Spencer
Cover design by George Cornell
Manufacturing buyer: Ron Chapman

ISBN   0-13-294488-X

Prentice-Hall International, Inc., *London*
Prentice-Hall of Australia Pty. Limited, *Sydney*
Editora Prentice-Hall do Brasil, Ltda., *Rio de Janeiro*
Prentice-Hall Canada Inc., *Toronto*
Prentice-Hall of India Private Limited, *New Delhi*
Prentice-Hall of Japan, Inc., *Tokyo*
Prentice-Hall of Southeast Asia Pte. Ltd., *Singapore*
Whitehall Books Limited, *Wellington, New Zealand*

To Gail

Contents

Part Three
OTHER CONCERNS

Preface

This text uses a "hands on" approach: in addition to talking about theatre history and describing the arts involved in theatre, it gives students the opportunity to "do" theatre. The value is clear. The question is how to fit such experiences into the classroom.

Let's begin by agreeing that the objective of such a course should be appreciation. The students will typically be non-majors and beginners. We can't assume that they will know anything about theatre, but they will have a great deal of undigested background taken from movies and television. A text such as this should allow a variety of styles of teaching and learning, but it should also lead to something. In this case, we will build to three experiences with scripts for which students will put together production plans. Thus, each chapter of this text but one provides materials for a production. In addition, there are bibliographies, discussions, and exercises along the way which should suggest attractive detours and long-ways-around. The final chapter, on criticism, helps in reviewing plays which are seen while taking the course, an invaluable adjunct to any introductory course in theatre. Finally, there is a list of plays to be read for study and pleasure now and in the future and a glossary of theatre terms.

The inclusion of practical exercises in acting, playwriting, and designing should be feasible even for large classes. A number of methods can be used: small, laboratory sections can be held in addition to large-scale lectures; assignments done can be handed in to the instructor for comment; and students can be randomly selected to read their work aloud in class or to do acting exercises for the entire group. Even without these opportunities to have one's work evaluated, the description of "hands on" exercises is itself a valid part of instruction in these arts.

I want to express my thanks to a number of people who have helped me shape this book. Frank McMullan, who was a friend and teacher at Yale, taught me a directorial method that I have used ever since. Kristina Hanssen, Gary Cotter, Robert Braddy, and Morris Burns are colleagues at Colorado State University. Kristina has told me what I know about costuming; Gary has spent hours listening to my scattered thoughts; and Bob has shared his ideas about teaching design, which he has done here with distinction for many years. Morris Burns has helped me by trying many of the exercises with his own students. Shuji Terayama is as accommodating and generous as he is talented. Tobin Jones, of the Language faculty, called his long hours of checking my translation of *No Trifling with Love* a "professional courtesy," but it was much more than that. Peter Arnott and I did the first performance of his translation of *Philoctetes* years ago in Iowa, with Peter in the title role. It's been a pleasure to work with him again. Shela Jennings is my wise editor and typist. She even wrote a haiku for the chapter on playwriting—wrote it, edited it, and then typed it. My thanks also go to the following, who reviewed the manuscript; David L. Hay; Charlotte Headrick, Oregon State University; E. J. Karioth, Florida State University; and Stefan Rudnicki, C. W. Post College. Finally, I want to thank all of those students who suffered through my experiments with the introductory course, gave me advice, and still professed to enjoy the course. And my theatre wife, who knows best how many weekends and evenings it takes to put on shows.

Porter Woods

Part One

MATERIALS FOR A PRODUCTION

P. L. Ghezzi, *Harlequin, Punch, Pantaloon*.
(Rome, Raccolta Teatrale Burcado.)

1

A Brief History
of Theatre

When one speaks of the development of theatre in the West, the usual theory is that it began in Greece with the rituals of the Dorians, ceremonies dedicated first to Papa Silenus and later to his son, Dionysus. We surmise that such an evolution from ritual to theatre is natural to humans and appears in most cultures when they reach a certain degree of sophistication. As a matter of fact, it is probable that theatre in the West and elsewhere had multiple origins, which were both psychological and social in nature.

We know, for example, that children learn through role play and imitation. In all cultures they demonstrate this tendency to "practice" adult behavior, and adults continue to rehearse new attitudes or prepare for special tasks through autosuggestion, or "adult" role play. We dress for special occasions, ritualize hunting behavior, make special faces (masks or makeup) for important social events, and formalize and elaborate upon important events such as the propitiation of the gods. Ritual and ceremony are the outward, social manifestations of personal and individual experimentation with new attitudes and roles in the society.

On the basis of these tendencies, we might develop the following scenario for the origin of drama among the Dorians. Let's imagine that they are basically herdsmen, that their social organization consists of clans and tribes, and that perhaps twice a year they meet to celebrate spring (as they move to higher pastures) and fall (when they are moving to the lower valleys). At these celebrations they repeat the stories connected with their early god, Papa Silenus, who is a god of fertility, and they thank him for getting them through the hard time of winter or ask his help for the impending difficult times. Perhaps early on they develop a tradition of a storyteller, whose task it is to tell the story of their god at each of these gatherings. There would be a tendency to repeat what had been said before, particularly if it had seemed effective. Embellishments would be added to further propitiate the god. This storyteller or priest would eventually have acolytes, youngsters who would learn the story from him and would assist in the ceremonies. Imagine that this is the practice from earliest times in Greece for these people who have arrived during the second millennium before Christ.

Papa Silenus was replaced by his son, Dionysus, sometime during the next thousand years, probably because of the increasing complexity of the Dorians' lives, and because during this same period they were repeatedly involved in conflict with the warlike people who lived in fortified cities along the coast and on the surrounding islands, the Mycenaeans. We might speculate that the ceremonies for Papa Silenus and Dionysus grew increasingly complex as rituals and that a sort of third-person, narrative tradition grew up which involved the acolytes in the ceremony. There is no way to date this development, but there is a logic to its occurrence if one accepts the truth of the tendencies noted. The young men might dress in goatskins, pretending to be creatures of the god, and help in the ceremony by singing portions of the story. At some point the magic step is taken: As in children's games and hunting rituals, there is a transition from the "he" to the "I." Imagine the boys asking the priest not what the god did at a given moment but "What did you do then?" This is a crucial moment in the development of theatre, but it is also a perfectly normal one, something we do quite easily in less formal moments of interactions such as children's games, storytelling, and our own daydreams.

The conflict between the Dorians and Mycenaeans resulted in the development of a third society, which ultimately was stronger and more vigorous than either of its parents. Out of this grew a number of smaller societies, one of which was the city-state of Athens. In this society, during the middle of the first millennium B.C., we see the rapid growth of drama. The theatre that developed in Athens had several highly individualistic features, reflecting the history of the people. The population was still divided into tribal groups, which perpetuated the earlier Dorian culture. The folklore accepted both the legends of Dionysus and the stories of the Mycenaean culture (for example Troy and Theseus). There are also examples of the continuation of the tribal ceremonies worshipping the god Dionysus during this early period of Dorian culture. By the fifth century B.C. in Athens, a new form of drama emerged and showed remarkable growth. It accepted Dionysus as the patron god, and was performed in places associated with worship of the god. Also, it was celebrated at one of the times of the year that tradition had established for such rites, and may have used singers and musicians who were trained for the earlier rituals.

The links are hard to prove, but several popular theories have grown up to explain the intermediate steps. One of these theories notes the evidence of choral contests held, for example, on the Acropolis before the fifth century B.C. Such contests celebrated the life and death and rebirth of Dionysus and probably involved a chorus and a leader, the latter of which might have played the first-person role of the god. Another theory notes that there were probably related kinds of ceremonies celebrated at the graves of heroes. Still another speaks of the possible contributions of an actor/director named Thespis, who is generally credited with the development of the first actor role as well as originating the chorus' leader, the linen mask, and traveling shows. However, he appears on the scene quite late (c. 535 B.C.). One can also speculate on a "great man" theory, which notes that it was indeed fortunate that Aeschylus appeared when he did to create singlehandedly a new form from what existed, that Sophocles came along at just the right moment to compete with Aeschylus and further develop the form, and that Euripides was there to be its final contributor just before the chaos of the Peloponnesian War. And there are more theories. The fact is that **Tragedy** started at this time and, while one theory can explain its name as meaning "goat song" and thus connect it with Dionysus, it is equally provable that there was very little reference to the god in the plays performed for the choral contests.

However, there was ample evidence of Dionysus' presence in the plays done in the midst of winter in the marketplace of Athens. These plays, which we nowadays identify as **Comedy,** were done when there were few strangers in the city, and seemed to grow out of another tradition. One theory has it that comedy developed from bachelor parties and parades, as evidenced not only by their broad humor but also by the fact that most of the extant plays end with a mock wedding. There was also a use of contemporary satire in these plays, quite unlike the apparent prohibition in tragedies of the day against allusions to contemporary events. Aristophanes could satirize Socrates and the major tragic playwrights and, sometimes in the same play, shift his tone and verse form and write a panegyric to Athens. By modern standards these comic plays were almost as broad and vulgar as the tragic dramas were serious and controlled.

The winter audience at the comic festival was more homogeneous, but even the Dionysian festival had an audience unlike one of today. All citizens were admitted free. But one must remember that Athens was not a city of free men. The percentage of slaves was perhaps as high as 50 percent and, of the rest, those not born in the city were considered alien (cf. *Medea*). The audience for plays, therefore, was a very homogeneous one, not only in terms of birthright but also in terms of education and material possessions. Yet to a modern American there is a feature of Athenian homogeneity that is often missing in our own culture. The key to this could be found in such understandings as their feelings about the god Dionysus. As a symbol, he possesses traits that we might feel are contradictory. He is both libertine and conservative, god of fertility and god of creativity, a figure of fun and a principle of the universe. The Athenians could accept him as embodying all these traits, and Euripides could write of the dangers of maligning or underestimating him (*The Bacchae*). Such plays tell us much about the audience. They could enjoy both the bawdy satire of the comic festival and the serious flavor of the tragedies.

One hundred years later, Aristotle would write about these plays and shape a theory about their structure and qualities. Also, he could guess at the power they must have had in a period when the playwright, and not the actor, was dominant in the theatre. Certainly, the era in which Aristotle lived was marked not only by a change in theatrical traditions but also by the development of a new audience. During the Hellenistic Age, the Greeks shaped a new society. Among the characteristics of this amazing new society, reaching as it did from the Aegean to the Indus, were its dedication to order and trade and its development of an entrepreneurial class. These people brought their culture to many of the same countries that had helped to shape Athenian society in its heyday. Now the Greek traders built health spas and theatre complexes in Asia Minor and elsewhere, and not only became cosmopolitan but went one step farther to shape a new society. Theatre in such periods of expansiveness is marked by these characteristics: (1) it reflects the concerns and interests of its audience; (2) it is generally about the lives of the

Greek, Roman & Early Christian Rome

	DRAMA	ARCHITECTURE	GENERAL	HISTORY
500 B.C.	525-456 Aeschylus 496-406 Sophocles 480-406 Euripides c. 448-380 Aristophanes 431 Euripides' *Medea* 429 Sophocles' *Oedipus Rex* 405 Euripides' *The Bacchae*	447-432 Parthenon built	776 First Olympic Games held 469-399 Socrates 427-347 Plato	480 Persians under Xerxes defeat Spartans. Athens sacked 478 Delian League established 451-429 Pericles rules Athens 431-404 Peloponnesian Wars 404 Athens falls to Sparta
400 B.C.	c. 342-292 Menander	c. 350 Theatre of Epidaurus built c. 330 Development of the Theatre of Dionysus 4th-1st centuries B.C. Hellenistic centers of culture built	384-322 Aristotle 341-270 Epicurus	357-336 Philip II of Macedon gains control of Greece 336-323 Alexander's conquests and death
300 B.C.				
200 B.C.	c. 254-184 Plautus c. 190-159 Terence			264-241 1st Punic War 218-201 2nd Punic War 149-146 3rd Punic War 146 Roman conquest of Greece
100 B.C.	c. 27-23 Vitruvius' *De architectura* c. 4 B.C.-65 A.D. Seneca	55 B.C. First permanent theatre built in Rome 30-12 Roman theatre built in Ostia	100-44 Julius Caesar 106-43 Cicero c. 100 Laocoön Group done at Rhodes by Agesander, Athenodorus, and Polydorus 70-19 Vergil 59 B.C.-17 A.D. Livy 43 B.C.-17 A.D. Ovid	60 First Triumvirate 44 Assassination of Caesar 27 B.C.-14 A.D. Reign of Caesar Augustus
A.D. 100		50 A.D. Theatre at Orange 70-82 Colosseum 114-117 Trajan's Column 120-124 Pantheon	121-180 Marcus Aurelius	70 Capture of Jerusalem by Titus 96-180 The reigns of the Five Good Emperors 98-117 Trajan's reign
A.D. 200				
A.D. 300			354-430 St. Augustine	284-305 Diocletian's reign 306-337 Constantine's reign
A.D. 400			404 Gladiatorial contests banned in Rome	395 Division of the Empire 410 Rome sacked by the Visigoths 455 Rome sacked by the Vandals
A.D. 500		532-537 Santa Sophia built in Constantinople	523 Theodora, a pantomime actress, marries Justinian I. 533 Wild beast spectacles banned	

Figure 1-1.

7

audience and, as is so often the case with a materialistic culture, is about marriage and money; (3) it avoids the serious and thoughtful, in this instance because such subjects do not fit comfortably into a regimen of bathing, exercising, and socializing, any more than tragedy fits the taste of vacationers in Las Vegas or Miami. Even on Broadway in our age, one sees the popularity of musicals and comedies. And satire, which we noted had thrived in fifth century Athens, is, as George S. Kaufman said, "what closed on Thursday."

The kind of drama that developed to meet this new taste is now called New Comedy. Its most famous practitioner was a playwright named Menander. He is known to us by references to his ancient reputation, the number of his imitators, and a few choice fragments of his writing. He was a student of a man trained by Aristotle, he was Athenian, and his plays are filled with allusions to people and places scattered through the Alexandrian Empire. His plays may not easily fit our notions of modern comedy, but they do fit the definition as it is used by Dante and Chekhov. His plays are comedies of manners filled with characters who represent, often stereotypically, the strata and variety of life in those times. In his writing we can see not only the origins of Plautan and Terentian comedy, but also foreshadowings of Molière, Shakespeare, Jonson, Shaw, and Neil Simon.

Roman Comedy

There seems to have been a native drama in Rome before the advent of Plautus and Terence and the New Comedy. The tradition of this drama began when early inhabitants of Rome had enjoyed clowns and rustic productions of various sorts created for local audiences. By the second century B.C. there was a custom in Republican Rome that political figures would sponsor carnivals (*ludus,–i*) for the populations of their districts. These celebrations were probably very much like our fairs, and there was undoubtedly a class of people who were employed to entertain at such events. We know that in the third century actors were considered lowlifes. They were probably like our "carney" people and the performers who ran medicine shows in the time of *commedia dell'arte*. Indeed, Punch and Judy shows, tumblers, and "the sting" are as old as theatre and as new as movies and television. The stages used then were perhaps platforms with steps at either end and a back curtain with openings. Plautus apparently did plays in such carnivals, and Terence complained in the preface to *The Mother-in-Law* at the failure of his play in its last outing, when the audience had abandoned it to watch a tightrope walker. In the following century, politicians began to cater to the public's taste for spectacle by building theatres even more elaborate than those of the Hellenistic era, though in this early period they frequently included a temple in the structure in order to overcome the prohibition against theatres as public structures. It was not long before the political realities of the Empire led to the building of giant coliseums in which pantomimes and spectacles, including sea battles and blood sports, could be performed for the masses.

When one considers the major playwrights of the Roman period, three names come to mind. They are Plautus, certainly the most vigorous and talented of the three; Terence, a member of a circle of wealthy, amoral Romans during his brief life; and Seneca, a brilliant, aristocratic advisor to Nero who would undoubtedly be surprised at his influence over subsequent generations of playwrights. Plautus and Terence were writing in the manner of New Comedy, often imitating plots, characters, and local color verbatim from Greek models, particularly Menander. However, Plautus has enormous strength and flair as a writer and his plays, which were apparently performed to music and included something like arias, have a life of their own which transcends their imitation of the Greek model. His language, as well, is witty and vivid. A common observation by scholars who know his skills is that Plautus not only is a great poet but also can be credited with creating characters who have survived the centuries to be imitated and recalled as often as any playwright's. Also, the Renaissance custom of using both Plautus and Terence in lessons for young scholars meant that they exerted tremendous influence over young minds for centuries, not only in terms of theatrical traditions but also in terms of language itself. Shakespeare is often credited as much as anyone with enriching the English language during one of its major periods of growth, but it should be remembered that in turn he was influenced by Plautus and Terence, despite Ben Jonson's comment that he had "small Latin and less Greek." Terence is most interested in language and nicety of construction. Indeed, one feels that he is writing for a coterie and not for the kind of audience suggested by what we know of popular theatre during his time. And Seneca's interest in theatre seems to have been devoted to "closet" drama—writing plays for mental exercise and for the entertainment of his friends. Seneca was also a Stoic. We find in his reworkings of themes from the greatest of the fifth century Greek tragedies a modicum of understanding of the original meanings of the plays, a profound lack of understanding of dramatic moment and place, and a striking predilection for the superstitions, stringent moral code, and heroic individuals without weakness which characterize Stoicism. A popular story has it that when Seneca was told by a messenger that his emperor, Nero, wished him dead, he halted his entourage of servants and friends, who were about to leave his summer villa, and gave a final feast, during which he slashed his wrists. Tacitus' version tells us the suicide died quietly in the company of his wife and servants.This is touching, but the heroes and heroines of his plays seem to stand on clouds, haranguing one another without real feeling, and die without bleeding. In place of action, we have debating. Ironically, Seneca's plays were extant when the Renaissance arrived, and his reputation as a philosopher, rhetorician, and scholar caused an age anxious to imitate the greatness of the past to ignore what they must have known were the weaknesses of his plays. This helps explain elements of Stoicism in the plays of many Elizabethan and Jacobean playwrights.

Roman drama changed after the construction of the giant pleasure arenas. There was a brief period when pantomime artists were popular, performing before huge crowds as dancers/actors/musicians, playing all the roles in dramas that were usually based on classical legends. But soon blood sports, races, and spectacles took over. The change that occurred then can always happen when theatre aims to please the taste of the worst possible audience. A great playwright might still write worthwhile plays and even educate the public, but the majority of playwrights will turn to situation comedies and biblical spectacles and other celebrations of the easily attainable. Wit becomes the banal. Meaning becomes the obvious. Adventure becomes the cruel. And comedy becomes slapstick.

Medieval Theatre

After Roman drama, there is very little that can be called theatre until the twelfth century. There still existed, of course, the same stratum of society described in early Roman drama: the tumblers, charlatans, clowns, and musicians who constituted a traveling show that reminded people of the pleasure of organized fun and make-believe. But during the period of almost a thousand years that separates this era from the next period of drama, Europe gradually sank into a time of insularity and fear. It was the age of feudalism, that most restrictive and backward of all human institutions, but it was also a period of the most astonishing faith and hope.

When we consider that Western drama apparently began in religious ceremonies, it seems appropriate that European drama was reborn in the church. As early as the tenth century in Europe, we have evidence from the books of prayer and liturgy from religious communities that there was a recurrence of the same metamorphosis that we imagined for the Dorians. The Easter celebration, for example, became more than a reading from the Bible. It could involve pantomime, the selection of parts and the creation of dialogue, and the performance of appropriate music. There was a direct emotional appeal in all this, one which the early Greeks would have understood.

The close of the Era of Faith in northern Europe is marked by the rebirth of mercantilism. Another scenario can be created. In a cathedral city in northern Europe, local trade has revived after years of inactivity. Ships ply between this port and others, and people in the countryside and the city have begun making goods for export. In the cathedral, the bishop must turn more and more to his wealthy parishioners for financial assistance to build a new spire or to provide for the priests. The social lives of the wives of the merchants are to a large degree centered in the church. They dress in their best finery for special services and vie for the opportunity to participate in the Easter pageant. When they began to take the pageant over, elaborate upon the service with secular additions, and make the service an opportunity for displaying their own wealth, the Church finally bans the service and throws it out of doors. In European cities this meant that the ceremonies were relegated to the porch of the cathedral and the marketplace and town square immediately adjacent, a natural meeting and business place for citizens and country people. The most common time for these celebrations was Easter, when the winter doldrums end and country people bring in the goods they have made during long winter nights for barter, when foreigners are on buying trips, and when the city folk are anxious for entertainment. The most frequent teachings in the Church of that time were passages from the New Testament and *exempla*, or moral tales, drawn from a variety of sources. Favorite stories from the Old Testament, the life of Christ, and *exempla* formed the sources for the plays, which comprised the Passion plays and mystery plays of this period. The town square would be bordered with platforms, bleachers for singers, and settings. The audience was a holiday crowd that would gather in the square. For as many as five days they would move about watching scenes performed in the Garden of Eden, Hell's Mouth, and the Palace of Pontius Pilate, and on the Sea of Galilee.

The texts grew longer and more elaborate, the costuming more expensive and eye-catching, and engineers were hired to create special effects. In such cities as Bourges, Lucerne, and Frankfurt during the fourteenth and fifteenth centuries, the Passion and mystery plays were the most notable theatrical events of the year and were a mixture of spectacle, trade fair, and religious observance. It is little wonder that in 1548 the French Parliament enacted a law against them. They had become increasingly secular and expensive, and one wonders if it hadn't been increasingly difficult for both church and state to collect taxes from citizens who insisted that they had already given.

In England these celebrations took a different form, and the primary reason for this was the planning of English cities in medieval times. Most were crowded neighborhoods with communal fields (commons) and trading areas on their outskirts. Many of the most famous cathedrals were located in the countryside. Thus when theatre evolved in England it took at least two forms. There were the medieval equivalents of fairgrounds in the towns of southern England, while townspeople of many other cities toured the plays through the streets on wagons, stopping at convenient intersections to play for people in the windows or standing in the streets. In England, as in other parts of Europe, there was an identification of certain guilds with appropriate stories from the Bible. We understand that water carriers often produced

Late Medieval & Renaissance

	DRAMA	ARCHITECTURE	GENERAL	HISTORY
Before	10th century. Ethelwold, Bishop of Winchester, "Quem quaeritis" trope 10th century. Hroswitha's translations of Terence	1163–c. 1245 Cathedral of Notre Dame built, Paris 1194–1260 Chartres Cathedral rebuilt 10th–13th centuries Mt. St. Michel	1182–1226 St. Francis of Assisi	1066 Battle of Hastings 1095–1291 Crusades 1137–1180 Louis VII of France's reign 1170 Death of Thomas à Becket
1200		1220–1288 Amiens Cathedral 1227–c. 1493 Toledo Cathedral 1248 Cologne Cathedral c. 1200–c. 1300 Rheims Cathedral c. 1261–1346 York Cathedral	1214–1292 Roger Bacon 1225–1274 Thomas Aquinas 1252 Inquisition begins using torture 1265–1321 Dante c. 1267–1337 Giotto	1215 Magna Charta
1250				
1300			1304–1374 Petrarch 1313–1375 Boccaccio	1309–1378 Popes at Avignon
1350		c. 1343–c. 1438 Doge's Palace, Venice		1348–1400 The Black Death ravages North Africa and Europe
1400		1378–1497 Canterbury Cathedral		1415 Henry V defeats French at Agincourt 1431 Joan of Arc burned at the stake 1453 Fall of Constantinople
14-50	c. 1460 Ste. Apolline miniature 1475–1554 Sebastiano Serlio c. 1486 Staging of classical play by Roman Academy	1420–1436 Brunelleschi's dome	1444–1510 Botticelli c. 1450 Printing developed 1452–1519 Leonardo da Vinci 1475–1564 Michelangelo 1483–1520 Raphael c. 1490–1576 Titian	1469–1492 Giuliano I and Lorenzo de' Medici rule 1474–1516 Ferdinand and Isabella in Spain 1498 Savonarola burned at stake
1500		1473–1480 Sistine Chapel built	1500–1571 Benvenuto Cellini 1518–1594 Tintoretto 1525–1594 Palestrina 1528–1588 Veronese 1532 Machiavelli's *The Prince* 1547–1616 Cervantes	1513–1521 Pope Leo X, patron of the arts 1517 Protestant Reformation begins 1527 Rome sacked by Charles de Bourbon 1534 England excommunicated 1545 Council of Trent
1550	1547 Valenciennes miniature 1558–1594 Thomas Kyd 1562–1635 Lope de Vega 1564–1593 Christopher Marlowe 1564–1616 Wm. Shakespeare 1572–1637 Ben Jonson	1506–1626 Building of Saint Peter's, Rome 1508–1580 Palladio 1552–1616 Scamozzi 1563–1584 The Escorial built 1570 Palladio published *Four Books of Architecture* 1573–1652 Inigo Jones 1576 Burbage built The Theatre, London 1584 Teatro Olimpico completed	1567–1643 Monteverdi 1596–1650 Descartes	1588 Spanish Armada sunk 1589–1610 Reign of Henry IV, France
1600	1600–1681 Calderón de la Barca 1606–1684 Corneille 1622–1673 Molière 1634–1691 George Etherege 1639–1699 Racine	1630's Royal Theatre at Buen Retiro 1632–1723 Christopher Wren	1606–1669 Rembrandt 1633 Galileo called before Inquisition 1635 French Academy established	1610–1643 Louis XIII, France 1618–1648 Thirty Years' War 1642–1648 English Civil War 1649 Execution of Charles I
1650	1640–1716 Wm. Wycherley 1670–1729 Wm. Congreve 1678–1707 Geo. Farquhar 1689 *Dido and Aeneas* by Purcell	1624–after 1679 Versailles Palace built 1675–1710 St. Paul's built	1667 Milton's *Paradise Lost* 1685–1750 Johann Sebastian Bach 1685–1759 Geo. Frederick Handel	1660 English Restoration 1660–1685 Reign of Charles II, England 1685–1688 Reign of James II, England
1700	1693–1739 Geo. Lillo 1707–1793 Carlo Goldoni 1730–1774 Oliver Goldsmith	1680–1691 Church of the Invalides, Paris 1705–1724 Blenheim Palace, Oxfordshire	1697–1764 Hogarth	1689–1702 William and Mary, England

Figure 1-2.

12

the story of Noah, for example. In general, just as in the cities of Europe, the pageants were both religious and commercial and grew longer and longer and more elaborate as time passed. Another tradition was concurrent with this one in England, however: the practice of the gentry to have entertainers as members of their households. These musicians and actors frequently were exchanged by their wealthy masters. There are similarities between the plays of the Easter pageants and the after-dinner skits or *interludes* done in castles and on estates. This custom also served as a means of establishing the tradition practiced in many countries, particularly Italy, of the wealthy acting as protectors and patrons for the arts. The third institution for the promulgation of drama at the close of the Middle Ages was educational: schools, colleges, and courts of law where the plays of Plautus and Terence and their local imitators were performed by students for pleasure and as a means of learning Latin.

The Renaissance

All of this was preparatory to the next significant social change in England and Europe. With the subversion of the Church's absolute power, not only by social-climbing merchants but also by the invention of the printing press, and the increasing power of kings, a new social order was coming into being. We have a tendency, reinforced by textbooks, to think of such matters as the rise of the Renaissance as events that suddenly occur one day, seemingly by fiat, and are then in force until the next chapter. Actually, the Renaissance took some three centuries to cross from Italy to Scandinavia. England was very slow to come out of the Middle Ages, and then only at the strenuous promptings of Queen Elizabeth, who was frequently angered by the contempt shown by European emissaries to her court. The Renaissance can be characterized as a period of growing materialism, individualism, and experimentation. One of the universal qualities of the age was its love for the ancient worlds of Athens and Rome and its fascination with the arts. In Italy, from the end of the fifteenth century through the end of the sixteenth, nobles and popes began reconstructing the genius of their ancestors and entertaining one another with what they thought, for example, were accurate recreations of Greek tragedy. Artists, carpenters, musicians, and performers were hired to present these dramas. Other artists and craftsmen were engaged in preparing spectacles, parades, and fetes that celebrated the weddings, crownings, and triumphs of the mighty. There was a great deal of money and time spent on these pursuits, and we have these nobles and their hired help to thank for opera, the baroque stage, and the notion that there are two theatres, one for the wealthy and one for the ordinary people. It took time for these achievements to reach France, and more time for them to arrive in England, and the path was frequently circuitous. One wonders how that preeminent loather of drama, Oliver Cromwell, would react to the fact that without his closing of the theatres and expulsion of the gentry, England might not have had baroque staging as early as 1660, when the lords and ladies returned from exile in Paris with their new taste for Italianate theatre.

There also existed in Italy, during the sixteenth century, companies of itinerant performers and clowns who were part of the tradition mentioned earlier, and while the wealthy and powerful were experimenting with revivals of classicism, these actors developed a form of popular theatre which came to be called *commedia dell'arte*. It was improvisational and farcical, and used stock characters, many of whom became widely known to Renaissance audiences from other sources as well. Shakespeare's clowns and Jonson's *Volpone* are both derived from the double tradition of Roman comedy and the contemporary *commedia*. Molière was a grateful student of their techniques when Italian comedians worked side by side with his company at the French court. The modern history of this tradition starts in the mid-1500s in Italy and led to the writing and innovations of Goldoni, who began as a *commedia* artist and finally brought Italian comedy into theatres, removing the masks and providing scripts, without destroying the vigor which was one feature of the older form.

English, Spanish, and French Theatre

In the interim, there are three fascinating theatrical periods to note: (1) the development of native drama in England from the end of the Middle Ages to the time of the Commonwealth; (2) Spanish drama from the late sixteenth to the early seventeenth centuries: and (3) French theatre from the time of the abolition of Passion plays to the time of Molière. The first, the English, grows directly from the three traditions noted, carnivals and pageants, the estate players, and the schools. In the film of *Tom Jones*, the young hero was shown stopping on his way to London at a wayside inn. When the gate was closed behind him and he and the other guests were safely behind the stockade wall, when his horse was stabled and his ticking sack chosen in the bachelors' quarters, he was in a safe, warm world which must have had great appeal for travelers. We know that it was not uncommon for traveling players to perform on platforms set up in front of these inns, with guests leaning from their windows, and servants standing to the sides or in the openings to the stables and other outbuildings. Blood sports could be held in such places as well. It is interesting to note that the positioning of the audience and the players at these inns is much like that of townspeople and wagons in the English medieval pageants. One conclusion is that invention is often shaped by what has been done before. For instance, when the first cars were made, many were equipped with tubes on the driver's side to hold whips. So it is with theatre, which is one of the most human of all institutions. There is speculation that when Mr. Burbage decided to build an odd structure on the wrong side of the river in London as a theatre and gaming house, he was probably influenced by performing spaces found in inns and colleges, as well as by his desire for privacy and for a type of building that could utilize ordinary timbers for sills and joists. There was a native "rightness" to the structure he built, just as there was a certain predictability to the kinds of plays performed by his players and written by his hacks. By and large, his playwrights were influenced by Plautus and Terence, interludes and pageant skits, a few native imitations of the Romans, and some versions of Italian romances. They also had a refreshing lack of knowledge of how playwrights in other countries were writing plays. A Ben Jonson might flash his erudition in the coffee-houses and at Blackfriars, a theatre for the upper class, but he joined his colleagues in the popular theatres in the pursuit of an art form that was exuberantly English, in many ways old-fashioned, and highly entertaining for the mobs who might come to a drama one day and be back for bear-baiting the next.

Spain's theatrical history can be traced back to the festival of Corpus Christi, when floats would be decorated and players hired to act out brief allegorical plays celebrating the Eucharist. The *carros* (carts) would be drawn up at several stops, creating settings, the plays would be performed, and then the procession would continue. We know of the tradition and the existence of the strolling players from such sources as Cervantes. The Golden Age of Spanish drama was a sudden blossoming of interest in drama in the sixteenth century. It occurred in Madrid and during the overlapping careers of two great playwrights, Lope de Vega and Calderón de la Barca. During the lifetimes of these two, the physical stage was developed from a simple platform in a courtyard with benches and a screened bleacher area for the women at the rear to a baroque stage. It is thought that on this earlier stage, as used by Lope de Vega prior to 1631, use was made of medieval set pieces and mansion structures of the sort that had been used for centuries, but Calderón and his patron, Philip IV, brought in an Italian architect and scene designer and built a permanent baroque theatre in a palace (Buen Retiro).

As for the French, after the abolition of pageants, several fraternal groups set about to find ways to circumvent the proscription. What they found in Paris were indoor tennis courts, loft-like buildings which could be rented or bought and adapted into theatres. The French seem to have built a platform at one end of a room which was typically some 120 feet by 40 feet, and made a horseshoe of boxes in the middle third with the shoe opening toward the stage, with benches within the shoe for young blades, and with a steep bleacher at the rear for the coachmen and bodyguards who were part of a wealthy person's entourage. The bleachers, by the way, came to be labeled *"le paradis"* and the denizens of that space were known as *"les enfants,"* or "the children of paradise." The earliest productions in these tennis courts were probably not unlike reviews or variety shows, but the popularity of the theatres and the growing self-image of the French during this era soon led to a more formal and impressive form of theatre. The sixteenth century was a period of political chaos, but by the next century the French were becoming a major political force on the Continent, and the arts reflected this new sense of importance. French scholars and artists turned to classical times for examples of what to do with public architecture, painting, and drama. Playwrights began to write in what they believed to be a classical mode, based on the writing of Aristotle and the interpretations of him by more recent scholars. What they agreed upon in principle was that theatre should observe the "unities" of time, place, and plot. What this amounted to was a kind of dramaturgy which sought balance and clarity through a single plot, and an action which took place in a day, occurring in a single location. However, what really resulted was constant debate between playwrights and critics and absurd standards of excellence, which frequently ignored the success of a play with its audience and material. In spite of the restrictions, the French were blessed with a series of remarkable playwrights in the persons of Corneille, Racine, and Molière, who all wrote successful plays seemingly in spite of the critical restrictions. The French theatre also began to change physically. First tennis courts were used; then buildings were erected strictly for theatrical productions. By the time of Molière's return to Paris, Italian designers and architects were employed to build baroque stages at the court. It would be these theatres and others that the English exiles would visit during their stay in France.

Let us interrupt this brief historical review to remark on several matters: (1) the evolution of audiences; (2) stage conventions; and (3) the modern communication revolution. It should be noted that theatre intimately reflects the taste and the social structure of a particular time and place. If theatre is being produced primarily for the very rich, one can be certain that the same kind of privileges are evident in the streets and the courts of law. Certainly there have been periods when there were two or more kinds of theatre being performed. The English Renaissance, for example, allowed both public houses and a Blackfriars. But generally there is one kind of theatre being done in a city, be it Rome, Athens, or Paris. The early Spanish, English Tudor and Jacobean, and late medieval European theatre were all "popular," and they anticipated the emerging rights of the masses. In many quarters this was seen as a threat. During Elizabeth's reign, for example, the town fathers fought a running battle with actors and producers over their right to do plays, which the former interpreted as the devil's handiwork. In some ways they were probably correct, particularly in terms of the danger of letting an apprentice feel that he had a right to entertainment and to know about the issues and attitudes of his time. The French Revolution grew from familiarity with the folly of French rulers as seen in popular entertainments and publications as much as from any concerted effort to protest for rights. In the ages that follow we will find the emergence of a heterogeneous audience, and also see the repeated suppression of theatre by governments, particularly in France and England, which feared not only the subject matter but also the danger of letting disparate parts of a society sit together to be entertained and instructed by a Beaumarchais (1732–1799) or a Hugo (1802–1885), for example.

Another matter frequently commented on in interpretations of the evolution of theatre is the "rise of realism." On one level, realism is simply a theatrical convention, a way of imitating life on stage. Because all theatre is make-believe, it is "not real" but only one way of lying about life. As we have noted before in the case of the Greek New Comedy, middle-class audiences prefer plays about themselves and have little liking for criticisms of their way of life (satire) or humor at the expense of the people they know and are (caricatures). Thus while we often hear critics speaking of theatre history as an evolution toward realism, it is possible to argue that this convention has been with us for a long time and is really a relative term. For example, we could argue that Molière was as much a realist for his audience as Neil Simon is for ours. Nowadays we speak of the Greek tragedies of the fifth century as classical, but one wonders if their strongest feature for the Greek audiences might not have been their "realistic" truth in terms of human experience, rather than the poetry, music, masks, use of dance, and ritual aspects, which make them seem formal and strange to a modern audience. One person's formalism, in other words, may be another's realism.

Finally, theatre not only reflects social change but may be an integral part of that change. For example, the invention of the printing press prepared the way for what in modern times has become increasingly rapid information exchange and the development of theatre and other entertainment media. Yet through all of this the underlying concerns of theatre have remained the same: the distillation of human experience or escapism and a reflection of the audience's interest in its own way of life.

To continue our overview of theatre history, when the English exiles returned to England, they brought with them an appetite for the comedy of manners and baroque staging. For the next four decades these plays were written and attended by the gentry, and the Restoration Comedy became a witty, amoral extension of a class' interest in itself. When it was eclipsed in England, it was replaced by didactic theatre and romantic comedy, and played to a much more diverse audience. In France there was a similar broadening of taste and audience. Voltaire (1694–1778) and others brought romantic adventures to the stage that more than violated notions of the unities of plot, time, and place. The staging kept pace with his broadening trend. Sets were made larger and more elaborate to allow for the stage effects required by spectacle. The producer/director was introduced to manage the increasingly complex business of theatre from rehearsal to performance. Such men as David Garrick (1717–1779) became prominent theatre figures. In the plays produced in England by John Rich and others there is an increasingly middle-class flavor. At this same time, during the eighteenth century, certain English producers began the process of resurrecting a very English playwright, long eclipsed: Shakespeare. It is interesting to note that during this same century, drama came to America, though it was largely imported and English. There were native writers even in the early 1700s, but America was uncertain of its own taste and talent until the mid-1800s.

In both England and France in the eighteenth and nineteenth centuries, the authorities tried repeatedly to control theatres with restrictive laws. In some instances they were persuaded by powerful producers who wished to limit competition, but there were also instances of governments being frightened by the subject matter of plays and the prospects of public assembly.

By the close of the nineteenth century, change was one of the most noticeable features of contemporary theatre. At mid-century, Madame Vestris was staging plays in London that were remarkable for their drawing-room realism, the collective ability of the actors in the company, and their rehearsal discipline. Henry Irving (1838–1905) was a famous actor of the period who was noted for what we would nowadays call psychological realism. In France there had been early eighteenth century experiments with fourth-wall realism by Diderot (1713–1784), which then led to the development of the "well-made play" by such playwrights as Scribe (1791–1861). The latter plays were filled with careful plotting, stunning reversals, and stories that revolved around marriage and money. These were the kind of dramas that Ibsen saw in the national theatre in Oslo and the young George Bernard Shaw reviewed in London.

One of the places on the Continent influenced by Shakespeare was Germany. During the early 1600s the scattered petty kingdoms of what was to become Germany were favorite touring places for English actors otherwise out of work, and in the eighteenth century there was a great deal of interest in translating and performing Shakespeare in Germany. The German tradition of state-supported theatre began in the same century in Hamburg. Imitations of English middle-class drama and Shakespeare were the most popular fare. There was an affinity established between English and German theatre. Not only Shakespeare but also lesser dramatists such as Lillo were very appealing to German audiences. French delicacy and taste were frequently indulged by German aristocrats intent on becoming patrons of the arts, but audiences preferred English realism and Tudor plays.

By the close of the century, two native playwrights, Schiller and Goethe, were central to the "Sturm und Drang" movement, the German romanticism of the eighteenth century. Throughout his long career, Goethe balanced the romanticism of his youth with his love of classicism. For most

18th Century & After

DRAMA

- 1700
  - 1707-1754 Henry Fielding
  - 1728 *Beggar's Opera*
  - 1729-1781 Lessing
  - 1732-1799 Beaumarchais
- 1750
  - 1749-1832 Goethe
  - 1751-1816 Sheridan
  - 1759-1805 Schiller
  - 1775 *Barber of Seville*
- 1800
  - 1802-1885 Victor Hugo
  - 1822-1890 Don Boucicault
  - 1824-1895 Alexandre Dumas, fils
  - 1828-1906 Ibsen
- 1850
  - 1840-1902 Zola
  - 1854-1900 Oscar Wilde
  - 1856-1950 Shaw
  - 1860-1904 Chekhov
  - 1862-1949 Maeterlinck
  - 1863-1938 Stanislavsky
  - 1871-1909 Synge
  - 1873-1907 Alfred Jarry
  - 1884-1964 Sean O'Casey
  - 1888-1953 O'Neill
  - 1888-1965 T. S. Eliot
- 1900
  - 1905-1980 Sartre
  - 1906- Beckett
  - 1914-1983 Williams
  - 1915- Miller
  - 1928 *Threepenny Opera*, Weill & Brecht
  - 1928- Albee
  - 1933 O'Neill's *Ah, Wilderness*
  - 1935 Eliot's *Murder in the Cathedral*
  - 1935 Odets' *Waiting for Lefty*
  - 1941 Hellman's *Watch on the Rhine*
  - 1947 Miller's *All My Sons*
  - 1948 Williams' *A Streetcar Named Desire*
  - 1949 Miller's *Death of a Salesman*
- 1950
  - 1956 Osborne's *Look Back in Anger*
  - 1962 Albee's *Who's Afraid of Virginia Woolf?*
  - 1968 Ragni and Rado, *Hair*

ARCHITECTURE

- 1715 Early beginnings of rococo
- 1785-1820 The Federal Style in U.S.
- 1792-1865 Capitol built in Washington, D.C.
- 1832-1923 Gustav Eiffel
- 1840-1865 The Houses of Parliament, London
- 1851 Construction of the Crystal Palace, London
- 1856-1924 Louis Sullivan
- 1869-1959 Frank Lloyd Wright
- 1883-1969 Gropius
- 1886-1969 Mies van der Rohe
- 1887-1965 Le Corbusier
- 1890-1891 Wainwright Bldg., St. Louis, first skyscraper
- 1913 Woolworth Bldg., New York
- 1925-1926 Bauhaus, Dessau
- 1930-1931 Empire State Bldg.
- 1933-1937 Golden Gate Bridge
- 1950's Le Corbusier's project in Chandigarh, India
- 1956-1959 Guggenheim Museum, N.Y.
- 1956-1958 Seagram Bldg., N.Y., van der Rohe and Philip Johnson
- 1956-1962 Saarinen's TWA terminal, Kennedy Airport, N.Y.

GENERAL

- 1714-1787 Gluck
- 1717-1779 David Garrick
- 1732-1809 Haydn
- 1746-1828 Goya
- 1756-1791 Mozart
- 1762 Rousseau's *Social Contract*
- 1769 Steam engine invented
- 1770-1827 Beethoven
- 1798-1863 Eugene Delacroix
- 1808-1879 Daumier
- 1809-1882 Darwin
- 1813-1901 Verdi
- 1813-1883 Wagner
- 1839-1906 Cezanne
- 1840-1917 Rodin
- 1841-1919 Renoir
- 1848-1903 Gauguin
- 1853-1890 Van Gogh
- 1859 Darwin's *Origin of Species*
- 1869-1954 Matisse
- 1872-1944 Mondrian
- 1874 First Impressionist Exhibit
- 1879-1955 Einstein
- 1903 Wright brothers' flight
- 1905 Einstein's articles on Theory of Relativity
- 1913 Stravinsky's *Le Sacre du Printemps*
- c. 1916 Einstein's General Theory of Relativity
- 1934 Fermi's work on neutrons and protons
- 1939 Lawrence's cyclotron
- 1942 Fermi splits the atom

HISTORY

- 1702 Queen Anne succeeds William III
- 1715-1774 Louis XV, King of France
- 1740-1786 Reign of Frederick the Great, Prussia
- 1762-1796 Catherine the Great's reign
- 1776 American Declaration of Independence
- 1789 French Revolution begins
- 1792-1804 First French Republic
- 1804 Napoleon crowned Emperor
- 1814 Napoleon abdicates
- 1815 Waterloo
- 1821 Napoleon dies
- 1830-1848 Louis Philippe, French constitutional monarch
- 1837-1901 Reign of Victoria
- 1848 Second French Republic
- 1870 Third French Republic (lasts until 1940)
- 1870-1871 Franco-Prussian War
- 1874-1965 Winston Churchill
- 1879-1953 Stalin
- 1882-1945 Franklin Delano Roosevelt
- 1889-1945 Adolf Hitler
- 1914-1918 World War I
- 1917 Russian Revolution begins
- 1922 Fascist revolution in Italy
- 1933 Nazi take-over in Germany
- 1936-1939 Spanish Civil War
- 1939-1945 World War II
- 1950-1953 Korean War
- 1961-1973 Vietnam War

Recent

Figure 1-3.

of his adult, creative years he was director of the Weimar Theatre under Duke Karl August. What he moved toward in his years at Weimar was a formal, ceremonial theatre, a theatre of rules. It is ironic not only that the enthusiasm of his youth was replaced with careful rules for acting gestures, but that he and Schiller were collectively less popular with the public during their lifetimes than a writer of melodramas and household happenings named Kotzebue, a second-rate playwright who was one of the lords of the audience during this period. However, this reminds us of the realities of popular theatre. He was as forgettable and popular as a dozen playwrights of our own stage. For example, who now knows the name of Boucicault, one of the first playwrights in America, or anywhere, to make a handsome living as a popular writer? Yet Boucicault's *The Octoroon* was one of the first American plays to deal with miscegenation, and its escape scene is perhaps the prototype for the famous sequence in O'Neill's *The Emperor Jones*.

In studying the history of the second half of the nineteenth century, one is struck by the enormous changes that took place in Europe. Victoria ushered in the era, the industrial revolution was its salient feature, and the end of an epoch was clearly visible in the social changes on the continent and in England between 1837 and World War I. Theatre reflected these changes in a strikingly accelerated manner. In France, Zola (1840–1902) and other writers used the novel and drama as a means of exposing the abuses of society. Zola's adaptations of his novels and stories to the stage created a new means of documenting social issues, and was labeled Naturalism. The audience was to be given the facts about an issue in terms of a particular case and allowed to come to its own conclusions.

Before the end of the century, certain writers appeared in theatre whom we still recognize today as major influences. Among these are Ibsen, Strindberg, Chekhov, Gorky, and Turgenev. Frequently, the ideas of these plays transcended their staging. As a matter of fact, one of the most famous theatres during this period, the first Théâtre Libre, was poorly equipped and small. The Theatre of Ideas and Innovation was thus launched. In rapid succession, new conventions were introduced, new acting methods explored, and new stage technologies introduced. It was a particularly exciting time in the arts. Not only was there an amazing increase in the number of theatres, the size of audiences, and the variety of plays and fads being introduced, but during the following fifty years new media were spawned from the traditions of theatre: radio, movies, and television. But the major style of all media has remained what one might expect, namely realism, and the major subject matter has been the celebration of the lifestyle and concerns of the middle-class. America gave the rest of the world the musical comedy. Freud and the Depression gave us a new understanding of psychology and Expressionism as legitimate subjects for drama. Beginning with such innovators as Alfred Jarry (1873–1907, *Ubu Roi*) and the Dadaists (1915–1923) there has been a steady stream of experimentation in theatre, always popular with a few and largely ignored by the masses until certain innovations became commercialized.

Stagecraft has changed in terms of the development of lighting, particularly with the Germans between the two World Wars, and we nowadays have plastics and vacuum shapers, which allow experimentation with materials. However, basic stagecraft remains something that Torelli, a major contributor to baroque staging, would immediately recognize if he were to tour a Broadway house. Theatre is still very much a reflection of society, particularly if one includes the new media that it and science have spawned. Theatre is clearly a popular art form, one belonging to the masses in our age or the well-to-do in less democratic times. The proof of a play is still in its success with audiences, though directors will continue to attempt to resurrect plays that have failed with their original audiences. Some critics will continue to attempt to prove to all of us that a particular play is much better than audiences thought it was. Occasionally they will succeed, as in such special cases as a *Waiting for Godot* or *Murder in the Cathedral*. But when one sees a well-done play that speaks to his or her conscience, experience, and/or funny bone, one should be reminded of how human theatre is, how close it is to our personal experience, and how much pleasure there is in sharing these things with other people in an audience and upon the stage.

DeWitt, *Interior of the Swan Theatre,* 1596. (Utrecht,
Bibliotheek der Centraal Museum.)

2

The Development of the Physical Stage

In a study of theatres and their audience spaces, stages, and stagecraft, there are two extremes to keep in mind. First, imagine a natural amphitheatre with a beaten-earth dance circle at its base (*orkestra*). Then, think of a well-equipped television studio with an audience area, a transmission station with facilities for producing live drama, and viewers sitting in forty million homes in America to see a "live" television special.

If one goes to a theatre on Broadway, on a university campus, or at a repertory company's home in a large city, there are many ways for a person trained in theatre to trace the development of the modern structure back to its most ancient predecessor. It is the purpose of this chapter to describe this development and its probable origins.

First, let us agree that the two parts of a theatre are a space for an audience and a space for performers. The primary consideration for the relationship of these two areas, which is equally important for a natural amphitheatre and the most sophisticated theatre, is the ease with which communication passes between them. The audience needs to see and hear the performers, and the performers need the immediacy of their spectators. Other considerations, such as easy access to seats, adequate lobby spaces, box offices, storage spaces and dressing rooms, workshops, and a myriad of special places for special equipment, as well as the adaptation of the acting space for scenery, can all come later. First, we need a place for audience and actors to communicate.

Historically, the first step probably involved the acting space. It is thought that in the Greek theatre the audience was seated in a natural amphitheatre on nothing more than plank benches until Alexandrian times, when the auditorium and stage house were formalized in stone. An amphitheatre allows good sightlines by wrapping the audience around the acting area and by providing a gradient so that spectators can see over one another. When such simple audience spaces were made of stone, it was possible to put in many more rows, because of the control of the sightlines and because the sound was focused by the auditorium's shape and the natural deflection of sound off stone surfaces.

Early on, the performance area, the beaten circle of earth, was probably bordered by a shed. Some speculate that in the case of the Theatre of Dionysus, the original temple to Dionysus was adjacent to the acting area and might have served as background. We can imagine a shed-like building being in place by the early fifth century B.C. This shed could have been used for storage and dressing rooms. There is also the possibility that the shed might have served as the first setting. Even today there are festivals that use real castles for Renaissance plays, and there is a famous Finnish outdoor play which reenacts the Russo-Finnish War in a region of forests, reconstructed camps, and battlegrounds, moving the audience from scene to scene on a railroad track and special bleachers. Everyone is familiar with the movies' use of actual sites for settings. There is a second type of scenery and setting

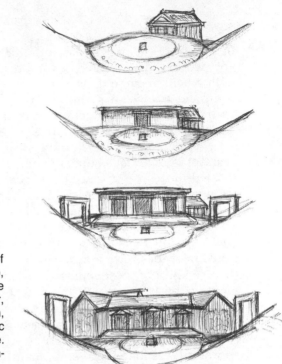

Figure 2-1. *Right:* Development of the Greek and Roman theatre. (Top, Primitive; Upper Middle, Early scene house; Lower Middle, King's door, platform, and entrances; Bottom, Side wings.) *Below:* Top, Hellenistic theatre; bottom, Roman theatre. (Roman theatre is taken from reconstruction of the Orange Theatre).

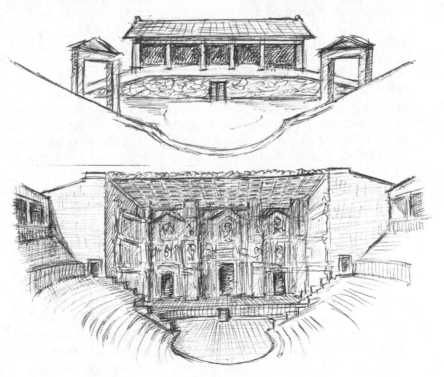

that is both realistic and symbolic. This type includes such places as church altars, legislative chambers, and a Tomb of the Unknown Soldier. The third type of scenery is entirely symbolic. The audience may see a section of a New York street (as in *Street Scene*), but its reality is clearly qualified by the proscenium that frames it. Thus, it might have been with the Greeks. The early shed perhaps had doors which could be used by the actors for their entrances and exits during the play. Later, these doorways might have been enhanced by making the middle one, for example, more like an ancient king's doorway. In a third step, the exposed walls of the shed might have been decorated or had temporary painted panels placed against them to further create the image of a palace and/or the environs of such a place.

There is some debate about the use of painted scenery in the fifth century B.C. Hellenistic theatres appear to have been constructed in such a way that *pinakes* (panels) could have been set against stage walls with architectural framing, and there are several theatre remains which have evidence of rows of movable, three-sided, rectangular prisms, which would have allowed three scene changes in a single performance. An earlier notion was that there was no painted scenery, but this idea was based upon the lack of extant paintings from the period. If one considers the level of sophistication of the architecture, sculpture, and drama of this period, it seems more than likely that there was painted scenery during the time of Aeschylus and Sophocles.

While the development of scenery helps a play's illusion and also solves certain "traffic" problems (entrances and exits), there were probably other changes and adaptations of the shed which were motivated by the need to give *focus* to the action. This is a second principle in the development of the Western stage. For example, as the playwrights created a second and then a third actor, the need for the separation of the chorus from the chief actors became more and more apparent. This division is clear in the structure of the tragedies in that there are scenes for the chorus, scenes for the chorus and one or two major characters, and scenes between main characters. The need for focus would explain what many believe happened next. A low platform was placed in front of the shed (*skene*) between the building and the *orkestra* and was called the *proskenion*. Even in the modern theatre, directors are trained to use stage levels as one of the means of drawing attention to an actor. Remember that this is not a problem in movies and television, because the camera can be moved to achieve focus. Imagine that in the Greek theatre the musicians and dancers remained in the *orkestra*, and the major characters used the upper level, except when the chorus shared this area for special scenes. We further speculate that two wings (the *paraskenia*) grew on either side of this platform. This would have helped to further define the acting area.

As for the auditorium, note the details in the photograph of the theatre at Epidaurus—its round *orkestra*, stairways (*climakes*), the broad, cross aisles two-thirds of the way up the house (the *diazoma*). This shows the formaliza-

Figure 2-2. The theatre at Epidaurus. (Courtesy of the Greek National Tourist Organization, Chicago.)

tion of the earlier house. Also, note the entrance archway, which stands between the auditorium and *skene*.

The developments that follow are associated with the Hellenistic Era, and can be seen in a number of theatre ruins from southern France to northern Africa and east to Turkey. The *orkestra* is frequently truncated by the *proskenion*, and this structure grows higher and higher, suggesting the disappearance of the chorus and separation of audience and actors, as well as the use of scenery.

Another feature of many of these theatres is the architectural unity of the stage house and auditorium. The beginnings of this tradition could be explained by the desire for greater cohesiveness, the repeated use of architectural motifs, and the use of one building material. There is another very practical reason for this development. Many such theatres are built on level sites and the planners were creating artificial amphitheatres. This is certainly a feature of the Roman theatres built in the first century B.C. (Figure 2-1 *below*, bottom). Note the *proskenion*, the *paraskenia* (the wings on either side of the acting area), the highly formalized *orkestra*, the enormous house, the unity of the entire structure in terms of design (particularly the integration of the entrance archways between the stage house and the auditorium),

Figure 2-3. The Theatre of Herodes Atticus, Athens. (Courtesy of the Greek National Tourist Organization, Chicago.)

Figure 2-4. L. Caullery, *Strolling Players Giving a Performance in the Country,* 1598. (Cambrai, Bibliotheque Municipale.)

and the elaborate permanent *scenae frons:* the forehead of the scene. Not shown in this illustration is the slot in the front of the stage from which the curtain was pulled to end a play, and the colored awnings, which were often stretched across an auditorium to shelter the audience and actors from the weather.

What followed this type of theatre was the huge coliseums in which audiences could watch pantomimes, horse races, and spectacles. After these were no longer used, all we have for centuries until the rebirth of drama in the twelfth century A.D. are the traveling players and charlatans who performed with nothing more than a trestle stage and a curtain.

Medieval Theatre

The next seven centuries would see the expansion of the Roman Empire, then the reverse tide of barbarians from the north, the Christianization of Rome, and the onset of what we now call the Middle Ages. Europe would become increasingly fragmented and finally slip into feudalism. Theatre would not be born again until the new materialism began to develop in northern Europe and Italy. In northern Europe the churches and town squares were natural gathering places, so when the early pageants were thrown out-of-doors by church authorities, they were staged in these spaces. Typically they took place in the spring at Eastertide, and were made up of many playlets based on stories from the Bible, each with its own setting. These playlets were arranged around a large town square, with the audience moving from site to site. By necessity, the players acted on platforms above the spectators, who might stand by the hundreds in front of the setting. We also know that it was the custom with these productions to make settings of painted cloth and thin lath. These represented such places as the palace of Pontius Pilate, Hell's Mouth, and Eden (see Figure 2-5). Such sets could be as small as one-quarter scale, reminding us of those children's forts that you stand in while playing. They were called *mansions*, and their construction is very much like the technique still used to build flats. The distortion or lack of perspective which you can imagine in mixing live actors with these small structures is like the paintings of the same period and the reliefs found on the walls of churches. Often the plays lasted a number of days, with lengthy interruptions, as performers would move about the square, readying the next setting and then performing.

The illustration shows a series of mansions in a row. In reality the various settings would be arranged on the sides of the square. There were other ways of performing these cycles. In England, pageant wagons were used, and in the southern part of the country, in Cornwall, plays were per-

Figure 2-5. The Passion Play at Valenciennes, 1547. (Bibliotheque Nationale, Paris. Executed by Cailleau and Jacques de Moelles.)

formed in circular arenas with mounds of earth on the perimeter for spectator seating. Costuming was a production value for all three types of pageants. In England the wagons became movable scenery. For example, the wagon used for the Noah story might be shaped like a boat and the Garden of Eden would be elaborately decorated, perhaps with traps into the lower part of the wagon for entrances and exits.

Renaissance Staging

The next important period in the development of the physical stage and stagecraft takes place during the Renaissance in Italy. Interest in Greek and Roman theatre had begun in the fifteenth century and had led to the establishment of centers of study, or academies. One of these, the Roman Academy, had a production mentioned in the 1486 edition of Vitruvius' *De Architectura* (the famous first century work on classical theatre). The academy's production had been under the supervision of Julius Pomponius Laetus (1425–1498) and had been performed in a courtyard. What the settings looked like for this particular show we don't know, but we can guess that it was done in a series of mansions, not unlike medieval structures, set on a five-foot platform. These were probably organized in one unit and had certain architectural features which linked them together instead of the diffuse, scattered arrangement described above.

The next step is represented by the production of *La Calandria* in 1513 in

Figure 2-6. Part of the setting for Terence's *Andria*, 1493. (From illustrated edition of Terence published in Lyon in 1493.)

Urbino. This production substituted a painted perspective background for the mansions and had three-dimensional structures that extended the scene and served, perhaps, as playing areas for musicians. The next phase seems to continue the exploration of how to make the scenic representation more true-to-life by use of a three-dimensional treatment. In 1545, Serlio published a treatise that dealt with both the ancient theatre and practical problems of staging and auditorium construction. His plan for an auditorium shows a further adaptation of ancient plans. He gives three designs for types of plays (comic scene, tragic scene, and satyric) based on Vitruvius' text, and advocates the continued use of the long, narrow acting area. However, immediately behind the stage there is a raked platform on which he places the scene. It is both painted and constructed in three dimensions, and uses forced perspective. Houses diminish rapidly to give the impression of distance in a short space. Of course, these are not practical buildings—the actors must stand in front of them.

An interesting tangent to the further development of staging is the Teatro Olimpico in Vicenza, completed in 1585. Amazingly, this wooden structure still stands. It is composed of a single scene for an adaptation of *Oedipus*. The acting area is the long, narrow Roman one, and the setting is seen through a *scenae frons* as three-dimensional, forced-perspective alley ways, which were never intended to be used by actors. This sort of theatre is obviously static, and the next development answered the increasing desire of patrons and artists for scenery that was changeable.

At some point during this development, the proscenium arch or frame

Teatro di Vicenza del Palladio

Figure 2-7. Teatro Olimpico, 1589. (From Cosimo Morelli, *Spaccato del nuovo Teatro d'Imola,* 1780.)

had become widely accepted. It may have begun with the use of curtains for masking or simply as a way to unify the impression of the scenery.

To answer the increasing demand for scenic transformation, the angle wings, which had been used to simulate three-dimensional structures, were replaced with *periaktoi.* These were awkward but could be moved. *A vista* scene changes (done while the audience watches) would eventually require something more of scenic artists, but their knowledge of perspective painting, the cosmetic qualities of candlelight, and the period's skill in carpentry and rigging would help in the search to find new ways of bringing movement and excitement into the theatre. One of the heralds of the new technology was Giacomo Torelli (1608–1678), who became the acknowledged master of stagecraft. One of his greatest contributions was the development of ways of moving flat wings, borders, and shutters simultaneously. Torelli was also a master of special effects, inventing stage illusions for fire, storms at sea, and special cloud effects, to name but a few.

By the mid-1600s the development of the baroque stage was largely

Figure 2-8. Anonymous engraving, sixteenth century. (Museo Teatrale Alla Scala, Milan.)

complete. Certainly in the years to come there would be innovations and adaptations, but the essentials were in place. The scenery had started as painted drops, and had progressed to angle wings, *periaktoi*, and finally flat wings. The auditoriums would go through greater changes over the following centuries because of the development of larger, more heterogeneous audiences. Torelli and other masters of spectacle would invent special effects over the centuries, but the basic technology was in place. While most early settings had been symmetrical (Figure 2-9), there would be later experiments in asymmetry (Figure 2-13), and these might require rearrangement of scenic units on stage, but not major changes. Eventually, most theatres would be built with the wing space, full basements, and fly lofts required by baroque staging. The chief impediment would not be rival forms for theatres but lack of funds. These innovations were very expensive.

It might be helpful to describe how such settings appear to a member of an audience, in a generalized, hypothetical case. Imagine that the show being done is a drama with five acts and three different locales. The action for the fourth act is ending and as you watch, the flat wings, the borders, and the back shutters, which represent the walls, raftered ceiling, and main door and stairways at the end of a huge, galleried room, begin to move. The candlelight is faint and flickering, and the scene seems to shimmer. Even as you watch, the room is disappearing upwards and to the sides as another scene, a tree-lined walk with interlacing overhead branches and a distant prospect of a mansion and hillside, begins to swim into view. The effect to a modern viewer would be very much like a "lap dissolve" in a movie. The earlier scene is gone at the same time and all the parts of the new one appear simultaneously. But how could this be accomplished with all of these scenic pieces? The lines that pull them are activated at the same time, perhaps by a single capstan in the basement, and the different lines to the wings, shutters, and borders are passed through pulleys and gears that equalize the speeds and distances. After it is struck, the set for Act Four remains stored in the wings and fly loft in readiness for the next performance.

Figure   2-9. *Deutsche   Schaubühne*, 1655. Wings, borders, and back-drop. (Title page from book.)

England, France, and Spain

In England, the Renaissance was late arriving, but before Elizabeth and her court ushered in a new era of patronage and acceptance of the arts, there were a number of places where theatre was done. Most were adapted spaces. For example, trestle stages were set up in inn yards or on the outskirts of towns, and in dining halls and great halls.

Pageant wagons were no longer widely in use by Elizabeth's time, but sumptuously decorated wagons were used in the Queen's coronation. The first truly English theatre grew out of all these traditions. It was a unique structure that could be adapted to both theatrical productions and blood sports. Unlovely, but capable of holding several thousand spectators, such theatres are best explained as inexpensive, multi-use facilities that capture the feeling one might have had leaning out of an inn window to watch players on a trestle stage below, or standing on a street corner in a crowded intersection watching a succession of pageant wagons. There were seats and appurtenances (or the lack thereof) for every pocketbook. The building, which Shakespeare described as a "wooden O," had a core which was open to the air, and performances were held afternoons in good weather. There are a number of theories about the structure of the stage in these theatres, and the most reasonable seem to be those that admit to a strong medieval influence on scenery and ways of performing. Not only do inventories of producers of the time mention *mansion* structures, but it makes good sense that the English would still be doing plays in that fashion. After all, Continental influences were not yet strong in any of the arts. We could also argue against the notion

Figure 2-10. Four views of the Swan Theatre, 1600–1638. (As arranged by Cesare Molinari in *Theatre Through the Ages. Top left:* Detail from Inigo Jones' 1638 drawing for Davenant's *Britannia Triumphans,* Duke of Devonshire's Collection. *Top right:* Panorama view, *Civitas Londini,* 1600, private collection. *Bottom left:* Visscher View, 1616, London, private collection. *Bottom right:* Paris Garden Manor map, 1627, London, private collection.)

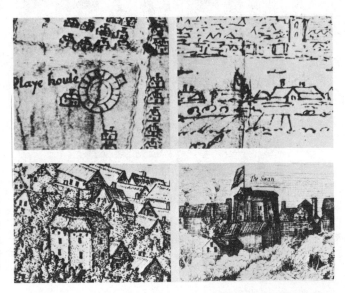

of the use or even the existence of inner balconies for performance, a theory which has been advanced by a number of scholars. Sightlines would be poor and in bright afternoon sunlight an audience would be unable to adjust their eyes. Think of the problem you have looking into shadows on a bright day. A. M. Nagler's notion of a neutral mansion structure or pavilion in the center of the stage seems a possible solution, plus the use of smaller mansions to suggest given places, and an overall emphasis on costuming, imagination, and action.

The crude sketch shown in Figure 2-11 was made by a Dutch traveler and is usually thought of as a rehearsal at the Swan. The figures at the rear might be workmen watching the rehearsal. For performance, imagine a pavilion-like structure set behind the couple on stage, with a practical platform on its top.

While these theatres were used by a mixed audience, Blackfriars, a converted refectory of a Catholic monastery "liberated" by Henry VIII from its former owners, was for the well-to-do. The plays done here were frequently based on mythology and Italian romances and were performed by the royal choir boys. We imagine a large room with benches and a raised,

Figure 2-11. DeWitt, *Interior of the Swan Theatre,* 1596. (Utrecht, Bibliotheek der Centraal Museum).

curtained stage at one end. There is no machinery or any of the trappings of the Italianate baroque theatre. In fact, Blackfriars helps us to visualize other theatres of which we have no positive records, and can only conjecture about. These are the French theatres, which were adapted from tennis courts after the banning of mystery and Passion plays in 1548. The only major difference would have been a horseshoe of boxes on the main floor of the French house, with the open end facing the stage, and a steep bleacher at the rear of the house for attendants and bodyguards of the wealthy. The benches in the center of the horseshoe in the French theatre would have been used by single men of fashion.

What we have in the tennis-court theatres of France is a gathering place for the upper class where one goes to be seen. Going to see the play was probably optional. We can imagine that in these houses the plays were frequently directed personally to the audience. Comments were made on stage based on local gossip; certain players had friends or patrons in the house; and even the intermissions were a social ritual. The most flagrant examples of this in all theatre were probably the plays of England's Restoration Theatre, when a king's mistress was an infamous actress. The plays contained allusions and satiric references to the private lives of the coterie audience, and there was hardly any difference between the dalliance and liaisons described in the plays and the behavior of the audience during intermissions. It was one of the most notorious instances of life imitating art and *vice versa*.

Another highly specialized theatre of this period was that of Spain, in the late sixteenth and seventeenth centuries, which was performed primarily in Madrid. There was a tradition of performances using decorated carts and hired actors for the festival of Corpus Christi, but popular, secular theatre developed in the sixteenth and seventeenth centuries with two important playwrights, Lope de Vega (1562–1635) and Calderón de la Barca (1600–

Figure 2-12. J. Comba, *The Old "Corral del Principe."* (Madrid, Museo Municipal de la Pacheca.)

1681). Lope de Vega's plays, in particular, were performed in courtyards in the center of Madrid's city blocks. We gather that these, too, as in the case of Tudor drama, were quite medieval in terms of the stage decoration, lack of baroque niceties, and their appeal to a heterogeneous audience. The audience was segregated, however. By Spanish custom, single and married women of good family were isolated from the ordinary people and the young men of fashion by being seated behind a screen at the rear of the courtyard on a steep bleacher. This was called, irreverently but perhaps accurately, the *cazuela* or "stew-pan."

There is an interesting similarity between the plays of Lope de Vega and those of Shakespeare. Both are poets of the people, writing equally well of commoners and princes. Both their audience and the sort of theatre used for the performances are also very much alike. Calderón, on the other hand, moved from this kind of theatre to the court and a new type of Italian theatre.

Seventeenth and Eighteenth Centuries

The major thrust in theatre construction, design of stage houses, auditoriums, and set design in the seventeenth and eighteenth centuries was increasingly Italianate and baroque. However, this does not mean that all theatres were equipped in this manner by mid-eighteenth century. As we have noted, such structures and the means to build them were expensive. We have many examples of public, popular theatres making do with less than a fully equipped stage, using outdated but less expensive staging techniques, and being housed in less than adequate buildings. It is equally true that the great theatres of modern times are usually the result of broad public support. Thus during much of this period we are waiting for social and political changes to catch up with the new theatre technology.

In both France and England, other problems were encountered in producing shows. The social aspect of attending theatre often got out of hand. Molière's actors and actresses were squeezed to the center of the stage by spectators who sat on the stage, often arriving late, and noisily had chairs brought in for their comfort.

In addition to the variable of cost, which so often explains the differences in theatres and scenic equipment during the late baroque era, there are two other important variables that explain the further development of the physical stage. One is the mounting inconsistency between preferred seating arrangements in a theatre and the realities of growing egalitarianism on the street. Most of the expensive boxes in theatres of the times afforded a very poor view of the stage but an excellent view of the audience and were also a place to be seen. Again, we have an example of the evolutionary aspects

Figure 2-13. Bibiena, interior of ogival church, with baroque mausoleums. (Museo Teatrale Alla Scala, Milan.)

of theatre. Even today in many houses in New York, for example, some of the most expensive seats are among the poorest for seeing a show. In a typical Broadway theatre, probably the best seats are the middle-cost, front-row seats in the first balcony.

The other important variable is the increasing interest in realism. In France, both Beaumarchais (1732–1799) and Diderot (1713–1784) were interested in a new stagecraft, different from the opulence of the reigning style. The sorts of plays both of these playwrights wrote in pursuit of realism often concerned ordinary people and took place in ordinary homes. Spectacle would continue, but there was quite clearly a movement toward another type of theatre for a changing audience.

In Chapter 1 it was mentioned that if a baroque-era scene designer and architect such as Torelli were to return to the present and visit a modern, commercial theatre, he would recognize his handiwork. First, however, he would have to get used to cable and electric motors being substituted for rope systems as well as a number of other adaptations for the proscenium stage. Essentially, however, he would see the same kind of stagecraft. What isn't the same is lighting and the revival of interest in very early audience-stage configurations, such as thrust staging and theatre-in-the-round. Let us deal with the major adaptations of proscenium staging and other stage configurations, as well as a number of experimental staging techniques and houses.

The staging techniques that have grown from baroque wing-border-and-back-drop configurations are the box-set, wagonning, revolve, and elevators. The major reason for the development of the box-set was the need for greater realism. One might describe a typical box-set and scene change in a modern theatre in this way.

Figure 2-14. Scene sketch. (Jeffrey McDonald, student, 1982.)

A colonial room. There is a fire burning in the fireplace up center. A short hall leads to a front door, stage right, and another hall goes up center to other rooms. A stairway is seen stage left. The ceiling is raftered, and a heavy chandelier hangs down over the table, center. Furniture is scattered throughout the room. When the scene ends, the curtain closes, and then in just moments it opens again to reveal an outdoor scene. The characters walk on and the action continues.

What happened? How were the interior and the exterior scenes changed so quickly? If this theatre is equipped with a fly-loft and grid, this could be what happened: As soon as the curtain closed, the crew came on stage. One unhooked the chandelier, another unlashed the fireplace from the wall to which it was attached. Others began moving the furniture. Electric motors pulled the cables that were attached to the back wall of the setting. The side walls were swung in as soon as the ceiling piece, which was also hinged to the back wall, swung down, and then these walls were walked in and the whole bundle was lashed and sent up into the fly-loft. The hallways, fireplace, and stairway were on wagons, which were then removed with the furniture stacked on them. The next setting was already in place. The lights came up on signal and the curtain opened.

In modern theatres, wagonning is a particularly popular technique for changing scenery. Imagine the same setting, only this time when the curtain closes, the entire floor of the setting, with the walls attached, is in motion. The set has been mounted on a large platform equipped with casters. Usually it is necessary to guide large wagons on and off stage with tracks or grooves. As one wagon moves upstage or into a wing, another is brought on with the next setting. And while this scene is being played, the next could be placed on the offstage wagon and the first scene struck behind a soundproof stage door.

A less frequently used device is the turntable or revolve. As implied by its name, it is a circular platform that turns to make scene changes. Several pie-shaped sets can be arranged on such a turntable. Changes can be made upstage on a section hidden from the audience, and additional scenic elements and furnishings can be added to a basic scene by bringing them in by wagons. Many theatre stages are built with a turntable permanently installed in them.

The most expensive stage would be like that found in the Metropolitan Opera House in New York. The stage is the floor of a huge elevator that can be moved to different levels for off-loading and resetting.

Most theatres have traps built into the stage floor, and usually have provision for wing storage, some sort of fly-loft area, and upstage spaces. All of these areas are, of course, outgrowths of the baroque stage. Only our lighting is truly modern. Earlier staging used candles, oil, and finally gas instruments. Candles were fitted with reflectors and lenses in the eighteenth century to give a more focused light when used in footlights, but it was not until the invention of arc lights and incandescent bulbs that lighting became a major means of creating stage effects. It must be noted that light in and of itself is not usable for scenery. Light must reflect from surfaces, and in the history of the modern theatre we see two uses made of the new lighting in its early experimental phase. In one, the better lighting made available to designers was simply used for the same purposes as gas light, candlelight or general illumination had been. There was greater range and control, but the aesthetic was the same. However, after the turn of the century there was a growing interest in saying less with more, the same sort of trend which one sees in modern art. Appia and Craig, to name but two designers, used lighting as an integral part of their design statement. Later, in the period between the world wars, European theatres experimented with even more subtle and complex optical and lighting effects. For example, they learned how to project moving scenery on a curving back wall (*cyclorama*). Nowadays, there are even companies that mix live and motion picture action on stage and use instant television replay.

A last technique that should be noted is one which several early designers helped invent. It is often used in musical comedies and other spectacles. A show opens with a street scene, in front of a drop; then the action moves to a hotel lobby; then to a scene in Central Park, then back to the shallow street scene. What is happening is a variation on the use of a backdrop. The narrow stage at the beginning is "in One." While this scene is played, the next scene can be set up, then the third behind it, and then the whole process can be repeated or variations by returning to "in One" or "in Two." In the Victorian theatre a variation on this was done with "olio" scenes in front of a drop. Actors would perform here between acts, allowing time for the stagehands to make set changes.

Other developments in theatre architecture and staging techniques either take us in entirely new directions or return us to where we began in this

Figure 2-15. An experimental design by Adolphe Appia, a pioneer in the use of simple, plastic forms, and lighting (*Oblique Shadows*, a setting for rhythm, 1909). (Adolphe Appia Archives, Swiss Theatre Collection, Berne.)

study of the physical stage. Theatre has been done in all kinds of structures, in all sorts of configurations. We have remarked on some of these: classrooms, dining halls, the salons of the wealthy, streets, and inn yards. Add to this list gymnasiums and warehouses. Modern church altars are often used as they were at the end of the Middle Ages, and natural outdoor amphitheatres still attract summer shows. The two most popular configurations nowadays other than proscenium are theatre-in-the-round and the thrust stage. Theatre-in-the-round is exactly what the name implies. Dinner theatres frequently use it. The problems of scene changes are overcome by the choice of play or production style, or in better equipped operations are helped by elevators. The value here is intimacy and excellent sightlines for everyone. The problems, in addition to that of how to change settings, have to do with lighting and a lack of variety of production styles. Lighting is difficult because anything other than lighting from directly above is going to shine in some spectator's eyes. The problem of variety comes from relying on actors as the focus of attention, and being minimally concerned with settings. Typically, a larger unit like a doorway or fireplace is suggested rather than realized. Furniture is usually low or see-through. In and of itself it is not a bad thing to place the emphasis on the actors, any more than it would be wrong to place it on scenery, if the show allows it, but during a full season or an endless one (such as some dinner theatres have), directors and designers like to have a broader palette from which to work.

The thrust stage is not only the most important innovation in modern theatre architecture and staging but also brings us full circle, back to the theatre of fifth century B.C. Greece. In England, Canada, and America, in

Figure 2-16. *Julius Caesar*, Stratford, Ontario. (Festival Theatre, Don McKague, photographer.)

recent years, it was popularized by Tyrone Guthrie, the producer and director, who first used it in his career at the Edinburgh Festival and then convinced the citizens of Stratford, Ontario, to build a Shakespeare Festival Theatre in this manner. This in turn led to the construction of the Guthrie in Minneapolis and the National Theatre in Chichester, as well as countless other thrust stages at university theatres and repertory companies throughout the three countries. Literally, it is an idea whose time has come again. Like most theatrical solutions, it poses as many problems as it solves. The major advantage in this case is the egalitarian seating (arranged in a 220° sweep at Stratford) with very few poor seats, and an emphasis on actors, costuming, and properties. The weaknesses are the lighting angles and, as with theatre-in-the-round, the danger of lack of variety in production. In the case of the three theatres mentioned, there are ingenious and handsome architectural solutions for the backwall of the stage. They are flexible to the degree that they can be adjusted to allow a great variety of openings and surfaces, but they also provide handsome architectural solutions for backgrounds. Guthrie's unspoken argument for this type of theatre was probably that he wanted to do something other than proscenium staging, but he has often written of the special chemistry that works on an audience when they can see one another across the house and then look back at the actors. He thought of the latter as a reaffirmation of the ritual aspect of theatre and felt that it had been too long absent.

Figure 2-17. The Festival Theatre, Stratford, Ontario. Designed by Tanya Moiseiwitsch. (Herb Nott, photographer.)

It is probably true that when the audience sat down in the Stratford, Ontario, Shakespeare Festival Theatre to see *Oedipus Rex*, they were emotionally and physically as close to the original event as any Europeans had been in 2500 years, including Frenchmen in the Comédie-Française, Italian audiences sitting in the Teatro Olimpico, and the Roman friends of Seneca enjoying a reading by the poet himself at his summer vacation home. We have already suggested that Torelli would recognize his handicraft backstage at a Broadway show. Sophocles, after having bridged the linguistic and cultural differences in Stratford, Ontario, might have allowed that it was a good way to produce the play if you couldn't be Athenian and if you couldn't do it out-of-doors on the south slope of the Acropolis.

A Selective Bibliography on Theatre History and the Development of the Physical Stage

Arnott, Peter D. *An Introduction to the Greek Theatre*. Bloomington: Indiana University Press, 1963.

Bieber, Margarete. *The History of the Greek and Roman Theatre*. 2nd ed. Rev. Princeton, New Jersey: Princeton University Press, 1961.

Bentley, Eric Russell. *In Search of Theatre*. New York: Knopf, 1953.

Berthold, Margot. *A History of World Theatre*. Tr. Edith Simmons. New York: Ungar, 1972.

Blum, Daniel C. *A Pictorial History of the American Theatre, 1860–1970*. 3rd ed. New York: Crown Publishers, 1969.

Brockett, Oscar G. *History of the Theatre*. 4th ed. Boston: Allyn and Bacon, 1982.

Cheney, Sheldon. *The Theatre: 3000 Years of Drama, Acting, and Stagecraft*. New York: Longmans, Green, 1953.

Gassner, John. *Masters of the Drama.* New York: Dover, 1954.

Hartnell, Phyllis. *The Concise History of Theatre.* New York: Harry N. Abrams, Inc., 1968.

Hewitt, Barnard W. *Theatre USA, 1668 to 1957.* New York: McGraw-Hill, 1959.

MacGowan, Kenneth and William Melnitz. *Golden Ages of the Theatre.* Englewood Cliffs, New Jersey: Prentice-Hall, 1959.

Molinari, Cesare. *Theatre through the Ages.* Tr. Colin Homer. New York: McGraw-Hill, 1975.

Nagler, Alois Maria. *A Source Book in Theatrical History.* New York: Dover, 1959.

Nicoll, Allardyce. *British Drama: An Historical Survey from the Beginnings to the Present Time.* New York: Thomas Y. Crowell, 1925.

———. *The Development of the Theatre.* 5th ed. Rev. New York: Harcourt Brace Jovanovich, 1966.

Southern, Richard. *The Seven Ages of the Theatre.* New York: Hill and Wang, 1961.

Self-Portrait, In Context, painting by John Offerman, art student, Colorado State University, 1982.

3

The Actor

The most important thing in acting is honesty. Once you've learned how to fake that, you've got it made.

George Burns, Winter 1980

Acting and actors have been with us from the beginning of theatre. When we discussed the origins of drama, we suggested that acting is innate to human beings and one of the natural reasons for theatre's development. We know, for instance, that acting or role playing is a way we rehearse our possible future, or a way to recall or reshape what has happened in our lives. At the core of acting is the irony of pretending to be something we aren't. The other irony in theatre is the action in which the characters are involved. Which is more important is moot. Both are the keys to theatre.

Acting is not a creative art form; rather, it is interpretive. We may think actors are involved in creativity when what they do is unlike what anyone else has done with a given role or if their portrayals are particularly revealing of a character's meaning. But acting should not be compared with painting or composing or playwriting. This is not to take anything away from acting, but only to describe what it is. If a pianist begins to improvise new compositions in mid-program, this isn't a piano recital, it is a composing recital, whatever that is. A clever improvisational actor can involve the audience in what is being created, not in what is being interpreted, and these are very different things for both the actor and the audience. A pianist, actor, concert singer, and conductor are all interpreters of someone else's or even their own work, and their excellence will exist not only in the beauty of their playing, speaking, singing, and baton technique but also in their ability to communicate their understanding of the intention of the work they are interpreting.

Some people have the notion that good actors live the roles they play on stage. Even one's private life might be taken over by a role one is playing, they think. This certainly happens, but rarely as often as it does in the popular fiction about acting. There are probably some pianists who think they are Chopin and conductors who believe they are Beethoven, but such hallucinations get in the way of interpreting the real composer. A good actor is aware simultaneously of the role being played and the reaction of the audience; in other words, what's being communicated and how it's being accepted. Good teachers have known about this since the first classroom. Parents have known it since children were invented. When the intention of a work of art is that it be communicated, then there is art in both its effective communication and its embodiment.

With realistic and even naturalistic acting, the audience will be aware of what is real and what is imitated. A common experience for actors is the immediate, "real" reaction of an audience to an actor dropping a line or stumbling when the script didn't call for it. I remember a noble experiment with the audience perception of an actor and his role in a production of

Molière's *Imaginary Invalid*. It was done by a midwestern repertory company and a famous actor turned director for this production. In the last third of the play, the leading man seemed to be having trouble with a very real cough. It came at awkward times, interrupted lines, and annoyed him. The play progressed to almost its last moments, and then the actor left the stage without warning. When one of the characters returned to announce that "Monsieur Molière" was dead, most of us, even those who remembered that the playwright had indeed died during a performance in that role, felt that the audience/actor relationship had been violated. Probably it would have worked better if the play had been called *The Death of Molière* or if the actor had done his coughing in the same vein as the rest of his performance.

If acting is not really being the character, then what is it? It is certainly more than knowing the lines and blocking or being properly costumed and made up. Often, in amateur productions, this is as far as people go, while in professional theatre it is not at all unusual, particularly with a revival of a famous play, for the cast to appear for the first rehearsal with lines memorized and ideas in mind for how they might play their characters. Assuming that we are speaking about intelligent, sensitive people, there probably has been a great deal of agreement about what acting is since the time of the Greeks. First, it is what we have just outlined: knowledge of a role and an understanding of how to communicate with an audience. Second, it is probably a choice of one or two approaches to acting that have existed since the beginning of drama. These are choices between the personal or the formal, the internal or the external, the classical or the "method." Put in simple terms, the external approach begins with an examination of the visible, external characteristics of a role. Often the roles themselves demand the approach. For example, you cannot very well portray a character in an opera who sings several arias without learning these arias and, hopefully, having the vocal equipment and training to handle them properly. The same is true of any number of periods in theatre. For instance, a player in Restoration dramas in England had to at least know how to counterfeit the behavior of the lords and ladies who were both the subject of these plays and their audience. In *commedia dell'arte*, the actors had to know the qualities of their characters in order to improvise in a scenario. Even today a distinction is frequently made between English and American actors. The popular notion is that the English know how to speak and be heard in a theatre, while the Americans mumble. This is a generalization, but it is true that the English place more emphasis on stage speech in their training of actors than do Americans. This could be partly attributable to our so-called American and "democratic" belief that all people should speak naturally and not use accents that might suggest that they are better than other folks. There is also a choice being made between internalizing and humanizing a character and polishing the external qualities. Many of our most famous stage actors, Henry Fonda and James Whitmore to name but two, have had distinctive regional accents. We accept them in a range of roles that many English theatregoers would find improper.

Sir Laurence Olivier has often been interviewed on the subject of his training and experiences as an actor. He believes that an actor must be concerned with what is obvious about a character. This includes gesture, speech, movement, and how the character interacts with others. In an interview with the *New York Times Magazine*, he spoke of the two approaches to acting:

> There are two types of actors—external and internal. . . . Those who start from the inside are more likely to find *themselves* within the parts they play. The others, the peripheral ones—like Alec Guinness and myself—start from the outside. They are more apt to find *the part* inside themselves. Those who start from the inside don't blossom until later and often the play is off before it happens.

As one of the great Shakespearean actors of our time, it is interesting to hear what Olivier has to say about these roles.

> Olivier sees the great Shakespearean roles as "cannibals." While playing Othello, he once described their consuming effect. "You give them all you've got and the author says to you: 'You've given all you've got? Good. Now, more. Good. Now, more. More, damn you. More, more. *More! More!*' Until your heart and guts and brain are pulp and the part feeds on you, eating you. Acting great parts devours you. It's a dangerous game."[1]

His method for developing a role is this:

> Olivier constructs a character by using selected traits, techniques, ideas, images. Assembled, they form the character in the round and this serves as a sort of shelter on stage. Then he moves inward.[2]

A representative of the other approach to acting is the American actress Uta Hagen, who has had an outstanding career in the modern theatre as both actress and teacher. In her book *Respect for Acting*, she immediately establishes her preference for internal acting. She chooses expressiveness and naturalness over artificiality and histrionics, but admits that good acting probably uses both, plus a "method" for objectifying one's approach. In an early passage of her book, she discusses the core of her method, which is to use one's own feelings and experiences even when approaching a character radically different from what you yourself are in everyday life. As she says:

> Once we are on the track of self-discovery in terms of an enlargement of our sense of identity, and we now try to apply this knowledge to an identification with the character in the play, we must make this transference, this finding

---

[1]Curtis Bill Pepper. *New York Times Magazine*, March 25, 1979, p. 58.
[2]Ibid.

of the character within ourselves, through a continuing and overlapping series of substitutions from our own experience and remembrances, through the use of imaginative extensions of realities, and put them in the place of the fiction in the play.[3]

Anecdotes about actors are always popular. They are sometimes true, frequently pointed, and always entertaining because of the people involved. Two concern Hagen and Olivier. It's been claimed that when Hagen was playing Blanche opposite Anthony Quinn in *A Streetcar Named Desire*, there was a failure on the stagecrew's part to go to a blackout and end the rape scene. Quinn whispered to Hagen, "What do we do?" Hagen, as a good method actor, was supposed to have replied, "Rape me."

Olivier's story, one of many, was about a particularly luminous performance of *Othello*. His friends were dashing backstage to congratulate him when they heard crashes coming from his dressing room. When they entered, they found Olivier destroying the furniture. They asked why, and he shouted that he knew it had been a great performance, but he was damned if he knew how to do it again.

A frequent confusion about acting is the idea that the "method" is a modern invention attributable to Lee Strasberg, Michael Chekhov, or Constantin Stanislavski, or all of them. Actually, the approach is probably as old as acting. For example, we have this description of an actor:

> He excelled particularly in the details of a role. He had a naturalness that verged on the familiar, even in tragedy, without thereby detracting from its grandeur. He was no less excellent in comedy . . . there was such great truth in his acting and so much naturalness that invariably he made you forget the actor, and he carried the illusion to the point of making you imagine that the action unfolding before you was real. . . . He never recited verse, but rather conveyed the situation, the feeling. He held pauses so long, and played so slowly that a performance would last half an hour longer when he had a part in it. Upon emerging from the wings, he became animated and spoke in low tones to himself or to the actor with whom he entered upon the stage, and by this means he appeared to live the part from the first verse he spoke. . . .[4]

The actor being described is Michel Baron, the chief tragedian of the United Company in Paris, sometime after 1720 when the actor had returned to the stage at the age of sixty-seven.

This writer recalls a visit to Lee Strasberg's Actor's Studio a number of years ago, when the acting coach's relationship with Marlon Brando, Marilyn Monroe, and Montgomery Clift was in everyone's mind. At this particular session, a young actor performed the scene from *Hamlet* in which he dismisses Rosencrantz and Guildenstern and then soliloquizes, "Oh, what a

[3]Uta Hagen, *Respect for Acting* (New York: Macmillan, 1973), p. 34.
[4]Charles Colle, *Journals et Memoirs*, as quoted in A. M. Nagler, *A Source Book in Theatrical History* (New York: Dover, 1952), pp. 288–289.

rogue and peasant slave am I. . . ." This actor was dressed in blue jeans, was very sincere about what he was doing, but conjured up a character who seemed to be agonizing over his motorcycle and was wondering if he was going to be accepted by Brando's Wild Ones. When it was over, Strasberg tore into what he had done. His basic point was that Hamlet was not an ordinary young man; he was a prince, and a prince living in a particular time and place. The key to his criticism was that the young actor had mistaken a way of doing roles with the style necessary for this particular role. It was obviously an eye-opener for the young man and for many of the would-be actors seated in the room. It also expressed a major point about all acting techniques: they exist to help the actor realize a role, but one must also be concerned with the tradition and meaning of a play and not let a means become an end.

Most drama done in America today is realistic and most of the actors we watch are familiar with the internalizing method we have discussed. So, let us do exercises based on this approach, following a procedure for training young actors that will give the reader a taste of this common approach to acting. The object is not to discover if you are a potentially fine actor, but to let you learn an aspect of appreciating theatre by doing what people in theatre do.

First, a word of explanation. This collection of brief scenes and improvisations is the result of a number of years of experimentation with beginning acting students. The more traditional way to teach acting uses short scenes from well-known plays, not the "open" scenes found here. The problems with the usual approach are these: (1) not everyone in class will read the scenes to be performed and critiqued; (2) even the students doing a particular scene might not read the balance of the play from which it was taken; or (3) in the case of a truly difficult scene, not all students do research on the play's meaning and production history; and (4) because of these difficulties, it is very hard to have a number of shared experiences with a class in terms of acting problems. Sometimes these difficulties with beginning actors are resolved by the use of theatre games. Here, they are resolved by using "open" scenes, written expressly for beginning actors, with nothing before or after the dialogue given. There are few if any stage directions, and character is revealed by the dialogue and situation. The scenes are "open" to student interpretation. On many occasions, all of the students in an acting class have been assigned the same scene (working with a partner) and invariably the result has been that no two scenes were alike in terms of characterization, mood, the type of conflict, or ideas of time and place. Furthermore, I have discovered real advantages in having everyone in a class know the dialogue being used and the problems posed by a scene. Scenes are well-prepared, and students can concentrate on basic acting problems such as honesty, subtext, and matters of characterization, style, and structure.

The improvisational scenes also given here are a familiar type of exercise and lend variety to the "open" scene assignments. Before starting these exercises, review the points made about acting in the preceding and the implications of our choice to do these exercises in the realistic and internalizing modes. We have noted that:

—Acting is interpretive, not creative.

—Actors should observe the people around them.

—Actors should root the character's feelings in their own experiences.

—Honesty is the cornerstone for the beginning actor, subtext follows, and characterization and style follow these.

—Acting is communication.

—Less is more.

Drama uses action and imitation. Its organizing principle is **Conflict.** Drama is always **Active,** that is we don't narrate, we do. Even when playing a muted or bored character, the actor should approach the role actively. Furthermore, unlike the reader of a novel, the playgoer cannot stop the action and have it repeated until a certain passage is understandable. Thus we are dealing with a very special form of communication in that it is swift and unrepeatable. It must be clear, direct, and lean.

Much of what we call acting is internal. Speech and movement are only parts of this act of interpretation and communication. Avoid criticism that is too specific and deals with externals. It is a tendency of beginning actors to think that a fellow actor's weakness has been the use of a gesture or the intonation of a word or, in other words, an external trait. If you start hunting for them you will find literally thousands of external details in the delivery of a line. It is much better to question what was meant by the actor (What did you feel? Were you being honest? How do you feel about the other character?) and let the surface affect take care of itself. Remember that in these exercises we are approaching acting from the "inside." When you critique, remember that *criticism* goes both ways: it is positive and negative. Don't be too intellectual. React, don't second guess. First, judge the acting and the success the actors have had with their major objectives. Matters of staging should probably not come up at all in early scene work. If you can't see or hear in the audience, move. The class is the audience for the actors. Certainly there will be some mannerisms, for example, that an actor uses over and over until they become annoying. These should be noted, but remember that in acting the victory doesn't necessarily go to the brave and the beautiful. Again, steer clear of comment on externals.

A final thought: make your scenes logical and clear. Work on the fundamentals. Do everything you can to promote the personalities and the underlying relationship of the characters. Try to communicate what is absolutely necessary, not everything that comes up in the rehearsals. This is the "less is more" principle. Almost everyone agrees that good acting is a matter of being a sharpshooter, not a scatter-gunner. Be objective about who you are, how you come across, because you are the "instrument" on which the character will play. Give the character a chance to come to life and don't worry about protecting yourself.

I. Honesty

In the following "open" scenes, we start with honesty. Let the characters you portray believe exactly what they say. They can show anger, love, doubt, but what they express is what they mean. In rehearsing these scenes you might play a game that is used in some acting schools: if you don't believe your partner's sincerity with a line, don't accept it. Make no response to the line of dialogue until it seems to be honestly motivated, and then take your turn at being honest. Find the characters and their situation in the rehearsals and emphasize honesty. The criteria for critiquing these scenes are: (1) How well did the characters project honesty? (2) How well did they communicate with one another and with the audience? (3) How much sense did the scene make in terms of its action, setting, and place?

N.B.: All of these scenes can be done with parts played by a man and a woman, two men, or two women. Certain lines and names may have to be changed, but keep other changes to a minimum. Some of the scenes use swear words. Omit them if you must, but they should be thought of as part of a character's personality.

Scene A

FIRST (*looking up*): Is that all you can think to say?
SECOND: Yes.
FIRST: How come?
SECOND: Because I know it and I mean it.
FIRST: It stinks.
SECOND: Sorry.
FIRST: Rotten, lousy, stinks.
SECOND: But it's the truth.
FIRST: Someday you're going to be damn sorry for this.
SECOND: I would be anyway . . . if I said it or didn't say it.

FIRST: Stinks.

(*A pause.*)

SECOND (*Rising from chair and crossing room to a window*): Lousy city, lousy house, lousy room, lousy people.

FIRST: Unh-hunh.

SECOND: Unh-hunh. That's what you said, right?

FIRST: You called it.

SECOND: Self-centered jerk.

FIRST: Look who's talking.

SECOND: Well, I'm on my way.

(*A pause.*)

FIRST: Okay.

SECOND: What do you mean, okay?

FIRST: Okay.

Improvisation #1

An aged employee of a company is asked to come forward at a retirement banquet to say a few words to the friends, associates, and employers gathered there. This group becomes the audience. It is a moment for honesty. The employee was not in a position of large responsibility. Plan very carefully what your character will say and how it will be said, creating your own script, and focusing upon "honesty" as a technique. Remember that, after thirty years, your character probably wouldn't tell them off.

Scene B

FIRST: Charley?

SECOND: What?

FIRST: Charley Smith?

SECOND: Mary? My god, you're Mary Shafer!

FIRST: Yes!

BOTH: What are—I haven't seen you—(*They laugh at the way they've interrupted one another.*)

CHARLEY: You talk. I haven't seen you in ten, twelve years.

MARY: That's right.

CHARLEY: How've you been? You're looking great.

MARY: Fine. No, I'm not.

CHARLEY: Not what?

MARY: Looking great. (*Then she forces a laugh at his look of discomposure.*)

CHARLEY: Same old sharp tongue, eh, Mary?

MARY: Same old "call a spade a spade," eh, Charley? But what are you doing here?

CHARLEY: Buying trip for the company I work for.

MARY: Where do you live now?

CHARLEY: Salem.

MARY: You went home.

CHARLEY: Yes.

MARY: And I'll bet you married Cecily.

CHARLEY: Married her and divorced her.

MARY: I'm sorry.

CHARLEY: I'm not.

MARY: Children?

CHARLEY: Several . . . how about yourself?

MARY: I never married. Figures, doesn't it? Everybody warned us about being too outspoken. But it does wonders for you in the business.

CHARLEY: You're successful?

MARY: Sure.

CHARLEY: Do you ever go home?

MARY: Never. There never was anything there for me.

CHARLEY: You're still a hell of a good-looking woman.

MARY: Bullshit!

CHARLEY (*laughing*): I'd ask you to have a drink—

MARY: But you won't.

CHARLEY: Yes, I do——

MARY: Then I won't accept.

CHARLEY (*laughs again*): Tough, tough, tough.

MARY: I liked you, Charley.

CHARLEY: And I liked you, Mary, but you scared me to death.

MARY: You were right.

(*A pause.*)

CHARLEY: They're flashing my green light, Mary.

MARY: Ciao, Charley.

CHARLEY: Ciao, Mary.

Scene C

ONE: Do you come here often?

OTHER: No.

ONE: It's a nice place.

OTHER: I suppose.

ONE: I like it more than most any other place I've been to.

OTHER: Really? This place?

ONE: You know. It maybe isn't the place as much as it is the recollection. Like it isn't someone's face in the sense of how good looking they are or something, but if it's that particular face. The one you remember. Right?

OTHER: I suppose so. Like the song says, "though your figure's less than Greek and you mouth's a little weak, when you——"

ONE: No, that isn't it at all. It's more like, "I've got you under my skin, I've got you under the hide of me, I've got you deep down inside of me——"

OTHER: That makes me think of surgeons. Deep down inside of me. Drivel.

ONE: Maybe it isn't drivel.

Figure 3-1. John Offerman, 1982.

OTHER: I say it's drivel, and I say the hell with it.

ONE: The hell with you, Lazue.

OTHER: In your ear, Lanier.

ONE: Up your . . . Let's cool it. Sorry.

OTHER: I'm sorry.

ONE: Shouldn't have forced a conversation on you.

OTHER: You didn't force a conversation on me. If I didn't want to talk, I wouldn't have talked.

ONE: Sure.

OTHER: Sure.

ONE (*pause*): Trouble with places like this. Too many strangers.

OTHER: Thought you liked this place?

ONE: For the memories, not the place.

OTHER: Oh. Not much to remember tonight for, hunh?

ONE: Doesn't matter. You can't force memories any more than you can force a homerun. If it happens, it happens.

OTHER: Lots of hitters go after homeruns. They strike out a lot, that's all.

ONE: That's what I meant. You always try to find significance in what you do, you strike out a lot.

OTHER: Better than a string of scratch hits.

ONE: For the hitter . . . not for the team.

OTHER: Yeah. But who said sitting in a bar was a team sport . . . hunh?

Note: You should be aware of the different shapes these scenes take. Characters will have the advantage, then lose it. Both characters may change as they interact, and notice how important the term **Pause** is when it's used. More about this in the chapter on playwriting, but the concept being demonstrated, even in these brief scenes, is that action and conflict lead to change. Be clear about these moments when you do your scenes. Key moments of understanding or the initiation of new approaches are usually referred to as **Beats.** In the following scene, these crucial moments will be indicated by a *. Deal with them. Also, in this scene don't play Mrs. Grayson as an old woman. Make her real, but don't worry about age.

Scene D

OLDER: I'm so sorry about your father, my dear. I only heard about it yesterday. So sorry.

YOUNGER: Thank you, Ma'am. Thanks.

OLDER: He was a wonderful man. Mrs. Grayson is my name.

YOUNGER: Thanks.

OLDER: What did he die of?

YOUNGER: Complications.

OLDER: What?

YOUNGER: Call it old age.

OLDER: Old age? You must be fooling. He was young enough to be my son.*

YOUNGER: Cirrhosis.

OLDER: What?

YOUNGER: A disease of the liver.

OLDER: Too bad. But it's a disease that takes many young men.

YOUNGER: Not too many. Just the heavy drinkers.*

OLDER: You didn't think I meant that, did you? I certainly didn't mean that.

YOUNGER: You asked what he died of.

OLDER: He was always a fine man.

YOUNGER: Even when he was on a binge?

OLDER: Particularly then.*

YOUNGER: What?

OLDER: I said, particularly when your father was on a binge. He was a fine man. Good company.

YOUNGER: Look, I really don't know you. I've been away for a long while . . .*

OLDER: And you just thought I was a nosy old lady.

YOUNGER: I don't know what to think.

OLDER: Your father was a nice drunk.* Some men are mean drunks. Your father was nice. I liked him.

YOUNGER: You've got to be putting me on.

OLDER: Every heard of Jimmy's? It should have been called Janie's. I was the bartender and owner for thirty years. I knew your father for most of those years. Long before you were born, before he moved away. It's nice to have him back after all these years. He wanted to be buried, here, hunh?

YOUNGER: Yes. It was his last request.

OLDER: Drunk or sober when he made the request?* Sorry, that's a hell of a question. You know your father was one of those men who can handle a sin with style. A lesser man would have just been another drunk. But not your father.

YOUNGER (*his reserve dissolving*): You really knew him?

OLDER: Honest! His only weakness——

YOUNGER (*beginning to laugh*): What was that?

OLDER: He was a grabber.* Not that I minded. What with the way I liked your dad and Jimmy dead for all those years. But he wasn't subtle.

YOUNGER: Now, come on——

OLDER: You've got something else to do? Funeral's over. No one else to look after, right?

YOUNGER: I was alone.

OLDER: Well, then let's get a drink . . .* and let me tell you some more about your old man. Okay?

YOUNGER: I think I'd like that.*

II. Subtext

The next step in beginning acting is to work with subtext. What we mean by this is that type of communication in which, to a noticeable degree, our character does or says one thing and means something else. There are a number of ways of approaching this, and we might use this technique: think of the real feeling or the underlying feeling you have about the other character and find out to what extent you can still say the lines with the surface meaning. The classroom audience will be particularly helpful in indicating how well you are communicating on the subtextual level. It will probably be necessary to adjust how strongly you feel the subtext, or how much you let it intrude through speech and gesture, to name but two of the ways we can show ambivalence. Generally, the less obvious we are on the surface, the better the acting in terms of subtext if we are also communicating our real objective.

Scene E

HARRY: I didn't ask you up.

JEAN: I know it. Thought I would anyway.

HARRY: I didn't invite you.

JEAN: Silly way to put it. "Invite." You "invite" people to teas or symphonies.

HARRY: The meaning's clear. I didn't.

JEAN: I know it.

HARRY: Then why don't you leave?

JEAN: I'd prefer to stay.

HARRY: Then I'll leave.

Figure 3-2. John Offerman, 1982.

JEAN: No, you won't. You've got your slippers on, a book on the table beside you, a beer in the fridge.

HARRY: But I'll leave if you're hanging around.

JEAN: Well, then, why don't you throw me out?

HARRY: Throw you out?

JEAN: Yes.

HARRY: Why should I do that? I don't want to throw you out. I'll leave.

JEAN: Unpleasant? Too unpleasant for you? Too goddamned unpleasant, throwing somebody out? It's your house, for chrissake. Just grab me by the scruff of the neck, and throw me out.

HARRY: Are you going to stay? I'd prefer not to hang around here and yammer.

JEAN: Take me in hand. Get me out of here. No?

HARRY: I figure you'll go when you're ready.

JEAN: Aren't you going to make me?

HARRY: I said I'd leave.

JEAN: What in hell is wrong with you?

HARRY: I'll put on my shoes . . .

JEAN: Try it. Just shove me to the door. Push me out. It could work. You don't want to spend the evening with me. That's for damn sure. So throw me out.

HARRY: There. I've got the shoes on. Take my coat now.

JEAN: **Throw Me Out!**

HARRY: I'll leave now. Please don't be here when I get back.

JEAN: Goddamned toad.

HARRY: Goodbye.

JEAN: I'll be here until you get back, blockhead. You ain't never gonna get rid of me.

HARRY: I'll walk about a bit . . .

Improvisation #2

Using the class as audience, do a nonhuman, a robot. See how close to human you can come. This is not the bionic man or woman, who were obviously human and whose nonhuman aspects are handled by makeup and trick photography. Your person is inhuman but seems human. Your subtext is that you have no feelings, no understanding.

Improvisation #3

A public apology which you feel you must give (or your family feels you must) and which you don't mean.

Scene F

SARA: Get the paper, will you dear?

MARY: In a moment.

SARA: The paper?

MARY: It's the end of the chapter. Just a page more.

SARA (*after a pause*): Well, I suppose I could get it myself.

MARY: Get it yourself? Oh, no! I'll get the paper. I'm almost done.

SARA: My leg's hurting terribly today, but the doctor says I should make myself exercise. I'll get it.

MARY (*looking up again*): Get it?

SARA: The paper.

MARY: What about the doctor?

SARA: He said I should exercise.

MARY (*engrossed*): Probably right.

SARA: Then I will.

MARY: Will what?

SARA: Get the paper.

MARY: Okay.

(*A pause.*)

SARA (*beginning to cry softly*): Little you care.

MARY: Shhh. I'm almost through.

SARA: So am I. And you'd never care.

MARY: Of course he cares.

SARA: Who cares?

MARY: The doctor.

SARA: I wasn't talking about him.

Figure 3-3. John Offerman, 1982.

MARY (*looking up from her book*): Of course you were. You said, he said you should exercise.

SARA (*petulantly*): I know what he said. He cares a lot more than you do.

MARY: Prove it.

SARA: What?

MARY (*puts down the book and goes to the door; returns*): Does he get you your paper, honey?

SARA (*puzzled*): No-o-o-o.

Improvisation #4

Two women, who are old friends, meet for afternoon drinks as they have for a great number of years. One woman can't help but feel superior to the other, because for the same number of years she has been the lover of the other woman's husband. Today the other woman has found it out, just before this meeting. She is torn between saying it and holding it back.

Improvisation #5

A very self-assured person who is trying to appear humble.

Scene G

SHE: Ham with your eggs, dear?

HE: Sure . . . Did you read the paper this morning? Charley got the promotion. My God, what's the world coming to. Charley Smithson can't count to twenty without taking off both shoes, and he gets a promotion.

SHE: He's a late bloomer?

HE: At least. Remember the party they gave last summer?

SHE: Party?

HE: Yeah, the one at the club. You spent a lot of time with him and Dorothy.

SHE: Oh, sure. The funny party. Not much fun but a lot of booze.

HE: Some people thought it was a great party.

SHE: I didn't.

HE (*looking up from his paper*): Why not? You seemed to be having fun.

SHE: Looking isn't being.

HE: Laughing, carrying on. As I recall I had a hell of a time getting you to come home. After I found you.

(*A pause.*)

SHE: I wanted to be found. You just didn't look in the right places.

HE: Or do the right things?

SHE: Maybe not always. But you've improved.

HE: Easier to live with?

SHE: Definitely.

HE: Thanks for breakfast. See you tonight. (*Pecks her cheek and leaves.*)

III. Characterization

Having worked on the basic techniques of honesty and subtext, let's attempt several "open" scenes in which you flesh out very special kinds of people. You should still begin with your own feelings and experiences translated into these roles, but take them a step or two farther in terms of the external reality. Old age, foreign birth, or social status can all be elements of characterization. We should begin with observation, but then, to be consistent with the approach taken so far, adapt it to what you'll be like when you are older, or try to find out what happens to your mouth and face when you attempt a particular accent. Imagine the reasons for people of a certain class behaving in a particular way, in terms of how you might adapt to such an environment. Don't do an old person's walk, but imagine how you would walk on ice if your neck were stiff. Also, be thorough in your research of such features as a German accent.

Scene H

ONE: Her name was Joannie. Did you ever meet her?

OTHER: Can't recall it.

ONE: She was a lovely girl. Tall, blond, moved like a dancer.

OTHER: Can't say I do remember her.

ONE: If you'd ever met her you would've remembered her.

OTHER: That attractive.

ONE: Yep.

OTHER: When was that?

ONE: Oh, about 1920.

OTHER: I remember 1920. Good year for me.

ONE: Same for me. We bought a Franklin. Remember the Franklin?

OTHER: Of course I do, but I can't say I ever liked that make too much.

ONE: Fine car. Beautiful paint job. So many coats of paint, you could see your face in it.

OTHER: Not as good as my Buick.

ONE: Of course it was. More of a custom-made car. Beautiful.

OTHER: But it didn't last.

ONE: Lasting doesn't mean anything.

OTHER: How come?

ONE: Lots of good things don't last.

OTHER: Like what?

ONE: Your spouse didn't.

OTHER: I didn't mean that. Manufactured goods, things like that.

ONE: Or clean rivers, like we had when we were young. Or that beautiful girl I was telling you about. Joannie. She got old just like the rest of us, I guess.

OTHER: What could be more natural?

ONE: But she was pretty and could dance.

OTHER: Franklin wasn't all that good mechanically.

ONE: Oh yes, it was. A piece of precision machinery.

OTHER: Precision machinery doesn't break down.

ONE: You ever know one that did?

OTHER: Lots.

ONE: I doubt that. They never made "lots." And those few they did make were like a lovely . . . young lady. Moved beautiful. Just beautiful.

Improvisation #6

An old lady or man is walking down a semideserted street in a large city, when out of the shadows stumbles a man or woman, physically deformed or emotionally different, blocking the older person's exit. They confront one another. This can be comic or tragic, but it is real for the participants, not a rerun of an old *Dracula* movie.

Scene I

SARAH: So I told him, if you want me to come to your church, you'll have to preach from the Good Book more and from the newspapers less. James didn't agree with me. Never did. So I told him that he didn't have no right to an opinion because he never took me to church anyway . . . and he said it was because it wasn't "revalent."

MARIA: Do you think they'd let us cook some? I miss cookin' so much. I was a good cook, and always cookin' for a big family. Seven, eight children. And the grown men. Every spring we'd butcher two hogs. The sausage . . . oh, it was so good. They should let us cook.

SARAH: Why don't you never listen to me? I wasn't talkin' about food and cookin'. I was talkin' about religion.

MARIA: I'm religious. Good for a person.

SARAH: You're right! And the Bible is God's revealed word. Right? "I am the truth and the light." The *truth*.

MARIA: Truth?

SARAH: That's what it says in the Bible and that's God's revealed word.

MARIA: Revealed?

SARAH: Like it says.

MARIA: So God wrote it in English?

SARAH: He can write in any language he please.

Figure 3-4.   John Offerman, 1982.

MARIA: But is God an English speaker? I mean I don't think it is said the way you said it, this God is truth and light.

SARAH: That's what it says.

MARIA: Verdad.

SARAH: What?

MARIA: Verdad . . . truth. If God spoke in Spanish.

SARAH: Of course he does.

MARIA: So how would he speak to us right now if he was to come up. Like the doctor, would he speak in English? I don't understand everything he says. Would God do that?

SARAH: Sure, if you was in an American-speaking hospital. Sure, God would talk like the doctors.

MARIA: But I don't like that. I wish the doctors spoke both. Especially when I get frightened and can't concentrate too good on what they are saying. And if God was like with us out here, why couldn't he speak so we both would understand him?

SARAH: Sure. He could if he wanted to. And so could Christ.

MARIA: But Christ didn't when he talked to the people, did he? It was in one language. There must of been Mexicans in the crowd at the mountain who didn't understand.

SARAH (*scornfully*): Mexican. Ha, ha, not there, foolish.

MARIA: Like for instance, Mexicans. Their Mexicans.

SARAH: If God or Christ had wanted people to understand them then they could do it.

MARIA: Then why isn't it that way in your holy book, especially if that's the word of God and the way he wrote it?

SARAH: Bullshit.

MARIA: Caca.

Scene J

Play the place, the weather, the time of day in the following scene. You will probably have to pantomime the baby carriage, as well. These are all skills which belong to characterization.

Scene: A spring day in a small park in an eastern American city. A young woman in a short-sleeved dress sits on a park bench idly rocking a baby carriage and looking out at the city below her vantage point. An old man or woman comes up and sits down beside her. She doesn't speak, but nods pleasantly. It is 1948.

OLD PERSON (*with a pronounced European accent*): It's a lovely afternoon, yah? I love sitting here on afternoons like this. You could say that this was my favorite park. Such a nice view, and a good breeze from the bay on hot days. Don't you think?

(*The young woman nods.*)

The city gets so hot during the day. Good if you can find a cool green place. August particularly . . . Are you from around here?

WOMAN (*she answers in a heavily accented voice*): No, I am not.

OLD PERSON: I didn't think I had seen you before. Is that your baby?

WOMAN: Yes.

OLD PERSON (*looking into the carriage*): Such a perfect baby. Not so old, right? Perhaps six months?

WOMAN: Eight.

OLD PERSON: And what is her or his name?

WOMAN: Hans.

OLD PERSON: Hans? That was my father's name. You are perhaps from the old country?

(*She doesn't answer. She seems to be drawing into herself.*)

So am I. But when did you come over? Before the war?
(*She nods her head.*)
After? Oh, after. I came before the war.

WOMAN: What do you mean? Did you escape?

OLD PERSON: Yes. I had some money and when Crystal Night happened, we made plans.

WOMAN: My parents weren't so lucky. (*Her bare arm turns to the old person and the tattoo is visible.*)

OLD PERSON: Oh, Mein Gott. Where were you?

WOMAN: Does it matter? I am here now.

OLD PERSON: But the rest of your family . . .

WOMAN: Gone. Please, must we say any more?

OLD PERSON: Of course not.

WOMAN: Yes, I love the view from here. It is like the Goethe poem, "Kennst du das Land . . ."

OLD PERSON: Yes. ". . . ein sanfter Wind vom blauen Himmel weht . . ."

WOMAN: Yes. And now we can talk. I would like that, but no more about the tattoo, right?

OLD PERSON: Yes. Because you have one but the baby doesn't. (*She nods in agreement.*)

Scene K

Just for variety, a scene for four wealthy women in a fashionable beauty shop. This is a very specific place. Also, the women should be carefully differentiated.

ONE: Pass me that magazine.

TWO: What?

ONE: The magazine you just put down.

TWO: Okay.

THREE: Is it true the Fowlers are getting a divorce?

TWO: That's what I heard.

FOUR: Is she here today?

THREE: I hope to hell not. We can't talk if she is.

ONE: Incompatibility?

TWO: What?

ONE (*addressing the others*): Incompatibility?

TWO: No, I heard she's toughing it out. Adultery.

ONE: Good lord. Why would she want to do that? Get it into all the papers.

TWO: She had proof and she hates his guts.

ONE: I can understand hating his guts, he's just naturally unattractive, but that's a messy way to go.

THREE: But you can get more in the settlement, and you're bound to get the kids.

ONE: Messy, messy.

TWO: I heard she wasn't all that pure herself. They were both playing around.

THREE: Where the hell did you hear that?

TWO: I didn't hear it, I saw it.

THREE: Well, you're not going to get me to tell my sources, but I think she had plenty of provocation for whatever she did, and she took it for one hell of a long time before she cheated on him and then only once or twice.

ONE: Jesus, I didn't know you two were that close.

THREE: We were and are.

TWO: Ta-ta.

THREE: What the hell do you mean, ta-ta?

TWO: Just that. You really get around.

THREE: Hand me that magazine.

ONE: Come on, let's not get into a fight. Let's keep it light. What's he like?

TWO: Who?

ONE: Hank Fowler.

THREE: You said he was just naturally unattractive.

ONE: I know. But the truth is I really don't know him, I'm just passing along what I've heard.

THREE: I'm the wrong one to ask. I like her.

TWO: I just heard. I don't know them all that well.

ONE (*to* FOUR): Do you know him?

FOUR: What?

ONE: I said, do you know Hank Fowler?

FOUR (*softly*): Yes.

ONE: Well, what's he like? Is he a horny son-of-a-bitch who deserves to get taken in a court of law by an indignant wife and an aroused constabulary?

(*All but* FOUR *laugh.*)

Well?

FOUR: No.

Figure 3-5.   John Offerman, 1982.

TWO: No, what?

FOUR: He isn't.

ONE: Isn't . . .

FOUR: He's probably the finest man I've ever known. Gentle, thoughtful, the kind of lover you'll never have. He just has one thing wrong with him, a vicious, aggressive, backbiting wife who never treated him like he was anything but dirt. He took it for ten years and finally rebelled.

THREE (*under dryer*): What did she say?

TWO: Shut up, Mabel.

ONE: Just shut up.

THREE: What's going on here?

(*A pause.*)

TWO: She knows him.

(*A pause.*)

FOUR: Just read your newspaper when you get it. It will all be there.

TWO: Honey . . .

FOUR: Don't "honey" me, you bitch. But I'll get out of here, so you'll feel free to talk.

Summary

Our final scene is taken from Shakespeare, whose plays represent the greatest challenge for theatre artists in our language. We will use the scene to review the techniques taught in this chapter. The opening speech uses honesty, the scene between Lady Percy and Hotspur uses both honesty and subtext, and the problems of characterization lie in the language, manners, and period of the play. You may want to do research. If so, begin by reading it in a critical work that gives backgrounds and carefully explains the language; then move on to criticism. Almost all libraries have good collections of the works and criticism of Shakespeare.

In other words, you can make this project as difficult as you wish, but, to begin with, approach it as a scene in which a character tells us honestly of his feelings about affairs in which he is involved. It then develops into an intimate scene between two attractive people. Kate knows her husband and realizes that she can't prevent his leaving, but she would like to delay the moment. Try not to be poetic, but adjust to the fact that you can't flatten Shakespeare into prose. Language is one of those elements of Elizabethan drama which is larger than life and is not to be hidden or ignored but to be cherished.

Henry IV, Part I, Act II, Scene III

Enter HOTSPUR, *reading a letter.*

But for mine own part, my lord, I could be well contented to be there, in respect of the love I bear your house.

He could be contented; why is he not then? In respect of the love he bears our house: he shows in this he loves his own barn better than he loves our house. Let me see some more.

The purpose you undertake is dangerous:

Why that's certain: 'tis dangerous to take a cold, to sleep, to drink; but I tell you, my lord fool, out of this nettle, danger, we pluck this flower, safety.

The purpose you undertake is dangerous; the friends you have named uncertain; the time itself unsorted; and your whole plot too light for the counterpoise of so great an opposition.

Say you so, say you so? I say unto you again, you are a shallow cowardly hind, and you lie. What a lack-brain is this! By the Lord, our plot is a good plot as ever was laid; our friends true and constant: a good plot, good friends, and full of expectation; an excellent plot, very good friends. What a frosty-spirited rogue is this! Why, my Lord of York commends the plot and the general course of the action. 'Zounds! An I were now by this rascal, I could brain him with his lady's fan. Is there not my father, my uncle, and myself? Lord Edmund Mortimer, my Lord of York, and Owen Glendower? Is there not besides the Douglas? Have I not all their letters to meet me in arms by the ninth of the next month, and are they not some of them set forward already? What a pagan rascal is this! an infidel! Ha! you shall see now in very sincerity of fear and cold heart, will he to the king and lay open all our proceedings. O! I could divide myself and go to buffets, for moving such a dish of skim milk with so honourable an action. Hang him! let him tell the king; we are prepared. I will set forward to-night.

(*Enter* LADY PERCY.)

How now, Kate! I must leave you within these two hours.

LADY PERCY: O, my good lord! why are you thus alone?
For what offence have I this fortnight been
A banish'd woman from my Harry's bed?
Tell me, sweet lord, what is't that takes from thee
Thy stomach, pleasure, and thy golden sleep?
Why dost thou bend thine eyes upon the earth,
And start so often when thou sitt'st alone?
Why hast thou lost the fresh blood in they cheeks,
And given my treasures and my rights of thee
To thick-eyed musing and curst melancholy?

In thy faint slumbers I by thee have watch'd,
And heard thee murmur tales of iron wars,
Speak terms of manage to thy bounding steed,
Cry, 'Courage! to the field!' And thou hast talk'd
Of sallies and retires, of trenches, tents,
Of palisadoes, frontiers, parapets,
Of basilisks, of cannon, culverin,
Of prisoners' ransom, and of soldiers slain,
And all the currents of a heady fight.
Thy spirit within thee hath been so at war,
And thus hath so bestirr'd thee in thy sleep,
That beads of sweat have stood upon thy brow,
Like bubbles in a late-disturbed stream;
And in thy face strange motions have appear'd,
Such as we see when men restrain their breath
On some great sudden hest. O! what portents are these?
Some heavy business hath my lord in hand,
And I must know it, else he loves me not.

HOTSPUR: What, ho!

(*Enter* SERVANT.)

Is Gilliams with the packet gone?

SERVANT: He is, my lord, an hour ago.

HOTSPUR: Hath Butler brought those horses from the sheriff?

SERVANT: One horse, my lord, he brought even now.

HOTSPUR: What horse? a roan, a crop-ear, is it not?

SERVANT: It is, my lord.

HOTSPUR: That roan shall be my throne.
    Well, I will back him straight: O, *Esperance!*
    Bid Butler lead him forth into the park.

(*Exit* SERVANT.)

LADY PERCY: But hear you, my lord.

HOTSPUR: What sayst thou, my lady?

LADY PERCY: What is it carries you away?

HOTSPUR: Why, my horse, my love, my horse.

LADY PERCY: Out, you mad-headed ape!
    A weasel hath not such a deal of spleen
    As you are toss'd with. In faith,
    I'll know your business, Harry, that I will.
    I fear my brother Mortimer doth stir
    About his title, and hath sent for you
    To line his enterprise. But if you go—

HOTSPUR: So far afoot, I shall be weary, love.

LADY PERCY: Come, come, you paraquito, answer me
Directly unto this question that I ask.
In faith, I'll break thy little finger, Harry,
An if thou wilt not tell me all things true.

HOTSPUR: Away,
Away, you trifler! Love! I love thee not,
I care not for thee, Kate: this is no world
To play with mammets and to tilt with lips;
We must have bloody noses and crack'd crowns,
And pass them current too. God's me, my horse!
What sayst thou, Kate? what wouldst thou have with me?

LADY PERCY: Do you not love me? do you not, indeed?
Well, do not, then; for since you love me not,
I will not love myself. Do you not love me?
Nay, tell me if you speak in jest or no.

HOTSPUR: Come, wilt thou see me ride?
And when I am o' horseback, I will swear
I love thee infinitely. But hark you, Kate;
I must not have you henceforth question me
Whither I go, nor reason whereabout.
Whither I must, I must; and, to conclude,
This evening must I leave you, gentle Kate.
I know you wise; but yet no further wise
Than Harry Percy's wife: constant you are,
But yet a woman: and for secrecy,
No lady closer; for I well believe
Thou wilt not utter what thou dost not know;
And so far will I trust thee, gentle Kate.

LADY PERCY: How! so far?

HOTSPUR: Not an inch further. But, hark you, Kate;
Whither I go, thither shall you go too;
To-day will I set forth, to-morrow you.
Will this content you, Kate?

LADY PERCY: It must, of force.

(*Exeunt.*)

Additional Exercises

The three plays included in this text can be used for acting exercises, but it should be done after they have been read and studied for production planning. Also, note the excerpt from *Hamlet* that opens the chapter on playwriting. The best source for additional scenes would probably come from the playwriting exercises for students in the same chapter.

A Selective Bibliography on Acting

Benedetti, Robert. *The Actor at Work.* Englewood Cliffs, New Jersey: Prentice-Hall, 1969.

Chekhov, Michael. *To the Actor: On the Technique of Acting.* New York: Harper and Row, Pub., 1953.

Cole, Toby and Helen Krich Chinoy. *Actors on Acting.* New York: Crown Publishers, 1970.

Hagen, Uta and Haskel Frankel. *Respect for Acting.* New York: Macmillan, 1973.

McGaw, Charles. *Acting Is Believing.* New York: Holt, Rinehart & Winston, 4th ed., 1980.

Skinner, Edith and Timothy Monich. *Good Speech for the American Actor.* New York: Drama Book Specialists. (Text and Cassette.)

Stanislavski, Konstantin S. *An Actor Prepares.* Tr. Elizabeth Reynolds Hapgood. New York: Theatre Arts Books, 1936.

_____. *Creating a Role.* Tr. E. R. Hapgood. New York: Theatre Arts Books, 1961.

_____. *My Life in Art.* Tr. J. J. Robbins. New York: Theatre Arts Books, 1948.

Henrik Ibsen in the Cafe of the Grand Hotel at Kristiania by Edvard Munch, 1898.
(Oslo National Art Collection.)

4

The Playwright

HAMLET: What! The fair Ophelia.

QUEEN: Sweets to the sweet: farewell! (*Scattering flowers*)
    I hop'd thou shouldst have been my Hamlet's wife;
    I thought thy bride-bed to have deck'd, sweet maid,
    And not have strew'd thy grave.

LAERTES: O! treble woe
    Fall ten times treble on that cursed head
    Whose wicked deed thy most ingenious sense
    Depriv'd thee of. Hold off the earth awhile.
    Till I have caught her once more in my arms. (*Leaps into the grave.*)

    Now pile your dust upon the quick and dead,
    Till of this flat a mountain you have made,
    To o'er-top old Pelion or the skyish head
    Of blue Olympus.

HAMLET (*advancing*): What is he whose grief
    Bears such an emphasis? Whose phrase of sorrow
    Conjures the wandering stars, and makes them stand
    Like wonder-wounded hearers? this is I,
    Hamlet the Dane. (*Leaps into the grave.*)

LAERTES: The devil take thy soul! (*Grapples with him*)

HAMLET: Thou pray'st not well.
    I prithee, take thy fingers from my throat!
    For though I am not splenetive and rash
    Yet have I in me something dangerous,
    Which let thy wisdom fear. Away thy hand!

KING: Pluck them asunder.

QUEEN: Hamlet! Hamlet!

ALL: Gentlemen,—

Shakespeare, *Hamlet* (Act V. Scene i)

The best-known definition of drama is found in Aristotle's *Poetics*. It separates drama from other forms of poetry in terms of its means, objects, and manner. A play, Aristotle says, imitates an action; its objects are good or bad men, and it avoids mixing narrative with action.

Most of us are used to the sort of author's voice found in novels and short stories, where narrative and descriptive passages are mixed with dialogue. The movies and television combine action with voice-overs and unusual camera angles and sudden shifts of time and place. The kinds of plays we will be using as examples in this discussion use stage time as real time, have relatively few locales, and will use a curtain or a blackout to indicate a change in time and place. Admittedly, the printed program for a production may give information which cannot be provided by the play itself, and the play we quoted from at the outset, *Hamlet*, uses special stage conventions to establish place and time. However, most theatre, even Shakespeare's, obeys Aristotle's warning about mixing action and narration in a play.

What your audience will expect when they come to a play you produce is: (1) that in two hours or slightly more they will be given a series of scenes in which stage time is real time; (2) that the action will tell a connected story that seems to be happening as they watch it; (3) that there will be characters to whom they can relate; and (4) that the action will lead to a climax and resolution, which will grow logically out of what has gone before. (Also, we make the assumption that the audience will realize that the actors and technicians are doing this performance for them.)

Given this description, how would one approach playwriting? There have been many books written about how to write a play. There is probably the same relationship between these prescriptions and playwriting as there is between most cookbooks and gourmet cooking. A play is not a series of answers to problems of technique, but such an approach helps us to define our problems and creates a structure in which to work, though it doesn't answer the need for subjective and creative responses to materials. In this chapter we will define many terms used in playwriting. We will show how to adapt a short story, and will discuss the most common styles of literature and how they are used in theatre—but don't make the mistake of thinking that these represent the art of playwriting.

Action, Conflict, and Character

First and foremost, think of playwriting in terms of **Action.** Some play scripts have surprisingly little dialogue. They are primarily descriptions of **Action,** as is the case with Samuel Beckett's short mime plays, *Act Without Words I* and *Act Without Words II.* Even the quotation from *Hamlet* with which the chapter opened is an action first and its character and plot values, as well as poetic utterance, come about because of what is happening. However, if you think that **Action** means the strenuous grappling of this particular Shakespearean scene, read Pirandello's *Man with a Flower in his Mouth* or Albee's *Zoo Story.*

Some of the greatest moments in theatre are those in which action and dialogue become one and the same. Language becomes gesture and action becomes statement. In his notes for *Camino Real,* Tennessee Williams alludes to such a moment:

> I hate writing that is a parade of images for the sake of images; I hate it so much that I close a book in disgust when it keeps on saying one thing is like another; I even get disgusted with poems that make nothing but comparisons between one thing and another. But I repeat that symbols, when used respectfully, are the purest language of plays. Sometimes it would take page after tedious page of exposition to put across an idea that can be put across with an object or a gesture on the lighted stage.

To take one case in point: the battered portmanteau of Jacques Casanova is hurled from the balcony of a luxury hotel when his remittance check fails to come through. While the portmanteau is still in the air, he shouts, "Careful I have —" and when it has crashed to the street he continues — "Fragile mementoes. . . ." I suppose that this is a symbol, at least it is an object used to express as directly and vividly as possible certain things which could be said in pages of dull talk.[1]

What is it that we are describing as **Action** or calling compressed or symbolic? It is clearly a quality, not a thing, and is as difficult to define as wind. You have to rattle leaves, move clouds across a sky, cause a drop in pressure, and ring porch chimes to define wind. The same is true of **Action.** It is what is done by characters or things on stage. It obviously should go beyond "running in place," "building a barn and tearing it down," or "sitting and standing." The playwright Maeterlinck experimented with what he called "static" theatre, and tried to convince people that a man sitting without moving or speaking could be dramatic. It was obviously a theatre game and would work if taken in the context of our usual expectations of **Action:** that it be overt instead of kinetic. We started with Hamlet and Laertes grappling in the grave of Ophelia and we could still be describing action by ending with the bedridden hero of *Whose Life Is it Anyway?*

In drama, what gives further meaning to **Action** are **Conflict** and **Character. Conflict** is a way of shaping action and **Character** is the means of expressing the **Action.** Let's imagine a scenario: two men are trapped in a room and hunting for a way to get out. There are people trying to keep them in. If we care about the men, we want them to get out. If, after setting up this action, we simply have the men push against the door to their cell and it opens and they are free, we are disappointed. Our expectations have not been fulfilled. We feel that it should take more time, and should involve something more than a direct line from the statement of the problem to the resolution ("We're stuck in this cell." "How shall we get out?" "Look, the door's open.") What we actually want are **Complications.** The bars and the door are electrified. There is smoke coming into the cell. The two men begin to argue with one another about which of them is responsible for their being there. But then they realize that danger is too close; they must cooperate. Finally, they seem to come up with a solution. It doesn't work. Time is passing. The poisonous smoke is rising in the cell. They think of one more solution, and it works! But to be satisfying, this resolution of the problem must answer certain needs. Is it logical? Did it grow out of information given about the people, the place, and the problem? It shouldn't just be fortunate or far-fetched. We make fun of the amazing appearance of a rescue helicopter or the cavalry. In order for an audience to feel its "vikies" (a term I first heard Lee

---

[1]Tennessee Williams, *Three Plays of Tennessee Williams.* Copyright 1948, 1953 by Tennessee Williams. Reprinted by permission of New Directions Publishing Corporation.

Marvin use to describe "vicarious thrills"), they must care about the people and believe in their rescues.

More Terms

There are many other terms, not the least of which is **Irony.** This may be the root concept, the one that all ritual, role play, and drama are about. The origins of the word are interesting. It comes from the Greek *eirein*, to speak, but the word also has the connotation of dissembling, that is to pretend or make something up. In Greek comedy the *eiron* was the frail, resourceful, sly comic who would trick the bragging soldier (*alazon*, later *miles gloriosus*). The pranks he played on this self-satisfied clod were called *eironeia*. His favorite trick was to make the soldier believe he was as weak as he appeared to be. Shall we say he was "crazy like a fox"? Nowadays, when we mention **Irony** we generally mean a situation in which the audience is aware of something unknown to a character on stage. A wonderful example of this happened in a sequence in the movie *Jaws*. The sheriff, a scientist, and the captain had been patrolling the shore waters, hunting for the giant shark. The other two had gone below when the sheriff started throwing out buckets of bait from the stern. Suddenly the shark rose from the water, enormous jaws and bulk filling the screen, and then dropped back into the water and disappeared. The sheriff staggered into the cabin and when the other two looked up, obviously unaware of his experience, he told them, "We're gonna need a bigger boat." Another kind of irony was used in the same film when, after establishing that the theme would be played every time the shark was to appear, it was played and the shark didn't present itself.

One is tempted to think that **Irony** is the context in which all drama occurs, because drama is a game played with the audience. Even the music used at the beginning of a film and the type of credits that appear suggest the nature of the particular game to be played. Can you imagine *Apocalypse Now* being introduced with *Pink Panther*-style credits and music?

In Western drama there are probably two types of plots. These are what John Gassner called "closed" and "open" dramas. The first are those tightly structured, sequential plots with their accepted ways of introducing characters, action, the causal connection of events, climax, and resolution. *Oedipus Rex* is a "closed" drama, as is *Death of a Salesman*. "Open" would describe such episodic plays as *Trojan Women*, *Tamburlaine*, and most television series that use the same characters and basic situation again and again. *Star Trek*, *All in the Family*, and *M*A*S*H* are excellent modern examples of this type of plotting. When "open" drama is well written, it develops the characters through a series of pithy, self-contained actions or episodes. It should be noted that this is also the technique utilized in the great epics of our culture, such as *The Odyssey*, *The Aeneid*, and *Beowulf*.

As we have already noted, in "closed" drama the action is completed in one play. The problem is stated at the outset, usually in terms of the characters, and then we move through complications and reversals to a climax and resolution. If you wonder why we have complications, just imagine where we would be if Hamlet were to make up his mind to attack or run in the first act. The play would simply end. In a well-constructed closed drama the reasons for the central character's indecision or the obstacles that prevent the solution of the problem must be reasonable, growing out of both the situation and the characters. What happens in *Oedipus Rex* is both logical and human. In a very real sense, character leads to action, and though there may be surprises for the audience, they are always possible in terms of what has gone before.

As we have noted, one of the three keys to successful drama is interesting characterization. This is probably not as important in comedy, where more emphasis is often placed on plot and stereotypes, though it never hurts for us to care about important characters. What makes a character interesting is not necessarily his or her positive qualities. The central figure may be a scoundrel, a rotter, a monster, but must be interesting to the audience. Hollywood has traditionally hedged its bets on films by accepting this truth and following a policy of casting popular actors in roles similar to ones that have done well at the box office in the past.

Suspense is simply delayed climax. Complications seem to be the easiest way to achieve this, but they can't be arbitrary, and they must make sense not only in terms of the situation that has been set up but also in terms of the behavior of the characters. I suppose you could graph **Suspense** by plotting the amount of pull it would take to yank a novel out of your hands every ten pages or fifteen minutes. Skillful authors create a suspense line that has ups and downs but generally tends to rise to the climax.

What of the subject matter for a play? Probably the choice is unimportant. We can all think of plays on the unlikeliest subjects that have caught audiences' attention because of the way they are written. Beginning playwrights often spend too much time hunting for the right plot or the most interesting characters. It's the wrong search. The fact that a story is about historically important people or cataclysmic events doesn't insure that it will be effective. *Our Town, The Time of Your Life, All the Way Home,* and *The Effect of Gamma Rays on Man-in-the-Moon Marigolds* are all plays on seemingly ordinary, nondramatic subjects, too low key to hold an audience's attention. All are also Pulitzer Prize-winning plays. There does seem to be one prohibition, however, and that concerns plays about beginning playwrights by beginning playwrights. Having said this I'm glad that James Joyce paid no attention to the general prohibition and wrote the novel *Portrait of the Artist as a Young Man.*

By way of summary, let's make a schematic of a typical three-act, realistic play. As we said before, our intention in this and the preceding discussion is not to provide you with a recipe for writing a play but to give you useful

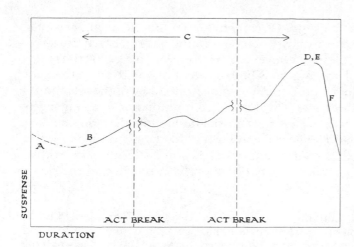

Figure 4-1. Graph of typical realistic play.

terminology for understanding the technique of playwriting. The play could be diagrammed in this way:

(A) represents the opening of the play with its exposition, introduction of the characters, and statement of the "problem." Generally, audiences are interested and excited at the beginning of a drama and willing to give it a chance. However, before (B), the inciting incident or the beginning of the action, there may be some flagging of interest, particularly if the exposition seems to take too long. (C) is the line of the action, seen in this case as rising action. The wavy line indicates the way our attention and interest rise and fall as complications interrupt the line from the statement of the problem to its resolution, and how we react as complications are resolved. It probably has to do with the nature of our nervous systems, but we could not sustain intense excitement even if a playwright were able to put it in a script.

Often, realistic dramas close each act with a strong action that is a "cliff hanger" type of ending. You might refer to a modern play, Jason Miller's *That Championship Season*, for this time-honored use of curtain lines. In most plays, near the end of the line of action there is an **Obligatory Scene,** a scene which we have been expecting. In some cases this could also be described as a **Confrontation** and it may or may not also be the **Climax** of the play. However, after the **Obligatory** scene or **Confrontation** and the **Climax** (D, E), what remains is the resolution and wrapping up, literally the "untying" implied by the term **Denouement** (F).

The Adaptation

One of the best ways to acquaint beginners with playwriting is to have them adapt a realistic short story. This not only is good for tyros but is also practiced by established playwrights. Of contemporary American playwrights, Arthur Miller has adapted plays by Ibsen, Van Itallie has rewritten Chekhov, and Edward Albee has adapted a novella by Carson McCullers for the stage. In other words, the art of adaptation is both a valuable way to learn the craft and to keep one's hand in. I would like to demonstrate some of the techniques of adaptation using a short story by Joseph Conrad, one of our language's greatest authors (whose works have now passed into public domain, incidentally). The story is entitled *Tomorrow*, and I would recommend that you read it in its entirety. Part of its charm and power lies in its leisurely narrative style, something which probably cannot be literally translated to the stage. First, a synopsis of the story:

> An old seafarer, Captain Hagberd, several years before had settled in the seacoast town of Colebrook. He built a duplex and rented one side to Blind Carvil and his unmarried daughter, Bessie. Over the years Hagberd has become something of a local character, what with his heavy canvas clothing and his vagueness about the realities of life. He is a private man, but he has an obsession which he has increasingly shared with the young woman from next door: that his son will be coming home "tomorrow." He has bought furniture and garden tools, for instance, which are stored in his house against that day. He has also infected Bessie with his dream and the young, single woman has come to believe that somehow her own future is tied to the imminent appearance of the son. Her father, Blind Carvil, is a petty tyrant, and mad old Hagberd and his shared dream are her only comfort.
>
> Then one day a young man comes down the street. It's Harry Hagberd, back to get what is his. The old Captain doesn't recognize him, or else refuses to, but Bessie is clearly overwhelmed by a dream come true. She cannot see, as we do, that Harry has no interest in her and is driven by hatred for the old man. But he is quite willing to borrow money from her, kiss her, and then leave. . . .

Almost half of the short story has been told before the appearance of the son. The characters have been described, as have the place and past events, and a number of brief scenes are presented that develop the relationship between the two old men, between Carvil and his daughter, and the Captain and Bessie. In a dramatic adaptation, these fifteen pages might come down to the following:

TOMORROW

CHARACTERS (in order of appearance)

CAPTAIN HAGBERD, an old, mad man

BESSIE CARVIL, his neighbor and friend, a spinster

JOSIAH CARVIL, her father, a blind man

HARRY HAGBERD, the Captain's long-absent son

> The yards in front of two ugly, brick houses which overlook the small harbor of Colebrook, England. Stage left, the porches and doors of the

duplex; center stage, the yards and a fence which divides them for a short distance from the houses; stage right, a road, Colebrook, and the world.

AT CURTAIN: CAPTAIN HAGBERD is puttering in his yard, spading, planning the arrangement and planting of the vegetables for his garden, and sharpening and cleaning his shovel. He looks toward the Carvil house (down left) occasionally, as though he expected someone. Finally, he stops and calls out:

Note the descriptions of the characters in the script. There will be other parentheticals within the script to help the actors, director, and designer, but basically the description of Captain Hagberd is a matter of the dialogue chosen for him from Conrad's story or adapted by the playwright. Conrad has taken his time to define this character. In one passage he wrote,

> He appeared, with the colour and uncouth stiffness of the extraordinary material in which he chose to clothe himself — "for the time being" would be his mumbled remark to any observation on the subject — like a man roughened out of granite, standing in a wilderness not big enough for a decent billiard-room. A heavy figure of a man of stone, with a red handsome face, a blue wandering eye, and a great white beard flowing to his waist and never trimmed as far as Colebrook knew.

There is no time for this sort of description either in the introduction to the play or in another character's speech about the Captain.

A number of scenes between the Captain and Bessie have developed their relationship before the arrival late in the story of Harry, the Captain's son. As Conrad clearly describes it, in the "intimacy" of their backyards the two are growing closer and closer. For the adaptation, it is necessary to find a point of attack that will allow one scene to serve for many without distorting the author's intention.

> CAPTAIN (*softly, then stronger, then softly*): Bessie! Bessie! Bessie!. (He waits a moment and then turns back to his work. A young woman steps out of the house. She is in her mid-thirties but is pallid, weary, and dry. She likes the old man.)
>
> BESSIE: Yes, Captain? Did you call me?
>
> CAPTAIN (*very pleased*): There you are! Your father?
>
> BESSIE: I'll just stay a moment . . . Have you been planting your garden?
>
> CAPTAIN: Yes, indeed I have!
>
> BESSIE: You decided where to put the potatoes?
>
> CAPTAIN: Yes.
>
> BESSIE: And the onions and carrots and radishes?
>
> CAPTAIN: I thought the two of us should decide that.
>
> BESSIE: Where will the potatoes go?
>
> CAPTAIN: Over there. Where the dirt is deepest and freest of stones. They need good loose ground to grow in and we can mound it up. It's still out of the shadow of the house in the morning.

BESSIE: And the rest?

CAPTAIN: You'd better decide. You have a woman's eye for nice things, like the flowers in your yard. You tell me where and when the time comes I can set up string for the rows.

BESSIE (*Moves about the yard, thinking*): Onions and carrots and radishes?

CAPTAIN: And a few pepper plants. They're pretty growing even if they don't usually ripen properly.

BESSIE: Let's make rows along this fence——

CAPTAIN: Bessie, how often do I have to tell you there will be no fence.

BESSIE: Oh, yes. Well, I'd put them over there, like they were flowers with a curve in the rows to go around those bushes and the radishes in the front because they're shortest and then the onions and the carrots. Put the pepper plants behind them, spaced out where they'll get the most sunlight.

CAPTAIN: And maybe a few lettuces between them and the potatoes?

BESSIE: Of course. They're so pretty growing.

CAPTAIN: We'll start tomorrow.

When Bessie turns and asks him to repeat what he just said, the old man says, "We'll start planting tomorrow. When Harry gets here." And then, significantly, "You'll be so good for him." She is embarrassed. "Captain, you shouldn't talk like that." But she is flattered and completely caught up in the old man's fantasy. "CAPTAIN: It's the truth."

The action continues with a scene in which Blind Carvil takes Bessie into the house with him, demonstrating the conflict between the two old men, and then Harry appears at the head of the street. When he speaks to old Hagberd in the yard, the Captain reacts violently. But we can't be sure whether he has really recognized the young man or not, and when Harry presses him, the Captain runs into his house. Later, there is a scene with Bessie, the obligatory scene, and then the final moments of the adaptation:

HARRY (*turning on him and driving him toward the door*): Sixteen years! You drove me out and now you'd drive me off again. And not a cent any time, you blood-sucking old skinflint!

CAPTAIN: Bessie, Bessie, this isn't our Harry.

HARRY: It's mine, I tell you. Every cent that went into this rabbit hutch of a house is rightfully mine——

(*The old man darts inside as* HARRY *advances.*)

——Do you see what he's done to me?

(BESSIE *is close to tears.*)

BESSIE: Please, please, please.

HARRY (*still furious*): You and the old man had it all figured. You were going to buy a husband and he was going to buy a son.

BESSIE: No!

HARRY: Well, you can't. (*He grabs her by the arms roughly.*) I damn near was sold on that week.

BESSIE (*taking the money from her jacket pocket when he eases his hold on her*):

Take this and go away. For god's sake. Leave us alone and don't ever come back!

(*He holds the money in his hand for a moment, thinking.*)

HARRY: You get it back from the old man.

BESSIE: No!

HARRY (*shaking the money at the* CAPTAIN's *window*): See this, old man? You can't buy me in, this time. And you can't buy yourself out. (*His smile returns as he turns to* BESSIE.) And now you need a receipt. (*He lifts her off the ground and kisses her passionately. He holds her for a long moment.* CARVIL *enters, groping for voices and sounds.*)

BLIND CARVIL: Buy? What does he mean, Bessie? Bessie?

(*The kiss ends and* BESSIE *stands stunned as* HARRY *backs off right, throws her a kiss, and then exits quickly and gracefully. She comes slowly to her senses.*)

BESSIE (*helplessly*): Don't go! Stop! Don't go!

BLIND CARVIL: Who? Bessie, who are you talking to? That stranger?

CAPTAIN (*coming out of his door furtively*): Is he off my property?

BLIND CARVIL: What did he look like?

BESSIE: He's gone. He won't ever come back.

CAPTAIN: Good girl. You frightened him away. Now we shall be all right. Don't be impatient, my dear. Just one more day.

BLIND CARVIL: Bessie! Bessie! Take me inside.

BESSIE (*weeping*): Keep quiet . . . I'll be there in a minute.

CAPTAIN (*utterly oblivious to her crying*): Tomorrow, Bessie. Tomorrow. *Our* Harry's coming tomorrow.

Curtain.

Styles in Drama

Another concern when writing adaptations or original plays are those generally understood types of literature that are usually referred to as "styles." Most of these also function as conventions in the theatre. We have already mentioned two, realism and naturalism, and there are several more, but before discussing them, let's publish the same warning. These are interesting concepts, but they should be used as a means to an end, not as the end itself. To be familiar with styles is to understand an important part of the vocabulary of our field. As has been said again and again, theatre is so diverse in terms of its skills and arts that we need a language which will cut across disciplines. The notion of styles of art is accepted in architecture, painting, musical composition, and writing of all kinds. The difficulty is not that these terms are not used broadly but that they are often used indiscriminately.

Realism is the most prevalent style in modern literature and drama. It can be said to grow out of a materialistic society's self-absorption. There have been a number of variations in the dramaturgy of realistic plays over the centuries, but basically what we have today comes from the well-made play of the eighteenth and nineteenth centuries and a tradition that goes back to the Greeks. The usual realistic play is characterized by features we have described in this chapter.

The term **Naturalism** has a confusing number of uses. However, in theatre we usually mean that type of drama which began in France at the close of the nineteenth century as a protest against certain social practices and the popular well-made plays of the time. What occurred was that a number of well-known authors (preeminently Zola) challenged the argument that certain people remained impoverished, uneducated, and miserably housed and clothed because of their innate inferiority. These reformers argued, instead, that one's environment is more of an influence upon the individual than genetic endowment. This was a revolutionary idea. What if the "haves" were morally responsible for the condition of the "have-nots"? What if providing education and adequate housing for the poor were to be thought of as justice, not charity? Naturalistic authors attempted to put these ideas into plays, short stories, and novels, using what they described as the scientific method to lay out the facts. Dramaturgically, what this meant was that plays seemed to start and end arbitrarily, letting events take place as they did in life, randomly and sometimes out of logical sequence. The authors tried to avoid pointing out the moral. It was impossible, of course, for these writers to come up with truly unstructured, objective plays that could serve as the raw data for scientific conclusions. Naturalistic dramas usually focused on the lives of the poor and were set in detailed, unpleasant surroundings. Several of the most famous are Gorky's *The Lower Depths*, Hauptmann's *The Weavers*, and O'Neill's *The Iceman Cometh*. In art, the so-called Ashcan School of American painters is an example of this style. In movies, *The Grapes of Wrath* and *On the Waterfront* provide two examples. The brilliant images of the Great Depression by Walker Evans in James Agee's *Let Us Now Praise Famous Men* give us an example of naturalism as interpreted by photography.

Impressionism has a very precise meaning in art. It refers to those European painters, primarily French, who experimented in the nineteenth century with a technique in painting that is the artistic equivalent of the physiological facts of how we see. They tried a number of ways to accomplish this, the most prevalent of which is seen in paintings by Monet and Renoir. It involved applying dabs of primary color to the canvas and allowing the eye of the viewer to mix the colors to the hues seen in nature. There was also an intense interest in views of nature, the ordinary seen as unusual, and a fascination with catching the unguarded moment. In drama, this same term is frequently used to describe those plays that attempt to capture the moment, downplay the well-written play and plot, and try to imitate the rhythms of everyday experience and conversation. Sometimes the term **Naturalism** is used for this type of theatre as well, but the principal difference would be the tendency of **Impressionistic** plays to describe the lives of any class of people and avoid a political point of view. The plays that would best exemplify this kind of convention in modern times would be by Anton Chekhov, though a case could also be made for Arthur Miller's *A Memory of Two Mondays* and *Death of a Salesman* (particularly in view of its treatment of fragmented time), and Tennessee Williams' *The Glass Menagerie* and *Summer and Smoke*. It should be mentioned that scene designers have often created settings for such plays that function visually in much the same way, that is they are fragmented, suggestive, and often make use of lighting and scrims to create mood and place. In support of **Impressionism** and in order to undercut the usual interpretation of the term as meaning something "like" life and not life, it can be argued that the way the convention works is probably much closer to the actual way in which we recall events or perceive them as they happen. We have an "impression" and rationalize from this according to our other needs. For example, people rarely recall falling in love in unpleasant surroundings, nor do they feel that significant events can be reduced to a literal transcription of the same event.

Expressionism should, literally, be dated from that period early in the twentieth century when Sigmund Freud began to exert a powerful influence over popular culture. Much of his writing does have the force of a lesson already anticipated by the reader. While the impulse toward **Expressionism** had always existed, Freud gave it a form and an importance not known before. In prose, Franz Kafka spoke to the same issues.

Basically, **Expressionism** is that form of drama which describes the feelings, usually morbid, of the writer. The author generally has some knowledge of their pathology and makes an attempt to communicate these feelings to the audience by striking responsive chords. Scenery and lighting are used to "flesh out" the world of feelings; the fragmenting of dramatic through-lines and characterizations create an atmosphere of free association, surrealism, and nightmare-like linkings of the probable and improbable. Early in the movement the remarkable movie *The Cabinet of Doctor Caligari* was filmed, followed by Buñuel's and Dali's small masterpiece, *The Dog of Andalusia*. There were a number of German expressionistic authors and several Americans. Probably the most remarkable American expressionistic play is Eugene O'Neill's study of terror and atavism, *The Emperor Jones*. In a strange way, one could explain the power of **Expressionism** as growing from the same impulse that makes Realism so popular: its purported description of reality. It was particularly appealing to people of the troubled twenties and thirties to believe that this art form and Freud's treatises on abnormal personality were closer to the truth of human personality and experience than other styles.

Romanticism has been with us since classical times. Its characteristics should be familiar. The point of view of **Romanticism** is anthropocentric, that is man is the center of the universe. Nature reflects man's feelings and concerns; this is the so-called romantic fallacy. For example, if a **Romantic**

describes the crucifixion (read the appropriate chapter in *Ben-Hur* by Lew Wallace), there will be a terrible storm at the moment of Christ's death. One might think that contemporary **Romantics** are all involved in searching for proof of ESP, extraterrestrial invasions of the world by intelligent beings in the times of the pyramids, and UFOs. It should be remembered, however, that there was once a tradition of political and cultural importance attached to this posture. In this tradition the hero was seen as an outcast, an individual who fought against society, a man who practiced love and career as he wished, but who had a fatalistic view of his ability to prevail in a society contemptuous of outsiders. Nowadays, this attitude may be found in an occasional Clint Eastwood movie, but the sense of elevated expression and significance is all but lost.

Anti-Form drama of the last three decades (sometimes referred to as Existential or Absurdist drama) clearly derives much of its meaning from a reaction to other dramatic forms. Except in the hands of a few master writers, this has usually meant drama that was more "reaction" or "parody" than a statement of new directions. In drama, as in other forms of writing, creating new forms carries with it the responsibility of creating new rules (training the audience). In the past thirty years, at least three types of **Anti-Form** drama have appeared. The first is demonstrated in the plays of Ionesco and Beckett, which, while highly individualistic, show both a broad familiarity with what has been done before and a common affection for vaudeville and modern philosophical notions such as nihilism. Secondly, in the sixties, in both America and Europe, there was a rebirth of the political or "message" play, which some critics have described as "the convinced convincing the convinced." It used a wide range of impromptu events, partially scripted happenings, fully dramatized plays, and "readers theatre" but always with the primary intention of communicating a political point of view. However, there is at least one example during this period of a group's using a known theatrical convention as a vehicle for their message. The San Francisco Mime Troupe, widely acknowledged as one of the most notable of the agitprop groups of the sixties, made its politics clear but also did splendidly by *commedia dell'arte* as a living art form.

The third type of play might be called philosophical drama, and it has been developed and used by a great range of modern playwrights but most notably by three Frenchmen: Genet (*The Balcony*), Camus (*Caligula*), and Sartre (among other plays, *The Flies*). These plays may have seemed different to audiences used to the nonphilosophical content of most popular drama, but they were part of a tradition going as far back as Sophocles. In the case of Camus and Sartre the message was existential, and one wonders if many of the "new" features of their plays were not simply the result of imposing new philosophical interpretations on character and events in otherwise familiar dramatic forms. Other Anti-Form plays have seized the public imagination briefly, have been discussed by professionals and teachers for a little longer, and then have disappeared. As usual with a popular art form, the proof of a new type of play seems to be in its power to find either an audience or advocates and keep them. I have rarely talked to a theatre director who hasn't thought of a way to produce and direct *Peer Gynt, Danton's Death*, or *Ubu Roi*, all masterpieces with long histories of unsuccessful productions. Because these plays have strong advocates, you can be certain that someday they will have successful productions and find an audience.

Summary

We have described what drama is, dealt with the most important terminology used to describe the technique of the realistic play, and given an example of one of the most useful exercises for beginning playwrights: the adaptation of a short story into a play. We have also discussed *styles* of art, with an eye to developing your ability to talk across disciplines as well as to understand the flavor, technique, and concerns of different types of art. We are now ready to attempt a series of exercises. I would advise that these be done before attempting an adaptation; consider them warm-ups. Most of them address the problem of creativity, which you might think has been lost in the shuffle during our discussions of technique. Respond to these exercises intuitively or "off the top of your head." Now you should try your hand at being subjective, not objective.

Exercises

Exercise #1.   First, a variation on the Japanese verse form called *Haiku*. Let's write poems that are condensed, allusive, more interested in evoking the spirit of the thing described than commenting on its meaning, and use signals from several of the senses. Our rules will be these:

A. Describe an action as it is happening;

B. Don't concern yourself with rhyme or metre;

C. Draw from all of your senses, not just the usual ones of seeing and feeling;

D. Don't be afraid to tie words together in unusual combinations;

E. Let's force all of this to happen by limiting ourselves to as few as seventeen syllables and no more than twenty;

F. Imagine that every word, each approach to describing the action, each unusual combination of words or phrases is an echo of the thing itself. In combination, they hopefully will make the action live.

For example:

1. You shrug goodbye
   As acrid, hazy cigarette smoke
   Sways in the hollow
   Where you were.

2. Rough neck
   Reaches hungrily
   For the glinting knife
   And shouts red
   When they touch.

3. Smell clay
   Earth, flowers
   Death
   Sweat

   Hear Rage,
   Swords

   Flower/Sweat/Rage
   Sink to
   Dust

The characters and meaning are implied, but the **Action** takes place as you read it. The poem speaks to and from the senses. Try your own.

Exercise #2.   Write the **Exposition** scene for an unknown play. Don't worry about explaining who is who, or what's coming next. The scene should be short, not overly obvious, well-motivated, and lead to our wanting to know more. Start with a provocative line. For example,

HE: Did you hear what she said?

or,

SHE: Why don't you come by anymore?

or,

HE: It wasn't always like this.

Exercise #3.   Apparently Henrik Ibsen often wrote plays backwards, starting with the climax and then working forward to the beginning. Start with the climax of another unwritten play. Write the scene. Don't explain to the reader who the people are or what has happened leading up to this. Don't edit or tell your critic/self how crazy it is. Just write a climax.

Exercise #4.   In defining **Denouement,** we described it as that moment in a play when the climax has ended and the matter is resolved and explained. It is that moment in a television mystery when the private investigator tells his assistants why he knew what he knew. Or when Watson looks up, puzzled, and says, "I say, Holmes . . ."

This could also be a profoundly sad moment, as it is in *Three Sisters* when the women of the title stand on their front door stoop and watch the soldiers march away, and their hopes for their own lives leave with them. Try your own.

Exercise #5.   Take these three fragments, the **Exposition, Climax,** and **Denouement** and see if there might be ways to connect them. Do they stimulate your imagination? Is there a thread you could pick up and use to connect the three? If you find that this gives you a start in writing your own play, you are in good company. It is purported that this is one of the ways Tennessee Williams composed plays: quilting together vivid scenes which had been written without critical concern for how they would work in a larger context.

Exercise #6.   Write the scene that preceded or followed the action of one of the "open" scenes done in the section on acting.

Exercise #7.   Or to be more specific, let's explore other aspects of playwriting. Try these:

A. **Irony.** Write a scene in which two characters are plotting against a third, then have the third character enter.

B. **Time.** Put the pressure of time on a scene. Something serious will happen in just a few minutes. Make your scene literally that long.

C. **Action.** Describe an action that has no accompanying dialogue. Make it as complete and real as possible.

Exercise #8.   Outline a situation and then have several actors improvise it and interact with you on how to put it down on paper.

Further Study: Adaptations of Novels and Short Stories

Listed below are a series of excellent novels that have been successfully adapted for the stage. Read both the novel and the play.

Herman Melville's *Billy Budd;* Louis O. Coxe and Robert Chapman, *Billy Budd.*

Muriel Spark's *The Prime of Miss Jean Brodie;* Jay Allen, *The Prime of Miss Jean Brodie.*

James Agee's *A Death in the Family;* Tad Mosel, *All the Way Home.*

Thomas Wolfe's *Look Homeward, Angel;* Ketti Frings, *Look Homeward, Angel*

Also look at short story collections, such as the following:

J. D. Salinger, *Nine Short Stories* (particularly note "Perfect Day for Banana Fish" and "Teddy").

The Short Stories of Ernest Hemingway (a famous collection of the American master's stories and two plays). *Fifth Column* is a full-length play and "Today Is Friday" is a brief scene. Among the stories, "Hills Like White Elephants" and "A Clean, Well-Lighted Place" fall right off the page into play adaptations, but others pose real problems of characterization and action for the stage.

James Joyce, *Dubliners.* (Very challenging.)

John O'Hara, *The Cape Cod Lighter* and many other collections. O'Hara was a master of a very special kind of dialogue that could suggest not only character and action but a person's social class and regional background. He is very difficult but challenging to adapt for the stage.

F. Scott Fitzgerald, John Steinbeck, Ray Bradbury, and many others have collections of short stories that should be read and used for adaptations. You may have seen PBS adaptations of works by these and other authors, but I have yet to see a favorite of mine, Steinbeck's "Johnny Bear." This story poses very special problems for adaptation, but it might work. Try it.

A Selective Bibliography on Playwriting

Archer, William. *Play-Making: A Manual of Craftsmanship.* Boston: Small, Maynard and Company, 1982.

Cole, Toby. *Playwrights on Playwriting.* New York: Hill and Wang, 1961.

Kerr, Walter. *How Not to Write a Play.* New York: Simon & Schuster, 1955.

Lawson, John Howard. *The Theory and Technique of Playwriting.* New York: Hill and Wang, 1960.

Mathews, Branden. *Papers on Playmaking.* New York: Hill and Wang, 1957.

Rowe, Kenneth Thorpe. *Write that Play.* New York: Funk and Wagnalls, 1939.

Smiley, Sam. *Playwriting: The Structure of Action.* Englewood Cliffs, New Jersey: Prentice-Hall, 1970.

Watercolor exercise. Eric Baker, student, 1982.

5

The Designer

When the curtain rises, it is the scenery that sets the key of the play. A stage setting is not a background; it is an environment. Players act in a setting, not against it. . . .

I want my imagination to be stimulated by what I see on the stage. But the moment I get a sense of ingenuity, a sense of effort, my imagination is not stimulated; it is starved. That play is finished as far as I am concerned. For I have come to the theatre to see a play, not to see the work done on a play.

A good scene should be not a picture, but an image. Scene-designing is not what most people think it is—a branch of interior decorating. There is no more reason for a room on a stage to be a reproduction of an actual room than for an actor who plays Napoleon to be Napoleon or for an actor who plays Death in the old morality play to be dead. . . .

Stage-designing should be addressed to the eye of the mind. There is an outer eye that observes, and there is an inner eye that sees.

Robert Edmond Jones, *The Dramatic Imagination*, pp. 23–26.[1]

Another artist in the theatre is the designer, often a composite figure who combines the skills of costume, lighting, and set designer. While designers seem to work exclusively with the visual aspects of a production, they are by no means divorced from considering the audience, the script, and the special concerns of the actors and director. In the modern theatre the successful designer is a cooperating artist with special skills and an understanding of the total art. The designer is neither a famous Renaissance artist who takes a brief holiday from other commissions to paint a mythological landscape for an Italian duke's pageant nor a preeminent modern painter who turns out sketches done in a characteristic manner to be transformed by craftsmen into drops, set pieces, and costumes for a new ballet. Nor is the designer one of those gods of the theatre who shapes all aspects of a production (as Gordon Craig did) and finally ends by playing a private game with puppets and models. Robert Edmond Jones described the craft eloquently and clearly in his book *The Dramatic Imagination*, a passage from which opens this chapter, but for most of us there are very large barriers to understanding what a designer does. For one thing, most of us last put pencil or crayon to paper to make a drawing in elementary school, and we were hurt when some of the more talented students laughed at our lack of perspective and the flat, stilted figures we drew. The other impediment is our lack of sophistication about environments and how to control them. This chapter will provide some suggestions for how you might overcome your fear of drawing, will show you the fundamentals of set design, and will also describe the modes of thought a designer uses.

We are on dangerous ground, but let's start our discussion of how a designer thinks by using three examples that might seem to suggest that design is indeed a branch of interior decorating, despite Jones' warning to

[1]Passage from Robert Edmond Jones' *The Dramatic Imagination* is used by permission of the publisher, Theatre Arts Books, 153 Waverly Place, New York, N.Y. 10014 — Copyright 1941, 1969, by Robert Edmond Jones.

the contrary. However, my assumption is that these three examples will draw on experiences we've all had or can imagine having.

First, pretend that you are walking down the corridor of a college dormitory. It's dinnertime and the rooms are empty and doors have been left ajar. The floor plans of the suites are identical, or at least mirror images of one another, and the basic furnishings, chairs, desks, beds, bureaus are the same. But unless it is a freshman dorm in the first week of school, each suite is very different, and if you know the people you can probably pick out their rooms. How? Is it by the clutter or lack of it? The pictures on the walls? The use of color?

Second, what if this were a monastery and the brothers who live in the cells have taken a vow of poverty? This would be reflected in the lack of personal effects in each cubicle. Can you imagine a single object on the top of each identical dresser that could suggest which brother is a music lover, a man from a large family, a scholar, an artist, an accountant? Don't use such obvious objects as records, family photographs, or books. Be imaginative.

Third, the advertisement in the paper might say, "Three bedrooms, two baths, dining-room/living-room combo, kitchen, private parking, and a beautiful view of San Francisco Bay." You have all the money you need to decorate and furnish this apartment. What will guide the choices you make? You cannot hire a decorator to make the choices for you.

What would be your objective in decorating this apartment? For the sake of this example, imagine that you have in mind a place where you can live comfortably, raise a family, and entertain friends. The choices are changing. Let's bring it into the realm of theatre and imagine that you are giving a large cocktail party in your apartment overlooking the bay. How would you like your guests to perceive the rooms and, through them, you? Is the living-room an extension of you or does it upstage you? And there are other matters, above and beyond decoration. What music will you play and how loudly? What drinks and appetizers will you serve? How will you pick your guests and how many will you invite? The questions are endless, but their intention should be obvious. The implications of your choices loom larger and larger. We are now talking about "staging" an event, and the rooms that you were simply decorating a moment ago are now serving as either focus or background to what's happening in them. This approaches what theatre design is about. Now you should understand a comment by another great American stage designer, Joel Mielziner, who several decades ago was the subject of a two part *New Yorker* interview:

> In recent years, Mielziner has been increasingly interested in the power of scenery to transmit psychological suggestion. The typical Mielziner setting is intended primarily not as an eye-filling spectacle but as an array of clues, hints, symptoms, innuendoes, keys to personality. One of the "house-lovely" magazines not long ago asked Mielziner to write an article treating stage design as a branch of interior decoration. He was outraged. . . . He pointed out to the editor

that the mission of scene design is to give the inside information, the lowdown, on the characters on the stage, while interior decoration tells nothing about its customers except that they have money enough to hire an interior decorator . . . .

Alva Johnston, *The New Yorker*, 1948[2]

Mielziner, by the way, was a designer who preferred to deal with all the visual aspects of a production whenever possible, from experimenting with fabrics under lights to checking on special effects in his own laboratory. His tools were not only line, form, color, texture, light, volume, and mass but also a knowledge of engineering and curiosity about new materials and techniques.

All designers should strive for this range of skills and must also have the ability to work effectively with other artists on a production. As we have said, a designer should work as hard with a script as a director and actor. A designer draws upon a broad range of knowledge and is an artist who can respond aesthetically to material in a play as well as a craftsman who can translate this into renderings or models and descriptive language.

The Design Statement

Years ago (1962) I saw the New Haven opening of a play by Gore Vidal called *Romulus*, which was adapted from *Romulus the Great* by Friedrich Duerrenmatt. There was the usual excitement and tension beforehand, and then the curtain opened to reveal an elaborate, amazing reproduction of a Roman courtyard. There was first a gasp from the audience and then spontaneous applause. This was the last real applause of what turned into a very tiresome afternoon, and I believe it was the last time I heard such an outburst for the setting of a straight play or drama. We hear that such reactions were common in the theatre of the 1800s and early 1900s. David Belasco could hold an audience's attention for ten minutes at the beginning of a play while the lights showed a change from dawn to morning on a stucco wall. I have a feeling that I've been lucky. Admittedly, I am used to spectacular settings and appropriate audience admiration in musicals. I will never forget the scenic effects of *Pippin* or the smoothness, speed, and magnitude of the scene changes in *How to Succeed in Business Without Really Trying*. Musical settings are often overdesigned, spectacular, colorful, and even imaginative, and the audience and production people accept this as a crucial value. Opulent scenery is still thought of as one of the keys to making grand opera grand, but for dramas, particularly realistic comedies or serious plays, the fact that a setting draws special attention is probably an evil omen for the production. For one thing, how would you like to be an actor on a stage that in and of itself can draw applause? Have you competed with a room lately? Do you recall the example we gave earlier of decorating an apartment? Do you want your guests to notice you or your living room? Do you want them to pay attention to what happens during the party or to the interior decoration? If you're feeling contrary and have been betting on the room, why not truly dehumanize the event and do what is done in discos? Make everything so bright, loud, and frantic that no one has to speak, much less notice anyone, and then add a smoke machine.

Some Common Mistakes

Another fact to be remembered is that plays exist in time, and a single setting which is supposed to serve an entire play and which makes a strong statement may become counterproductive after awhile. Have you ever sat in a room with a crooked picture or with a record player stuck in the same groove, softly repeating a phrase again and again? What may start as an amazing setting may become an obtrusive boor by Act Two. Also, sets filled with gimmicks that call attention to themselves (walls that pull out and change, floors that lift and sink, furniture that becomes other things) can be fine for a time but then can become what the play is about. Too much detail can be distracting. Too little can confuse viewers by drawing their attention.

One of the most frequent mistakes made by beginning actors, directors, and designers is what might be called the True-to-Life Paradox. This paradox states that what is real and actual in everyday life is not necessarily either on the stage. What we really have in play production is an understanding between audience and performers about the rules of the game to be played. For example, in real life a person might pause for five minutes before answering a difficult question. On stage, five seconds of silence is an eternity. In real life, any of us can think of a truly ugly room or backyard, but it does not follow that a stage replication which is true-to-life will communicate squalor or disruption. Ugliness is a statement in the theatre and must be expressed through the means available and as part of an understandable convention. One of the strongest means available on stage is the imagination. The believable reaction of actors to a backyard scene when they stand in a doorway, with the yard imagined, is probably stronger than any representation of its reality. The next time you read or see a production of *Death of a Salesman*, notice how Arthur Miller portrays the Lomans' backyard.

When Andy Warhol makes a two-and-a-half-hour movie that is a single, unmoving shot of the Empire State Building, is it art? Or a movie? Of course not, but it is a shrewd comment on taste and what some people really don't know about art. If you sit through the whole performance and then complain that nothing happened, the answer is that you got exactly what you deserved. Why didn't you walk away?

Life is not art and art is not life. It is fascinating, however, that the greatest art in the theatre, as in music and painting, deals with the grimmest subjects. It has been said that the purpose of great art is to make the hideous beautiful. Cruelty, pathos, and ugliness are not exorcised from great theatre but are understood and controlled.

Stage Conventions and Design

We have already mentioned the importance of using the audience's imagination, but you should realize that this has been formalized over the years. In fact, theatre could be described as a game played by performers, producers, and audiences. The rules of this game are usually called conventions. Realism and naturalism are neither "real" nor "natural" in the theatre, but are merely conventions it uses. For example, one of the plays provided in this text is Sophocles' *Philoctetes*, the story of a warrior abandoned on a deserted island by his shipmates. When it is prophesied that the Trojan War can be won by the Greeks only with the help of the warrior and his bow, his enemies return to bring him back. Your approach to designing a setting for this play might be a naturalistic one, though there would be considerable problems with a script that is rather formal and depends on extrahuman agencies to resolve its problem. Naturalism, however, might lead you to constructing a super-realistic setting of rocky ledges and plants, which could truly exist in such a place as the play describes. The central character's costume might suggest the rags that are the only remnants of the clothing he had when he was abandoned, or it might be made of the skins of the small animals and birds that he kills for food in this lonely place. Lighting effects and sound effects should fit this concept. But when all this is done, the place is not real and only the youngest or most naive members of the audience would think it so. As a matter of fact, a value often found in the conventions of realism and naturalism as practiced by amateur or mediocre artists has nothing to do with theater: the notion that the cost and care taken in making a setting, for example, is noteworthy. Most of us have learned by now that the price of making a movie, for example, is no guarantee of its entertainment value. The real effectiveness and art of a production has to do with principles already stated and at least two more, unity and appropriateness.

Unity

All elements of a production should work together and enhance one another. They should be like the paradoxical apple that is more than the sum of its parts. We have suggested that a setting must answer the needs of the action with furnishings, entrances, and backgrounds that are facilitators of action; it should not become what the scene is about but should instead provide a meaningful environment; and it should also provide clues to the mood and meaning of the play. Every part of a production potentially contributes to the production's overall effect or detracts from it. A flamboyant costume in the Lomans' kitchen in *Death of a Salesman* will mean something entirely different than the use of the same costume in a children's play. Orchestral music used as background for a naturalistic production of *Philoctetes* may undercut the meaning of the detailed, accurate setting described above. The casts of *Waiting for Godot* and *The Elephant Man* should not be able to interchange their theatres, sets, music, and costumes.

This point bears further amplification. There are a great many human activities that embrace this principle of unity. For example, graduation exercises involve dressing in a subdued manner, the use of special clothing identifying the people being honored, playing special music, the making of statements by adults, and using large, neutral spaces or rooms to house the audience and participants. There is not an excessive use made of decorations. Our contention is that even if we hadn't needed to invent graduations yet, when we got around to it they would probably take this form. This is also true of formal dances, baptisms, and a hundred other social happenings in which we need and desire unity of impression.

Appropriateness

Appropriateness could be another word for unity but let's use it as a term to describe the subtext or underlying meaning of aspects of a production. The first production of Chekhov's *The Seagull* was a disaster, partly because the audience was embarrassed and then amused by what they took to be the inappropriate truthfulness of the actors. They were used to theatricality, and they were seeing the first, struggling attempts at naturalism in acting. The theatrical cartoonist Hirschfeld has a wonderful series of cartoons in which he toys with the idea of miscasting roles: Barry Goldwater and Lyndon Johnson as Vladimir and Estragon in *Waiting for Godot*, Carol Burnett as Blanche in *A Streetcar Named Desire*, and Barbra Streisand as Lady Macbeth. Have you ever seen *Bambi Meets Godzilla?* There are some people who cite this short movie as the funniest parody of Disney ever done. Or they tell you about *The Dove*, a takeoff on Ingmar Bergman, specifically his film *Wild Strawberries*.

In theatre, inappropriateness can be almost anything that has missed the artists' attention and serves to create the wrong impression. It may be an actor in a costume that doesn't fit the period represented by everyone else on stage, a mispronunciation of a word, or an actor putting his hand through a stage window that doesn't have glass but was supposed to be closed. Most inappropriate happenings in a production are due to carelessness or a lack of understanding of how stage conventions work. These agreements with an audience demand that a designer and other artists take pains. Often it is the visual aspects of a production that will strike the audience as inappropriate. In the 1940s it was commonplace for movies to portray a "poor working girl" as someone with a luxury apartment and a huge wardrobe. How many jet contrails have you seen in Westerns supposedly set in the 1800s? Lapses such as these are even more noticeable when the audience and the production are "live."

Sometimes a designer or director is faced with the need to lie in a production. A director may have to cast young actors in old roles or a designer may be working with conventions that suggest rather than accurately describe reality as we know it. This leads to another interesting fact about how conventions work in the theatre. Generally, if you are going to lie in the theatre, tell a "whopper." There are countless examples of homely actors who have successfully played dashing roles, minimal set designs which have suggested whole empires to audiences, and scripts which have pretended to know the innermost thoughts of the mighty. In such cases any sign of hesitancy would immediately destroy the illusion. Movies can be very "real," but they have enormous difficulties with the unreal or suggestive. Fog doesn't make a setting impressionistic, but asking the audience to use their imaginations can create that meaning.

Is a Designer an Artist or a Craftsman? A Digression Applying to All Theatre Artists

Most of us have watched the floats in the Parade of Roses in Pasadena. We're impressed with the visible signs of expense and care taken, but are they art? Or is this beauty? No matter what the television commentators say, I think not. As a matter of fact, Japanese floral design probably has a more legitimate claim to being called an art form. One reason that float making is a craft and floral design as practiced by the Japanese is an art lies in the relationship of the finished work to the artist. We have mentioned forms of expression that are suggestive as well as those that are obvious. What we have meant by the latter term was art which signed its meaning. The most obvious form of emblematic art would be that which is imitative (for example, a rococo building or salon that is an elaborate copy of a baroque structure). We could also mention signs of expense as being emblematic. We may sigh at the money spent for a float, a wedding, or a house, but we must realize that there is no necessary connection between cost and value as art.

Another feature of being an artist, as opposed to working at a craft, is an awareness of what has been done in the field, the continuity of training, and the setting of standards and goals. When experimentation and curiosity end, then an art tends to become a craft. Crafts tend to repeat themselves and grow only gradually, if at all.

Both craft and art involve skill, however. I prefer to think of it schematically as a pyramid (Figure 5-1). The apex of the pyramid is an individual who not only is capable of repeating what has been done before, in terms of historical interpretation and possessing the necessary skills, but is also able to see new ways of doing things on the level of both craft and ideas. The craftsman tends to repeat what's been done before or use the craft to answer the often nonartistic needs of buyers. The artist-manqué falls short or is frustrated in the desire to be an artist. Such a person tends to have faults in the direction of seeing art as a matter of style and emotion, not craft, and certainly not as a balancing of art and craft. Most of us have guilt feelings about an expert piece of sports equipment that we never learned to use or a fine instrument that has remained unplayed. We've all been or known athletes- and musicians-manqués. The true artist in any field is one who combines both craft and creativity, knowledge of tradition and a willingness to experiment. In my heart of hearts I would like to call football's Lynn Swann an artist, but I realize it doesn't fit. He's graceful when he catches a pass, but not artistic. Swann's intention and training make him skillful and his physical attributes make him graceful, but Baryshnikov is the artist. The leap made to catch a pass is not the object of what a wide receiver does. It is a means to an end. A great dancer's leap is both process and objectification of that activity. It can be repeated, but it is also a part of a "phrase" that in turn is part of a

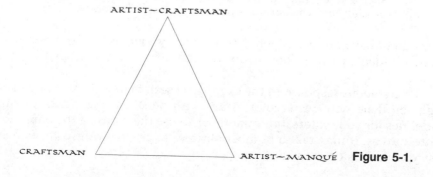

ARTIST-CRAFTSMAN

CRAFTSMAN   ARTIST-MANQUÉ   **Figure 5-1.**

history of other artists and teachers as well as, conceivably, a new way of doing what has been done before.

Choosing the greatest artists is a matter of degree, but those who qualify to have the term applied all have these attributes. Think of Stravinsky, Michelangelo, Picasso, but also think of thousands of people of lesser fame who are still artists in the best sense of the term and derive the same pleasure, if not the same notice, by embodying these characteristics. Many of the people in the theater—designers, directors, actors, playwrights, producers—are artists. Theatre, to be well done, demands it.

Pencil to Paper

Now that we've talked about design, let's attempt it. First pencil, then watercolor, watercolor and tempera, and finally model building. Don't concern yourself with creating finished scene designs or pictures suitable for "framing." Our purpose, as elsewhere in this text, is to at least give you something to imagine and talk about, and better yet, to do and see the results. There are several excellent texts on drawing that capitalize on new theories about right- and left-hemisphere control. You might enjoy reading *Drawing on the Right Side of the Brain* by Betty Edwards because of the help it and other good books will give you in abandoning the accustomed way of seeing things, which is a major problem when you sit down to sketch. Now take a pencil and paper and respond to this image. (Exercises #1, #2, and #3 are handouts for Design I, taught by Robert Braddy, Designer, Colorado State University Theatre.)

> *#1.* As the lights come up, we discover in the gloom a dank dungeon prison. A number of cells open onto a passageway. The floor is strewn with straw and other bits of filth. A few odd pieces of furniture are scattered here and there. The air is foul. There are many dark corners and there are heavy shadows created by the low stone vaulting. Large, smoking candles render a misty, oily light.
>
> Soon a young rake-hell will be brought down into this place to ponder his life of dissolution. The period is the 16th century. The place, Vienna.

If you don't have an idea of what 16th century Viennese prison architecture might be, don't rush to look it up. Imagine it. Note the clues the passage gives.

One student response to the exercise is seen below. The second exercise might be done with watercolor. Start with pencil, if you wish, to suggest guidelines for your colors, but remember to use the white of the paper for the lightest areas. It may take a number of times to get the watercolor to behave. Test your colors on throwaway paper.

Figure 5-2.   Pencil sketch exercise. Jeffrey McDonald, student, 1982.

#2. As the curtain opens, we see the throne room of a castle in Scotland. It is a large chamber with a high, vaulted ceiling. Its stonework is cold and damp with the night's fog. The furniture and accoutrements of a room of this sort are present. Although these objects are in evidence, the room is by no means lavish or rich, and we sense that it is rather more empty than full or cluttered.

The hour is well past midnight. The attendants of the castle have left one or two low-burning torches to provide light for anyone who might pass through.

In another part of the castle, a murder has just been committed. Shortly, we will see the murderer feeling the first sharp pangs of guilt as he enters the throne room.

Again, we have included student responses, and we would caution you not to dash off and reread *Macbeth.* Try for the flavor of the place, the time of night, and the ominous quality.

These results from a single class, including several artists and a number of students who had rarely put pencil or watercolor to paper since elementary school, are very interesting. Even in black and white you can probably pick out the student who has at least rudimentary watercolor technique (Figure 5-3), but I also like the drawing that shows awareness of the way that light and shadow interact (Figure 5-4), the one with the excellent use of highlights that surprisingly throw the throne into darkness (Figure 5-5), and the experimental work in which the student is exploring unusual plastic

Figure 5-3. Watercolor exercise. Jeffrey McDonald, 1982.

shapes (Figure 5-6). They may not be expert, but they all have power and originality.

Another unusual aspect of all the watercolors is the awareness the artists have of the volume of the stage itself. Look at them and imagine where you are sitting in the theatre. How well can the actors move in these spaces?

Next you may wish to start experimenting with mixing watercolor tube pigments with black or white tempera for shadow and light. Or outline with pen and then add color as tints. This technique has been used in the solutions of the next exercise.

> *#3.* Show a very poor room now occupied by a person who once had wealth and status. And then show the room of a person who has limitless wealth and time to make the room expressive of his or her taste.

In both of these drawings the artist is introducing another element by answering the exercise. Any answer is inevitably a comment on the people who inhabit these places. Notice the man's briefcase in the bare room and the drapery in the woman's room, which almost seems an extension of her own clothing.

Materials. By now we can see the need for certain materials and antici-

Figure 5-4. Tracy Geipel, student, 1982.

pate those that we will need for the next exercise, which is the construction of a model for a stage and rudimentary stage settings. In addition to drawing paper and watercolor paper, cardboard and the backs of posters can be used with tempera, because of its covering ability. Here is a list:

Soft pencils and felt tip black pens
Drawing paper and watercolor paper (pads)
A watercolor tray with fewer colors and generous amounts and/or tubes of watercolor
Tempera, at least black and white for lightening and shadowing
Exacto knife set
Steel ruler
Gesso
White glue
A broad brush and a narrow brush
Masking tape, narrow

Figure 5-5.   Laszlo Palos, student, 1982.

Figure 5-6.   Shirley Ross, student, 1982.

Figure 5-7. *Poor Man.* Eric Baker, student, 1982.

Figure 5-8. *Rich Woman.* Eric Baker, 1982.

#4. Construct in $\frac{1}{2}''$ scale an open top box, 15 actual inches wide, 15" deep, and 10" high. The front of the box should be cut out to form a proscenium $12\frac{1}{2}''$ wide and 8" high, from the bottom. Paint one side black, then mount on a board or cardboard to create a stage house and apron. (See Figure 5-9.)

#5. In order to become used to objects in space, cut out the shape of a chair, a man, and a woman, all to scale and with a stand attached to each. Place the box on a table and find a place for your chin where the floor of the stage model disappears and your view is centered. Placing a scale on the side of the proscenium allows you to see how objects will vary in size depending on where they are placed.

#6. To further explore the space and draw some conclusions about sight-line limits, make a pen-and-ink sketch of three walls of a room to the same scale. Cut it, tape the sections together flexibly and place this in various positions in the box stage.

Notice that the illusion of realism, for example, works better when the setting comes down to the proscenium, without a gap, with the side walls at an angle larger than 90 degrees in order to give the best sight-lines to the largest number of seats in the typical auditorium. Also, note that if the setting is too far upstage, people seated in a balcony or a steeply raked main floor would be unable to see the top of the rear wall. If the setting is too far downstage, people in the front rows might see too much of the top of the setting. These vertical limits are sight-lines as well.

At this point we could launch into a discussion of perspective and teach you, among other things, how to translate a groundplan into an accurate three-dimensional drawing or model, but our intention is to have you *observe* objects in a theatrical space.

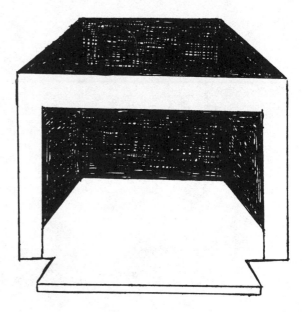

Figure 5-9. Pattern for stage.

Figure 5-10. Interior pattern.

Lighting

Lighting as a branch of design in the theatre is a relatively new field. Lighting before the end of the nineteenth century usually meant general illumination. In the baroque theatre a call for more light would be answered with more candles, lowering chandeliers on pulleys, and lenses for magnifying and focusing footlight candles. We can see the enormous technical advances in all aspects of lighting over even the last forty years in instruments, lamps, control systems, projectors, and color media. Lighting takes place in a theatre and so you might wonder if this would affect lighting techniques and theory. The answer is "yes," in many expectable ways as well as in some new ones.

Lighting has four properties: intensity, color, distribution, and movement. By the first we mean how clearly or how well we can see something on stage, but we must bear in mind that this can be subjective. If you are coming from darkness into partial light, you may have a stronger impression of being able to see clearly than if you are dealing with degrees of intensity beyond this point. Objects seen in front of dark backgrounds will give the impression of stronger lighting than those seen in front of light backgrounds. Also, remember that it may take more light to illuminate one object than another. As for theatrical conventions involving intensity of light, there is a tendency to associate comedy with bright light and tragedy with dim, shadowy illumination.

Color in lighting may be caused by one of three things: the color of the objects being illuminated, the color of the light itself, or color media. All light, be it natural or artificial, has color as a component. For example, think of sunlight, moonlight, and incandescent light. One of the conventions that has developed around this property is the idea of colored light being "warm" or "cold" depending on its position in the color spectrum. Colors, according to this convention, may be used for psychological effect in productions.

Distribution has to do with the form and direction of light. We may see light falling in a shaft or rationalize its direction by noting the shadows created. We speak of "spot" light and "pools" of light, but remember that we don't see light. We only see objects that reflect light or cause shadow.

Movement, light's final property, is regulated in the modern theatre by sophisticated dimmer systems. They can make light come and go, rise rapidly, or fade slowly, and are certainly a far cry from the chandeliers on pulleys used in an earlier age.

Nature has prepared us for a wide range of phenomena, and the lighting designer must be aware of this. Two effects are particularly familiar. The first is the level light of sunrise and sunset, when objects seem to grow flat and their colors seem purer. There is an anecdote about a young boy walking with his grandfather on a summer evening. The last rays of the sun vividly illuminate a hillside and a flock of sheep.

"Look, Grandfather, at how white the sheep are."

"Yes," the old man replies, "but only on this side."

The second effect is that of midday, when the sun is at a higher angle and there is a great deal of ambient, diffused light. Shadows are less directional and softer, if they exist at all. The first kind of light can be created in the theatre by a single, eye-level light coming from the direction of the audience, who are, after all, the ones you want to see the scene. The second effect is usually created by pairs of lights at ninety degrees to one another and at 45 degrees to the stage floor. These lights, plus spill from other pairs aimed at other areas and the reflection of light from objects on the stage, help to create the impression of light in nature.

An analogy can be drawn between this kind of lighting and one of the ways to reinforce sound. Instead of taking the human voice and amplifying it from a speaker so that it overrides the performer's voice, we can reinforce it by sending the signal to a number of speakers around an auditorium and running them at relatively low levels. When properly done, the actor's voice is still the most noticeable—it is directional, but it seems to have more resonance and brightness. The same technique can be used with lighting.

Another type of lighting used on stage is motivated lighting. An example of this is the lamp in a setting that is supposed to provide illumination. Actually, it will be only a part of the overall lighting, but the controls will be handled in such a way as to give the impression of the light being turned on and off from a wall switch, for example. The stage lighting, though stronger and better distributed than it would be naturally in the room, nevertheless supports the convention.

Exercise #1

Look at the student renderings in this chapter, as well as other photographs and drawings in the text, and decide the nature and direction of the light sources.

Exercise #2

Using penlights or flashlights, illuminate objects in the model stages you constructed.

Exercise #3

How would you light a hallway leading from a box-set living room? How would you create the effect of a setting sun on the semitransparent drapes of the set? A summer sun? A winter sun? Can you suggest morning light and evening light in the setting?

As you attempt exercises of these sorts, you will note that up to a certain point, it is easier to control light when you are at a distance from the object to be lighted. The closer you are the more difficult it is to light a stage. A small, low-ceilinged stage will probably require more instruments than a large stage. This is why most well-designed theatres have optimal "throws" for instruments. There are three basic types of instruments used in theatres: (1) ones which provide soft focused, pooled light; (2) those which create focused, "tight" light; and (3) unfocused "floods" for general lighting. In addition to these three types, there are specialized instruments such as projectors and follow-spots (movable, powerful instruments for focused light).

Exercise #4

Shine the light of two flashlights on a person's face in a dark room. Shine it from below, at eye level, steeply from above, from behind, and then in various combinations. What are the different moods and effects that you created? Which of the combinations is most like the lighting used in portraits? In particular movies?

The lighting designer is often asked to come up with special effects. I remember a production of *Julius Caesar* at Stratford, Ontario's Shakespeare Festival. (Look at the photograph of the theatre at the end of Chapter 2, Figure 2-17, and particularly notice the railing on the balcony.) At the end of the play, Octavius Caesar, who is destined to become Caesar Augustus, speaks of Brutus. In the growing darkness the actor climbed onto the railing, and spoke:

> According to his virtue let us use him,
> With all respect and rites of burial.
> Within my tent his bones tonight shall lie,
> Most like a soldier. . . .

The lights began to fade to complete darkness except for one eye-level instrument that seemed to come from our direction. It began to dominate the stage until the actor's profile grew flat and seemed to be a Roman coin floating in the void, as he concluded:

> To part the glories of the happy day.

Then to blackness.

Costuming

The last but not the least of the artists in theatre is the costumer, a visual artist who makes statements through line, color, texture, and mass. Usually the costumer designs makeups as well. Costumers must have the same grounding as the other theatre artists in the complete art, with particular attention to period, style, the ways in which all the elements of a production interact, and the special concerns of actors. Some of the specific skills that must be learned are tailoring, pattern making, dying, mask construction, and makeup.

There is magic in costuming. All of us have worn special clothing for a dance, a graduation, a wedding, or Halloween, and our feelings were very much those of an actor in a period play who needed the right costume to complete the character. I recall the excitement of a cast of mine when the elegant costumes from the 1967 Broadway production of Bertolt Brecht's *Galileo* arrived from the rental firm, complete with the names of the original artists on labels in the collars. Note that our show's designer had checked the sizes, colors, and designs of this set of costumes before choosing them for our production. This is always a necessary precaution.

Figure 5-11. *Left:* Costume rendering for *Marat/Sade*. Kristina Hanssen, costumer, Colorado State University Theatre, 1980. *Right:* Photograph of actors from *Marat/Sade*. Production at Colorado State University, directed by Morris Burns; Robert Braddy, designer.

Thinking of Brecht, there is his story of the little actor, a bit player in *Threepenny Opera*, whom he watched, unobserved, while the young man tried on hat after hat in the wardrobe room, hunting for just the right one for his character. The setting, lighting, and properties may flesh out the environment, but costuming "dresses" or completes the character.

Not only can costuming be metaphoric, but it may also have to be flattering, or allow for extreme movement, or make a strong statement of period and class, place, or style. These would be problems even if the actor were to appear in a neutral space, but most stages are anything but neutral. There are settings and lighting to worry about, as well as the visual statement made by other characters. To cope with such problems, costumers develop their concept for a show in concert with the stage designer and lighting designer, plan a palette for a show, and check materials under lights when in doubt about how they might "read" on stage. They know the flow of a show and can avoid having certain costumes on stage at the same time. In conclusion, we can say that costuming can either be the major metaphor of a production or a subtle statement of the reality of a show. It is always a principal means for projecting the meaning of a character.

Summary

We started with Jones' famous statement about the function of a setting as an environment in which an action takes place, not the meaning of a production. Lighting was described as one of the ways we complete this statement, while costuming was seen as both an aspect of design and a major means of fleshing out the actor. These are all visual arts involving special techniques and understandings, but they must function together to help shape a successful production.

Selected Bibliography

Barton, Lucy. *Historic Costume for the Stage.* Boston: Walter H. Baker Co., 1963.

Bellman, Willard F. *Scenography and Stage Technology, an Introduction.* New York: Thomas Y. Crowell, 1977.

Corson, Richard. *Stage Makeup.* 6th ed. Englewood Cliffs, N.J.: Prentice-Hall, 1981.

Edwards, Betty. *Drawing on the Right Side of the Brain.* Los Angeles: J. P. Tarcher, Inc., 1979.

Jones, Robert Edmund. *The Dramatic Imagination.* New York: Theatre Art Books, 1958.

McCandless, Stanley. *A Method of Lighting the Stage.* New York: Theatre Arts Books, 1958.

Mielziner, Jo. *Designing for the Theatre.* New York: Atheneum, 1965.

Parker, W. Oren and Harvey K. Smith. *Scene Design and Stage Lighting.* New York: Holt, Rinehart & Winston, 1974.

Payne, Darwin Reid. *Materials and Craft of Scenic Models.* Carbondale and Edwardsville, Illinois: Southern Illinois University Press. London and Amsterdam: Feffer and Simons, Inc., 1976.

Pilbrow, Richard. *Stage Lighting.* New York: D. Van Nostrand, 1971.

Russell, Douglas A. *Stage Costume Design.* Englewood Cliffs, New Jersey: Prentice-Hall, 1973.

Selden, Samuel and Hunton D. Sellman. *Stage Scenery and Lighting.* New York: Appleton-Century-Crofts, 1959.

Fouquet's miniature of performance of *The Martyrdom of Ste. Apolline.* (Musée Condé, Chantilly.)

6

The Director

Just as an actor explores his or her own experiences to find specific, concrete examples to support a character's feelings and behavior, a director draws on feelings and knowledge of people, places, and ideas. All of the theatre arts, when seen in these terms, are alike. We have the balancing of art and technique; movement toward focus and simplification; and the use of subtext, the suggestive, and the metaphoric. And how does irony work? We make the audience find themselves in the material because we understood it, and subtly but insistently promoted it.

The Director

A theatre director has responsibilities in the modern theatre ranging from that of producer to that of acting coach. Usually, in academic and professional theatres, the director is a member of a team that includes the technical director, the designer, the costumer, and, in some instances, the playwright. A director works with a business manager or department head on budget, schedule, advertising, and the hiring or selection of staff and performers for a given show or season. A director conducts rehearsals and, during the run of a show, coordinates his or her activities with those of the house manager, stage manager, and heads of crews. Many like to be in the house for every performance and most keep very close watch on their productions. Abe Burrows, of Broadway musical comedy fame, was known for his unannounced visits to theatres where his productions were playing. Standing in the back of the house, he would check a scene against his watch to see that the performance was running on time.

In other words, the director may be responsible for everything from rehearsing a show to supervising the box-office unless the tasks are otherwise delegated. In the historical sketch in Chapter 1, it was noted that eighteenth century directors handled both the artistic and business affairs of their companies. Nowadays large theatrical companies usually have both a business director and an artistic director.

Sometimes a director will become associated with the work of a particular playwright. Over the last thirty years in America there have been several examples of this: Alan Schneider with Edward Albee, Elia Kazan with Tennessee Williams and Arthur Miller, and Jose Quintero with the revivals and premier productions of hitherto unproduced plays by the late Eugene O'Neill. There have also been playwrights who were distinguished directors. Few Americans realize that Bertolt Brecht was both the leading director and founder of the Berliner Ensemble, one of eastern Europe's great theatres after World War II.

Two Types of Directors

Directors usually take one of two extreme approaches to their art. Those who take the first approach see their task as that of interpreter, an artist who is aware of the backgrounds of a play, the type of audience for whom it was originally written, and its strengths and weaknesses as a script. This type of director may update a play in terms of language, costumes, and settings, but will do it for good reason and with an awareness of cultural equivalents. Such directors see their role as that of midwife, someone vitally interested in the survival of the child, but not necessarily its parent. The extreme of this approach would be those directors who hesitate to do a contemporary play unless they have seen an "approved" production. They tend toward archae- ological productions of older plays whether or not they will have meaning for their audience, and believe and use everything they read in the acting edition of a play.

The other major group of directors would be those who create their own plays from other people's works.[1] They are less interested in historical and artistic accuracy than they are in the use of a play as a vehicle for what they wish to say in the theatre. I remember Tom O'Horgan's *Gammer Gurton's Apocalyptic Needle* as an exuberant, exciting evening in the theatre that had very little to do with the medieval play upon which it was loosely based. However, a production of *Timon of Athens* directed by Michael Langham and produced by the Shakespeare Festival in Stratford, Ontario, in the early sixties, seemed to effectively split the difference between these two ap- proaches. The action took place in what appeared to be Egypt and the Sinai, in the present. The end result, which was enhanced by a musical score by Duke Ellington, succeeded in making one of Shakespeare's most difficult and flawed plays entertaining and pertinent without destroying its shape and meaning.

Another example of the balanced choices a director must make may be epitomized by the difficulty one has in finding translations of Greek tragedies that will work on the modern stage. Should a director pick a scholar's work because it is accurate, or a poet's translation because it sings? Until recently, the choice was a hard one. Did you want an archaic, Victorian one, a modern, prosy one, or the adaptation of a William Butler Yeats or Robinson Jeffers?

Another example of our misunderstanding and misuse of earlier drama would be the "mellerdrammers" so often used as summer entertainment in vacation spots. Too often such productions are nothing more than parodies of earlier acting and stage conventions. Anyone who has come to believe that they are accurate reflections of an age that didn't know how to tell a good yarn or was overly sentimental should read Belasco's *The Return of Peter*

[1]See Richard Gilman, "Directors vs. Playwrights," *Saturday Review of Literature*, April 1982.

Grimm or see Gillette's *Sherlock Holmes* or *The Secret Agent*. Admittedly, some melodramas are based on poor plays, and perhaps a poor play deserves what it gets, but does an audience?

It is my feeling that beginning directors should start with the interpretive artist's point of view, the first approach we mentioned, and begin by trying to understand a play's meaning and history. After this step has been taken, the novice director should attempt to understand the audience for whom the production is planned, and then bring the two together in as entertaining and meaningful a manner as possible.

What Happens During Rehearsals?

The purpose of this chapter is to prepare you for the next section of this text, in which you will develop production plans for three plays, functioning as dramaturg, actor, designer, and director. Our emphasis in this discussion will have to be on the director's responsibility to develop a production plan that can be shared with other creative people. Therefore we are stopping short of the rehearsal phase, but the fact is that this is where most texts on directing begin: the art and craft of developing a production during rehearsals. So, let us touch briefly on these matters.

What happens after a play has gone through the conceptual and planning phase? The actors and production staff may have already been selected. This is the case with repertory companies, where actors are hired for a series of roles during a season. In college or university theatres, precasting is often avoided and these decisions are deferred until the last moment, but once rehearsals begin, many of the same steps are taken. There is a read-through. The director may acquaint the actors with the production concept and show them the ground plan and setting and costume renderings. Arrangements may have to be made for the special needs of roles such as fencing lessons, diction coaching, and dance instruction. Some directors describe the characters' personalities and relationships in detail before the actors take the stage. Others consider this a preemption of the actor's task. Many actors are suspicious of a director who "talks a play to death." Judge for yourself, but rehearsing a play should ideally be a cooperative process of discovery. However, we've all had the experience of enjoying a production, whether movie or play, that came out of anything but such a process. Young actors who plan to make a career in theatre should talk to professionals and hear tales about directors who have very little interest in what might motivate an actor to do a certain thing on stage, but expect it to happen and leave it to the actor to work out. And that excellent piece of naturalistic acting you might have seen last year done by a famous touring company may not have been created by application of the "method" but by rote with a demanding director teaching how he wanted the play done, nuance by nuance and gesture by gesture.

However, as a general rule, we would hope that putting a production together would be a cooperative effort. A director should be concerned with answering problems about the shape of the production, and actors must focus on developing their characters. Actors need feedback and the director becomes an audience of one, but is careful to keep the stage of development in mind so that the actor doesn't rush to solutions. Much of good acting is behavioral and requires repetition and deepening by degrees, not by leaps. Sometimes this is referred to as "layering," and this process may also make an actor vulnerable, so a director must not take advantage of the special relationship shared with the cast.

Sometimes actors protect themselves during this germinative stage of a production, but it's the exception, not the rule. A story is told about Lee J. Cobb in the original production of *Death of a Salesman*. Week after week, while everyone else was making progress, Cobb mumbled and withdrew. The other actors were becoming quite concerned when one day a new person appeared at the rehearsal. He resembled Lee J. Cobb, but when he spoke and moved his name was Willy Loman.

What is most often discussed in books on directing is blocking, movement, stage pictures, ways to solve common production problems, and suggestions of how to give a play coherence and cohesion. This approach in many instances grows out of a notion of how to teach fundamentals effectively, but with some writers it is actually a theory about how audiences see plays.

There is a notion among filmmakers that, when planning a film, one should never use slides or photographs because they deny the nature of the medium, which is the interplay of light and shadow in motion. Even in a well-designed series of slides or "stills" of locations and actors for a proposed film, in which attention is paid to rhythm, duration of image, close- and long-shots, the effect is very different from that of seeing a motion picture. For one thing, a "still" is still. If it moves or takes on some other sort of life, it is because of an outside agency. Perhaps, they say, the best way to plan or teach film is to use short, inexpensive rushes or an entirely different medium like layouts of pen and ink sketches.

This has interesting implications for how one might approach stage direction. Stage focus, so important to a medium that cannot "zoom" in on a subject, is more than stage composition, blocking, or the use of levels. It may be an active piece of behavior, such as "taking stage." In the chapter on acting, we discussed the need to think of acting as more than a composite of external characteristics. This could be said of directing as well. Stanislavski, whose fame as an actor was based on cameo or character roles, said it was imperative to put aside his last portrayal and start fresh with the next. Perhaps directors should do the same and avoid reliance on rules and set solutions, thinking instead in terms of process. However, in the final analysis, these matters are best explored by studying directing and then doing a number of plays with an open mind.

Developing a Production Plan

Our main purpose in this chapter is to describe a way in which a director can develop a production plan. A provocative study of this art is Frank McMullan's *The Directorial Image*. Again, the description of what an artist does in the theatre will be found to be a process, not a checklist.

The first step, McMullan suggests, will be an open-minded reading of the script. The object here is to come as close as possible to the experience an audience will have. It is not easy to read a play with an open mind and to make oneself finish a script in one sitting, but this should be the goal. Hopefully, when you read the scripts at the end of this text, you will be able to see them through the eyes of an actor, a designer, and a director. Jot down your reactions, but don't slow down. Don't spoil the cumulative effect of a script contained in the emergence of theme, mood, and character, and the suspense created by complications. First readings of a play are very special.

I doubt that you will know any of the plays included here, and this is intentional. There is truly no right or wrong way to respond initially to a play, but there is a human tendency to mistrust our perceptions when we are beginners. This also explains why there are no production shots or renderings. Hopefully you will feel freer to imagine your own.

Returning to McMullan's steps, after reading the play we would next study its dramatic structure, analyzing how it would work on stage. (Refer back to Chapter 4.) Also, we should decide how the production should be shaped to appeal to our particular audience. But remember at this point not to give a sigh of relief as you leave behind the subjective responses you've had to the material and start the objective and analytic part of the process. You may be aware of a thought teasing at the edge of your consciousness about some aspect of the play, an idea for the production which you cannot put on paper, or some free-floating connection which you cannot pull down to earth. Don't hurry to tie up these loose ends. Remember that you are not dealing with absolutes, and that having everything explained and decided may simply mean that you have put an end to creative thinking. Later, given the chance, some of these intuitions may lead to other research and thought, and become part of your metaphoric conception of the play. Indeed, it is much more likely that these elusive aspects of a script will contribute more to the image you will have of a play than the rational and quantifiable ones.

The next step in the process is an analysis of the production "values" of the script. Some of these values will have already been touched upon in your analysis of dramaturgical concerns and others may relate directly to your emerging notions of how to produce the play. According to McMullan, the values are:

Mood
Theme
Character
Plot
Dialogue

All of these will be present in most plays, but McMullan's point is that different plays emphasize them in different ways, and create different configurations. For example, John Synge's *Riders to the Sea* has a clear and inevitable plot and its characters are representational, though not stereotypical. However, the play's principal values are its mood and the beauty and authenticity of its dialogue. An Agatha Christie play, like *Witness for the Prosecution* or *The Mousetrap*, may use two-dimensional characterizations and predictable settings and have nothing to say about deeper meaning, but employ the intricate twists and turns of the plot as its major theatrical value. In this case, plot is a game played with the audience. Arthur Miller's *The Crucible* emphasizes theme on two levels: that of the historical occurrences described and that of the modern application of the occurrences to the McCarthy era. Neil Simon might be described as a master of comic dialogue and Samuel Beckett as an adroit juggler of theme, mood, and dialogue, using vaudeville as a showcase for philosophy.

The next two steps in this process of developing a production plan are obvious extensions of those already taken. Having listed the key values of a script, we ask ourselves how they relate to one another. What does this configuration tell you about the style and structure of the work? For example, *Riders to the Sea* will demand a production style that emphasizes the reality of its world, from accents to clothing to the furnishings of the cottage's sparse interior. An acting style is called for that makes the inevitable believable without resorting to either overacting or flatness. McMullan's other term for such patterns of values is *points of focus,* and one can see how this approach helps a director plan a production as well as find an image that unites all of the concepts. When he has completed his discussion of *Riders to the Sea*, McMullan arrives at an overall image of "a craggy rock with the sea lapping at it and wearing it away." (*The Directional Image*, p. 212.) If I were the designer I think I would want to hear more, but this is clearly a beginning.

During this process we have been moving from clarification and simplification to conceptualizations and then to metaphoric extensions, which

Often designers and directors will develop a production plan with the help of "thumbnail sketches." Robert Braddy, the designer at Colorado State, is particularly adept at using this technique to help his directors. He and I did a production of *Hamlet* on a stage with hardly any fly space, trapping, or wing space. As you can see in Figure 6-1, we started with steps and moved on to steps and hanging units and then to arches, and finally (G) the setting rendered here evolved. It functioned as both a space stage and full stage, and there was a show-drape. In addition there were two special curtains, one that came in downstage to create a shallow setting and another that closed off the sky vista to create the throne room. The end product was a functional and elegant set.

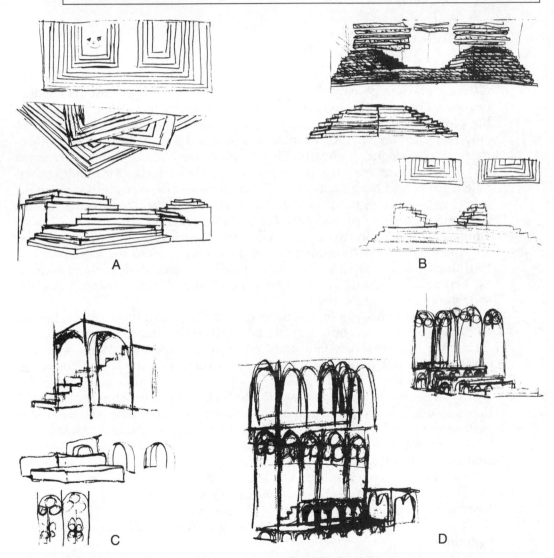

Figure 6-1. Thumbnail sketches and final rendering for *Hamlet*. Robert Braddy, designer, Colorado State University Theatre.

Figure 6-1 (*Continued*)

E

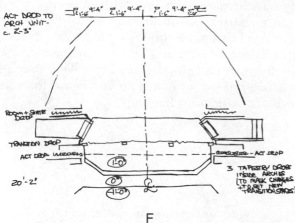

F

G

in turn can feed back into our understanding of the material. It is a good way to deal with complex materials, especially those that combine both objectivity and subjectivity. We have seen this same process occur with the actor, designer, and playwright. The plot of a play is seen in clearer and clearer outline and the shape of the action comes into focus. Theme and mood emerge. The words which we choose to express these understandings should be the best ones possible.

It's been said that poets are the inventors of language. Sometimes this is literally true. A Shakespeare or a Lewis Carroll "makes up" words, but the point that's really being made is that writers can place a word in a new or fresh context. Great directors have this same power with an entire play, because they find new meanings or sharpen old ones. Can one really separate our current enjoyment of Shakespeare from the staging concept that Tyrone Guthrie developed from both the historical facts and his concept of how these plays should appear on a modern stage? Can you divorce Peter Weill's script for *Marat/Sade* from the Peter Brook production? Or Shaffer's *Equus* from its original production concept created with John Dexter?

The Production Meeting

You should now be ready to share your understandings and feelings about the play with your cocreators. Undoubtedly there are some loose ends, and ideally these should be explored until you have settled on your production concept. However, the usual case is that you and the other artists have a number of different perceptions of what the final production might be. The production discussions will have to take you to the final step of an overall production image. Lighting designers, costumers, stage designers, actors, and directors may have common languages because of the similarities of their disciplines, but the use of imagery is one of the effective ways to talk across disciplines. Textures, tonalities, and sounds are all part of this language as well as music, movement, and poetry. It always seems easier for us to speak of what the play is about in rational, quantifiable terms, but I have seen production meetings that were bogged down in such discussions come alive when someone played a recording of music which helped express the feelings they had about the play, or listed a series of seemingly disconnected images that had come to mind while reading the script. By the way, a series of seemingly disconnected images is to be preferred to no images at all, but a single, strong image related to all aspects of the play is the ideal, though it might not be found until the planning phase ends, if then. The attainable goal is the willingness of fellow artists to speak to one another in these terms.

A final word about images and metaphor. As we have been insisting, this is neither vague nor sloppy thinking, but it is certainly different from what most of us do day in and day out. Remember that although computers have been built that can handle the most complicated mathematical functions given the correct information, no one has programmed a computer to write good poetry. The principal quality of this mode of thought and expression is not that it is abstract, but that it is suggestive. It makes connections between words and ideas and between ideas and images that provoke new lines of thought. When Dr. Samuel Johnson sought to define metaphor for his dictionary, he put it this way: "the application of a word to an use to which, in its original import, it cannot be put. . . ." Actors, designers, directors, and playwrights should all be aware that good art has inner tensions which, by working in concert and in opposition to one another, create the work itself. Dissonance in music, contrast in painting, subtext in acting, detail in opposition to mass in architecture are all manifestations of this. Conflict and resolution are the facts of a great play. It is intriguing to speculate that even the smallest unit of a complex work of art, like rectangular bricks in a rectangular building, help to reflect and shape the ultimate form of the entire object.

Other Kinds of Research

In the next chapter, there are materials that demonstrate what a director does to further explore the world of a play. We have already seen the need for historical understanding and a knowledge of the development of the physical stage, but there are other types of research that also should be done. For example, some of us like to check other artistic works of the same period and place. These could be novels, plays, the music with which the playwright must have been familiar, as well as paintings, furniture, and clothing of the time. Through this research we develop a more detailed understanding of the history and feeling of the period. Rod Steiger, the actor, has a reputation for deep reading on all the historical roles he plays. I know a student who converted a long-awaited European tour into a summer in Ireland because he wanted to prepare himself for the lead in *Playboy of the Western World*. There will be materials that lead to unexpected connections, and what we read today may give us insights for a play produced a decade from now. The excerpt from *Pincher Martin* by William Golding, which is included in the materials for *Philoctetes*, is historically incorrect, misplaced geographically, but it speaks strongly to me of the main character's isolation and loneliness. Some of us are "eye-minded" and it is useful for us to browse through art books and photographs, and to recall movies we have seen. I know of playwrights who not only write extended biographies for their characters, but also find pictures for them: a face, an expression, anything to pull them out of the imagination and make them real. When you're studying a Greek tragedy, why not find a picture essay that shows the lives and faces of modern-day fishermen living the same life as that portrayed in a fifth century B.C. play?

This sort of research becomes a matter of habit for people in the theatre and is not necessarily linked to a particular production. Just as actors should train themselves to be observers of people, directors should become voracious readers, learn to absorb environments, and become students of the allied arts. Sometimes linking one's own background to a play is an exciting way to finding the core of a production. In this passage from *The World According to Garp*, John Irving describes his character's search for just such a core to his writing while living in Vienna:

> He put "The Pension Grillparzer"—as they say—aside. It will come, Garp thought. He knew he had to know more; all he could do was look at Vienna and learn. It was holding still for him. Life seemed to be holding still for him. He made a great many observations of Charlotte, too, and he noticed everything his mother did, but he was simply too young. What I need is *vision*, he knew. An overall scheme of things, a vision all his own. It will come, he repeated to himself, as if he were training for another wrestling season—jumping rope, running laps on a small track, lifting weights, something almost that mindless but necessary.[2]

We have attempted to include a wide range of materials for *Philoctetes*, but they are not meant to be complete, only representative. Look them over, then follow your own intuitions and system for research.

A last thought about the directorial image. A well-known example is taken from stories and documents concerning the Broadway production of *A Streetcar Named Desire*, written by Tennessee Williams, directed by Elia Kazan, and designed by Joel Mielziner. In Kazan's notes about the production, Blanche is spoken of as a butterfly in a jungle, and one story has it that this description evolved into a mutually agreed upon image of a moth against a naked lightbulb. I think we can all see the appropriateness of such images to the theme and dramatic action of the play, which involves the struggle of Blanche against her environment, her brother-in-law, and madness. Like a moth or butterfly, Blanche is both threatened by and attracted to the dangers of her situation. The image also gives a strong visual clue to Mielziner's scenery. It had an aura of decay, clutter, and faded beauty that could dissolve when the front lights dimmed revealing an old woman passing behind the house selling "Flores por los muertos." The costumer, Lucinda Ballard, dressed Blanche in yellowed lace, which gave her an air of languishing dignity. The image itself seemed to have its moment on stage when the moth-like Blanche, fluttering about the flat, tried to give her small corner some

[2]John Irving, *The World According to Garp* (New York: E. P. Dutton, 1978), p. 110. © 1978 by John Irving. Reprinted by permission of E. P. Dutton, Inc., and Literistic, Ltd.

romance and mystery by hanging a Japanese paper lantern over the naked light-bulb. Not all images will fit or inform a play this well, but the effort to arrive at one and the willingness to share it with the other members of the production staff are crucial.

Afterword

What remains to be done after the cocreators have decided on a design for the setting, ground plan, costumes, adaptations of the auditorium or stage, lighting design, and sound and music for the production? The cast and crew may need to be selected, and the periods of construction and rehearsal must begin. Often these three phases—the study of the script, the planning of the production, and the actualization—overlap. Sometimes in community and college productions, casts and crews are selected just prior to rehearsals, and this may force a director to rethink production values or hold them in abeyance. However, there are also plays that demand much prior planning and early commitment to blocking patterns and creating special effects. For example, period plays can make severe demands on actors in terms of costuming, accents, and stylized behavior. It may be necessary to select a cast early and arrange for a longer period of preparation.

As we have said, it is not at all unusual for professional actors to appear for the first rehearsal with all the lines of their parts memorized, but often directors will insist that lines be "set" only after relationships, reactions, blocking, and special moments have been developed. Unlike the high school or church drama many of us have experienced, the smallest problems for professional, college, and many amateur productions will be the memorization of lines and blocking. The role you have and the play in which you appear will be understood as a much more complex and interrelated experience. Lines will become part of the behavior of the characters portrayed, units will merge into the flow of the entire play, and theme and mood will become concerns of the entire company. Some directors use such techniques as a preshow review of the action verbs associated with each unit, putting the cast through a condensed experience of the play before the curtain rises. This is very much like the preparation used by sports psychologists when they help Olympic performers imagine all the steps of their routines before they mount the rings or point their skis downhill.

Let's summarize, in outline form, the steps taken by a director in preparing a production:

I. Work done in private:
    A. Reading the play with an open mind, hopefully in one sitting;
    B. Analyzing the play's structure;

    C. Thinking of the play in terms of your audience;

    D. Finding the play's values;

    E. Deciding the play's points of focus;

    F. Developing a directorial image;

    G. Continued reading, research, and pursuit of intuitions about the material.

II. Work done with cocreators:

    A. Communication of ideas and feelings about the script, the sharing of images, and the development of a unifying image for the production;

    B. Development of a groundplan;

    C. Selection of period, style, and other considerations with the visual artists (designer, costumer, and lighting designer);

    D. Coordination with a composer or selection of recorded music and sound effects;

    E. Discussions with the playwright, if available, and decisions on the ways in which the writer will participate in this phase and the next;

    F. Coordination with the staff on schedule, budget, and delegation of authority for the rehearsal and construction period.

III. Preparation and evaluation of the production by the director:

    A. Casting;

    B. Rehearsals:

        1. Read-throughs;

        2. Identifying units and working them;

        3. Run-throughs;

        4. Technical rehearsals, dress parade, dress rehearsals;

        5. Performances and brush-ups (when needed);

    C. In some cases, an evaluation session with the cast and coworkers after the show closes;

    D. Strike (before or after C).

Summary

The crucial features of these steps are that each belongs to the same process, each is necessarily flexible, and two of the three phases must be done with other people. It could be argued that even phase I involves remembering group activities such as being part of an audience, producing other plays, and critiquing past plays.

    Group activities, particularly those that undertake complex and creative tasks, are often mistrusted, but the folklore about groups coming up with camels when they meant to invent horses is mistaken when it comes to theatre. You might want to examine the careers of Gordon Craig and William

Butler Yeats for signs of what can happen to men of genius when they attempt to be all things to a production. One of the characteristics of a poor production will be signs of a lack of cooperation. This is evident in shows in which actors and setting are competing for attention or when costumes say the wrong things about the characters. Music inappropriate to the mood of the show and actors in the same production who seem to be acting in entirely different plays are also sure signs of discord.

There are several requirements for the production meetings, planning sessions, and problem-solving discussions. In this chapter we have dealt primarily with the director's preparation, but it goes without saying that all cocreators must do their homework. They must all feel free to make contributions to these sessions and must be equally committed to solving problems, particularly those of budget and calendar, and dedicated to making the production as successful as possible. Probably the worst matters of business for such meetings are "hidden agendas" or no agenda at all.

It can be argued that all theatre is spendthrift and irrelevant. There are better ways to make money, safer ways to express oneself, and careers that are more important in the eyes of the world. It may seem trivial to say that what you do gives pleasure or understanding to an audience, or to have to admit that your last production meant very little even to the few people who bothered to attend. But remember, as you go through this process of planning and carrying out a production, that theatre is an institution that flourishes after a culture has dealt with its day-to-day needs. Drama is one of the important means we have for sharing cultural understandings, and doing theatre is something that gives almost everyone pleasure at some time in their lives, whether they admit it now or not. Finally, in the "real" world of governors, industrialists, and generals we often hear that the projects yielding the greatest satisfaction are those that involve large numbers of people with diverse skills and interests, require the setting of goals and methods for accomplishing a complex task, and ultimately combine both the practical and the ideal. Helped produce a play lately?

A Selective Bibliography on Directing

Berry, Ralph. *On Directing Shakespeare: Interviews with Contemporary Directors*. London: Croom Helm; New York: Barnes & Noble, 1977.

Black, Malcolm. *First Reading to First Night: A Candid Look at Stage Directing*. Seattle: University of Washington Press, 1975.

Canfield, Curtis. *The Craft of Play Directing*. New York: Holt, Rinehart & Winston, 1963.

Chekhov, Michael. *To the Director and Playwright*. Compiled and written by Charles Leonard. Westport: Greenwood Press, 1966.

Clurman, Harold. *On Directing*. New York: MacMillan, 1972.

Cole, Toby and Helen K. Chinoy, eds. *Directors on Directing: A Source Book of the Modern Theatre.* Rev. ed. Indianapolis: Bobbs-Merrill, 1963.

Dean, Alexander and Lawrence Carra. *Fundamentals of Play Directing.* 3rd ed. New York: Holt, Rinehart & Winston, 1974.

Gregory, William A. *The Director: A Guide to Modern Theatre Practice.* New York: Funk and Wagnalls, 1968.

McMullan, Frank A. *The Directorial Image: The Play and the Director.* Hamden, Connecticut: Shoe String Press, 1962.

Selden, Samuel. *First Principles of Play Direction.* Chapel Hill, North Carolina: University of North Carolina Press, 1937.

Part Two

PLAYS FOR PRODUCTION

Pebbles on a Greek beach. (Courtesy Greek National Tourist Organization, Chicago.)

7

Sophocles:
Philoctetes

This chapter will provide you with your first opportunity to develop a production plan for a script. You should refer to the preceding chapter on directing for general guidelines and the outline of steps to be taken, and you should look back at all of the earlier chapters of this text, which have been designed to help you with this task.

However, to assist you with this first play, there is an introductory, "backgrounds" section. The play itself is reprinted here with an imaginary director and designer reacting to the play as if for the first time. There is also an interview with Peter Arnott, the translator, about the play and problems of translation. There are visual materials of the sort you might find in your own research, and a series of quotations from William Golding's *Pincher Martin*, which speak about the feelings of a man trapped on an uninhabited island. These are examples of the sort of research you should do when developing a production plan, and should not be construed as the only possible choices to be made for this play. In the following two chapters, as you deal with other production projects, there will be fewer and fewer specific examples. The materials used in succeeding productions will have to be increasingly your own.

Section I: Backgrounds

Philoctetes (first produced in 409 B.C.) is one of Sophocles' later plays and demonstrates his growing control over his materials. For example, he seems to have made a conscious decision in setting the action on a barren island (unlike versions of the legend, no longer extant, by Aeschylus and Euripides). The play combines a story of divine order with one of personal morality and growth, the sort of theme found in Sophocles' masterpieces, *Oedipus Rex* and *Oedipus at Colonus*. Furthermore, the chorus is well integrated into the action, rather than being a commentator that is somewhat uninvolved.

This play was first presented as part of a trilogy and satyr play performed at the Festival of Dionysus, a celebration for citizens of Athens. The plays were performed in a large natural amphitheatre. It was probably equipped with a scene house, and perhaps with a raised acting platform, but still had improvised seating. The production would have seemed colorful and rather elaborate to modern viewers, not unlike opera. Speeches were accompanied by music, there was dance, and perhaps some scenic decoration in the form of panels which were set against the scene house wall. Masks were used as well.

The audience, made up of family groups, was deeply involved in the performance. We have evidence of their being upset by plays that commented on unpleasant contemporary events, and their being frightened by the horrific and moved by the pathetic. They cheered the actors and playwrights who won awards, and spoke out strongly against the performers and writers who offended them, in the "gripe" sessions which typically followed the days of performances.

The actors were trained in dance and voice. They frequently demonstrated their range and versatility by playing several roles in the same play. Later, after the heyday of Greek drama, the actors would rule the stage for a time and chop up the great plays in order to piece together their favorite speeches to show off this same versatility.

Thus the concerns of the actors, playwright, patron, and audience at the first performance of the *Philoctetes* must have been these:

How well do the musicians play?

How well does the chorus sing, dance, and yet still fit the character of the mariners they are supposed to be?

How well do the principal actors handle their roles?

How beautiful and/or appropriate are the settings, costuming, and masks?

How well is the play structured and the verse written?

Does the production move us?

Figure 7-1. Sunset, island scene. (Courtesy Greek National Tourist Organization, Chicago.)

There were many other concerns, but these must have been foremost. Modern readers misunderstand several important features of such plays. For instance, the Athenians did not have copies of *Bulfinch's Mythology* at home. Their legends and myths were still part of an oral tradition. In this and in other ways, the enjoyment of such plays was not based on the aesthetic appreciation of an "informed" audience but on the emotional, human responses of people who wanted to be entertained. The Elgin Marbles and innumerable art books have helped promote the notion that the Athenians were austere, controlled, and Aristotelian, if you will. However, there are indications from recent chemical and microscopic examinations that the Greeks decorated their statuary art with semi-precious stones and painted them with vivid colors.

Philoctetes

SOPHOCLES

(Translated by Peter Arnott)*

ODYSSEUS: Here we are, Neoptolemos. The coast
   of Lemnos,
This no-man's land, this bare excrescence in
The waters. Son of Achilles, it was here
I set down Philoctetes years ago—
Acting only under orders, understand.   (5)
We never had a minute's peace for prayer what
   with his
Wailing and moaning, calling down bad luck
On the whole expedition. But enough of that.
There's no time for discussion. This is urgent.
If he finds I'm here, I've squandered all the
   hours   (10)
I spent devising stratagems to trap him.
So get to work. The rest is up to you.
Start hunting. See if you can find his cave.
It has two entrances, to catch the sun
From both directions, when it's cold outside.
   (15)

And in the summer it's a channel for
The breeze to circulate, and bring him sleep.
There should be a spring below, on the left-
   hand side.

DIRECTOR: Odysseus, the take-charge guy, is obviously more experienced than the boy Neoptolemos. Note lines 10–11. Could this be the key to the play? The situation, judging by this speech, is that of an older, crafty man using a young, naive man to find and bring back Philoctetes. Also, there is bad blood between Odysseus and their quarry.

DESIGNER: Lines 1–3—here is the first description of the place. Line 14—the description of his cave home.

DIRECTOR: Most of this first speech suggests his craftiness.

*Translation © 1983 by Peter Arnott. Used by permission of Peter Arnott.

At least, there was. So go and reconnoitre.
Quietly, mind. Does he still have his home
   there? (20)
Or has he moved? Then, I'll tell you the rest
Of what you must know, and we'll go to work.

NEOPTOLEMOS: Odysseus, sir! It hasn't taken long
   To find it. I can see the cave, I think.

ODYSSEUS: Above or below? I can't see from
   where I am. (25)

NEOPTOLEMOS: Up here. There's not a sound.
   No one's at home.

ODYSSEUS: Take a look. He may be asleep in
   there.

NEOPTOLEMOS: I am. It's empty. Nobody in sight.

ODYSSEUS: Are there any signs of human
   habitation?

NEOPTOLEMOS: Yes. A pile of leaves. A rough and
   ready bed. (30)

ODYSSEUS: You're sure there's nothing else?
   The place is empty?

NEOPTOLEMOS: Well, there's a wooden cup. A
   clumsy
   Bit of work. And a heap of tinder, too.

ODYSSEUS: Yes, that's his lair. You've found it,
   right enough.

NEOPTOLEMOS: Hey, Odysseus! There are some
   rags as well (35)
   Hanging out to dry. His dirty bandages.

ODYSSEUS: This must be where he lives. It's
   obvious
   He must be somewhere round about. He
   couldn't
   Hobble far with an old wound like that.
   Maybe he's gone to hunt for food, or an herb
(40)
   To ease his pain, if such a thing exists.
   Tell your man to stand guard. I mustn't let
   him
   Take me unawares. He'd rather have me
   Than all the Greek army put together.

NEOPTOLEMOS: He's going on ahead to guard the
   trail. (45)
   Let's hear the rest. What do you have in mind?

DIRECTOR AND DESIGNER: Line 25—could he be hiding in the bend of the rock?

DIRECTOR: Line 25—keys to the man, Philoctetes, and how he lives. Suspense.

DESIGNER: There is a definite feeling to this place.

DIRECTOR: Summarizing lines 37–82: Odysseus is very much in charge. Reiterates the fact that there is bad blood between him and Philoctetes (42–44). Line 45 seems to refer to one of the sailors who has gone to stand guard. Lines 47–50 are wonderful examples of Odysseus both cajoling and bullying the boy. He must feel very superior to him. And this goes on in the long speech following.

DESIGNER: "Herbs"? (Line 40) What does the island look like? Traditionally it is Lemnos, but Sophocles has made it uninhabited. Would it be more effective to think of it as a confined space? And the guard standing on a height?

ODYSSEUS: My boy, this is where you have to prove yourself
    Your father's son. And not in strength alone.
    What I have to say may shock you. All the same,
    You came here to assist me, and you must. (50)

NEOPTOLEMOS: I don't understand.

ODYSSEUS: You have to spin a tale
    To win Philoctetes over. Lie to him.
    When he asks you who you are and where you come from,
    Say, the son of Achilles. Tell the truth that far.
    But tell him you hate the Greeks and all their works   (55)
    Because you listened to them when they begged you
    To leave your home for Troy, insisting that
    You were their only hope of taking it;
    And then, when Achilles died, they didn't judge you
    Worthy of inheriting his armor,   (60)
    When you claimed it as your right. Tell him they gave
    The armor to Odysseus. You can call me
    All the bad names you can think of, I don't care.
    But if you refuse, you'll incur the wrath
    Of the entire Greek army; for without the bow
        (65)
    Of Philoctetes you will never capture Troy.
    Why should it be your job, you ask? Because
    You can get close to him. I can't. He'll trust you.
    You sailed out as a volunteer. Nobody
    Drafted you. You didn't join till later.   (70)
    I have no such excuse. If once he sees me
    While he still has his bow, good-bye Odysseus.
    And you'll go with me. No, we must be smart.
    His bow is irresistible. We have
    To find some way to steal it. Yes, I know, lad,
        (75)
    It goes against the grain to say such things
    And play a dishonest part. But make the effort.

DIRECTOR: Odysseus' speech and the attitude it betrays are strictly "any means to accomplish the end." The boy, however, is the son of a dead hero, a man who was noble to a fault. How will the boy respond to this trickery?

The prize is worth it, and the end
Will justify the means. Forget your scruples
And put yourself in my hands, just for one (80)
Short day. And when it's over you can be
A paragon of virtue for all time to come.

NEOPTOLEMOS: Odysseus, there are things I do
    not care to hear.
Far less to do. I do not have it in me
To act against my conscience: and my father
                              (85)
Never had this reputation either.
No. I'm prepared to take this man by force,
But not by trickery. We outnumber him:
Besides he's crippled; we can beat him easily.
I know I'm under orders to assist you   (90)
And hate to back out now. But, sir, I'd rather
Play fair and lose him than play foul and win.

ODYSSEUS: Yes, you're your father's son. A
    gentleman.
When I was your age, I preferred to keep
My mouth shut, and let my hands do the work.
                              (95)
But then I learned what the world is all about.
A man is judged by what he says.
It makes no difference what he does.

NEOPTOLEMOS: You're asking me to lie. Is that an
    order?

ODYSSEUS: Trick Philoctetes. That is all I ask.
                             (100)

NEOPTOLEMOS: Why trick him? Why not put the
    facts before him?

ODYSSEUS: He'll never listen. And you couldn't
    make him.

NEOPTOLEMOS: Where does he get this terrifying
    strength?

ODYSSEUS: His arrows are fatal and they never
    miss.

NEOPTOLEMOS: Then it's not even safe to get close
    to him.   (105)

ODYSSEUS: Except by guile. That's exactly what
    I'm saying.

DIRECTOR: Line 92—Odysseus said "the end justifies the means." Neoptolemos has strong feelings about this underhanded way of dealing with the situation. Conflict between the two men. Lines 94–98 demonstrate how far apart they are on this: Odysseus seems to be saying that as a youth he was deceitful but didn't speak out. Neoptolemos' comment about lies and orders (99) is very revealing. The exchange certainly indicates how Odysseus can handle the boy's objections.

DESIGNER: Line 104—talk of arrows. They are poisoned, always fatal. What would they look like? A Bushman's skinny, fire-hardened shaft or the heavy, harpoonlike arrows sometimes used nowadays for big game hunting?

Line 106—lie to protect your skin. Why is that necessarily the situation? And then the boy puts it naively but pointedly, "But I could never look him in the eye." (109) A man's opinion of you is important. Is this too youthful a view of nobility?

NEOPTOLEMOS: Don't you believe it's wrong to tell a lie?

ODYSSEUS: Not if you have to lie to save your skin.

NEOPTOLEMOS: But I could never look him in the eye.

ODYSSEUS: If you can profit by it, force yourself. (110)

NEOPTOLEMOS: How do I profit, if he goes to Troy?

ODYSSEUS: Troy cannot fall unless we have his bow.

NEOPTOLEMOS: Then am I not to take it? But they said —

ODYSSEUS: You, with his bow. Not one without the other.

NEOPTOLEMOS: If that's the case—we have to win the bow. (115)

ODYSSEUS: Accomplish this and you will have two prizes.

NEOPTOLEMOS: What do you mean? I'm open to persuasion.

ODYSSEUS: A prize for intelligence. A prize for courage.

NEOPTOLEMOS: Very well, I'll do it. I have no more scruples.

ODYSSEUS: Are you sure that you remember my instructions? (120)

NEOPTOLEMOS: No need to worry. I'm committed now.

ODYSSEUS: Stay where you are, and wait for him.
  I'll leave you. He mustn't see us together.
  Oh, the sentry. I'll take him back on board.
  If I think you're taking longer than you should (125)
  I'll send the same man back to you,
    disguised—
  Wearing the outfit of a merchant skipper
  To keep up the deception. He'll have a good story.
  Pay attention, and watch out for hints.

DIRECTOR: Odysseus' line (110) seems sarcastic. Perhaps he's tiring of arguing with the boy.
More exposition in terms of the problem (111). But Odysseus is slippery when spelling it out.

DIRECTOR: When the boy is persuaded, it seems to happen too suddenly. Slow the moment down. Emphasize Odysseus' impatience, arrogance. This is Neoptolemos' commander. He is angered by the boy's reluctance to act.
The whole matter of taking the guard and the use of disguise is interesting. We should wonder what he's up to.

DIRECTOR: The chorus seems to be fond of Neop-

You have your orders. I'm going on board.
                                                    (130)
Hermes, to whom all liars pray,
And Athena, my strength and comfort, help us
    now.
CHORUS: We're on strange ground here, master,
So, tell us what to do.
The man is bound to be wary.   (135)
How much should we let him know?

A king is the regent
Of god on earth.
He sees beyond
The wit of others.   (140)
To you has descended
The wisdom of ages.
It is yours to command
And mine to obey.
NEOPTOLEMOS: First, you would like to see for
    yourselves   (145)
His dwelling place, by the water's edge.
Look, there it is. Be on your guard
When he comes back. Watch for my signals
And do whatever the moment suggests.
CHORUS: Lord, it has been my abiding care   (150)
To watch for your good. So tell us.
Whereabouts does he make his home?
Where can we find him now?
If you don't tell us soon
It may be too late.   (155)
I fear he may pounce
On us unawares.
He must be somewhere.
Where can it be?
Walking the island   (160)
Or lurking inside?
NEOPTOLEMOS: You see where he has his sleeping
    place,
A cave with the entrance at either end.
CHORUS: Poor man, but he's not inside?
Where is he?
NEOPTOLEMUS: Gone to find food. If we looked
    around   (165)

tolemos and wants him to do well. Should they be young men, too? Through him they will succeed. The ancient notion of fealty to your ruler and his responsibility to you is very strong in this scene. And suspense. Philoctetes is coming? They have forgotten to place another guard to replace the one Odysseus took.

DESIGNER: The high ground is empty. Upstage entrance for Philoctetes?

DIRECTOR: Line 133—the impression of the chorus being made up of young men is reinforced in these speeches. No one is taking the initiative. Someone should post guard so that he won't "pounce upon [them] unawares." Neoptolemos is retelling what he has been told about Philoctetes. He speaks of his life, his bow and arrows, and his loneliness and pain. These are character details for the young man, made more important because we know what Odysseus said of Philoctetes to him and where he placed his emphasis. Odysseus saw him as a thing, an obstacle, a powerful enemy. Neoptolemos is prepared to see him as a human being, potentially a friend, someone to be pitied.

DESIGNER: Line 163—again the mention of his cave. It must be visible to them from where they stand now. Also, it seems that they are staying close together and are unable to see from where they are: an enclosed area? A depression? Note the comment of his "track" which suggests again "herbs," low, coarse plants, and thin, rocky earth. Note "by the water's edge" (line 146).

We'd discover his track. As I heard the story,
This is the way he keeps alive.
Hunting game with his bow and arrows.
And always in pain. He can find no cure.

CHORUS: I pity the man   (170)
  Without kith or kin.
  Without a soul
  To live with him.
  Alone all his days
  In sickness and pain,   (175)
  Each moment bringing
  Its burden of care.
  How has he born his misery so long?
  The gods go to work.   (180)
  The more a man profits,
  The more he must pay.

  He was born to the purple
  And passed among men
  As second to none.   (185)
  And now has lost all
  That makes life worth living.
  Solitary his days.
  He lives with the beasts
  Of field and mountain   (190)
  With pain for his partner, and famine too.
  No ease can he find,
  When he bellows his pain.
  There replies but the distant
  Mocking of echoes.   (195)

NEOPTOLEMOS: I have heard his story, and know
    it well.
  It was heaven's will, if I am any judge,
  That he suffer the malevolence of Chryse.
  His present exile and his suffering
  Are surely heaven's dispensation too.   (200)
  He has a bow, god's gift, invincible.
  But heaven has decreed he shall not use it
  Till time has run its course, and the day
  Appointed for Troy's destruction has come.

CHORUS: Quiet!   (205)

DIRECTOR: A suggestion of the implacable architecture of the universe. "Man is made to suffer."
Line 196—Neoptolemos tries to stem the pitying talk of the men regarding Philoctetes. The man probably has gotten what he deserved. This will act as irony later when we see how susceptible the young man is to the very same pity for the unfortunate man. The cry of the tormented man helps to build suspense. In a moment we will see him. The translator emphasizes the sailors' panic and sudden lack of discipline with the humorous line "the song he sings is no shepherd's song" (line 217). It is anything but. A nice moment just before Philoctetes heaves himself into view.

DESIGNER: There are a number of clues to the environment of the play in the chorus' lines. For example, the loneliness of the echo, the existence of famine on the island and the mention of the "lonely hostile sea." The bow of Heracles is mentioned again, and it is becoming more and more important to the play as a hand property.

NEOPTOLEMOS:
  What is it?
CHORUS:
    I heard the noise
Of something human, a tortured cry.
What was it? Here! No, that was the way!
A voice! Yes, a voice! He must have cried
As he stumbled along the path.   (210)
There's no mistake. It's sharp and clear.
The scream of a man in pain.

  Come, lad!
NEOPTOLEMOS: What shall we do?
CHORUS: Think fast!
  No need to look further. He's coming to us.
                                         (215)
Home from the hills. But the song he sings
Is no shepherd's song but a cry of pain
That heralds his coming, wrung from his lips
By the agony of each dragging step.
By the sight of an empty, hostile sea.   (220)
PHILOCTETES: Strangers, ahoy.
  What country do you hail from? What sort of
    men
  Would put in at a place like this?
  An empty island, harborless?
  What country or what family am I   (225)
  To name you by? You dress like Greeks.
  And all things Greek are very dear to me.
  But let me hear your voices. What! Are you
  Afraid of me? You take me for a savage!
  I am castaway, so pity me;   (230)
  I live here all alone, with no
  Companion but my pain. If you are friendly,
  Give me an answer. It would not be fair
  To part without a word.
NEOPTOLEMOS: Well, in the first place, since you
    ask,   (235)
  We're Greeks, my friend. You can be sure of
    that.
PHILOCTETES: What joy to hear a human voice.
  To have someone to talk to after

The terms we are developing to describe the place: barren, solitary, stony, isolated. A place of echoes surrounded by the empty, pitiless sea. In regard to costuming, Philoctetes takes them for Greeks from the way they dress. But what does he look like? "You take me for a savage?" He probably looks like one. His clothing long ago was worn out by the rocky surfaces of his island, and used for bandages for his wound. He must have clothing, but all that is available to him are the pelts of small animals and birds. His arms must be free to use the bow and reach easily for the quiver. There should also be a differentiation between Neoptolemos' clothing and the sailors', one which clearly states the difference in position in a highly stratified society.

DIRECTOR: Hemingway wrote about the mysterious moment of contact in battle in the short story "Old Man at the Bridge." He described the silence before the first tanks appeared at the other side of the river. This scene has something of that feeling, though the ominous quality of the strange man is quickly dispelled by his almost pathetic desire to talk and find out who they are, and his hope that he has not been forgotten. His cry, "You never heard my name?" is almost childlike in its plea for human contact. Note also that Neoptolemos has followed instructions and begun the deceit suggested by Odysseus. It is important not to make Philoctetes too pathetic too soon, however. Let him retain some of his mystery and force. He is, after all, a legendary figure.

So many years—and such a one
As you. What was the urgency   (240)
That brought you here, boy? What need?
What kindly wind?
Tell me your story. I must know your name.

NEOPTOLEMOS: I am an islander from Skyros,
    bound
For home. My name is Neoptolemos,
Achilles' son. And now you know it all.   (245)

PHILOCTETES: Names dear to my heart. And you
    are the boy,
Reared by your father's father, Lycomedes.
Where did you sail from? What business
    brings you here?

NEOPTOLEMOS: Our present voyage began in Troy.

PHILOCTETES: Troy? But how? You weren't with
    the fleet   (250)
That went to Troy when war broke out.

NEOPTOLEMOS: You were a part of that great
    enterprise?

PHILOCTETES: Boy, don't you know who you are
    looking at?

NEOPTOLEMOS: How could I? I've never seen you
    before.

PHILOCTETES: You never heard my name? You
    never heard   (255)
About my fall from grace, my sufferings?

NEOPTOLEMOS: Never a word. This is all news to
    me.

PHILOCTETES: Oh, this is cruel. How the gods
    must hate me
If no word of my fortunes has trickled home;
If Greece has forgotten the sound of my name.
                                              (260)

The devils! To abandon me, and make
A private joke of me; and all the while
My malady grew more voracious daily.
I'll tell you who I am, Achilles' son.   (265)
You may have heard of me. I am the man
To whom Heracles bequeathed his bow and
    arrows;
Philoctetes, son of Poeas, whom the two

DIRECTOR: Line 258—this long speech is our first introduction to the man, Philoctetes. It has several features. He vividly recreates what went before, and this is ironic because we have already heard another version of the same story. The difference between the two stories may be accounted for by one being truth and the other a falsehood. Or it may be Philoctetes' self-pity. We are in a position identical to Neoptolemos'. We can't tell what's true and what isn't. Again, the problem is that if Philoctetes seems too full of self-pity, it will undercut the need for us to feel sympathy.

Commanders of the army and Odysseus
Cast out, more shame to them, and left alone
                                            (270)
To die by inches from a snake-bite, venomous
And mortal. Yes, boy, they abandoned me
To my disease. Our fleet was on the way
From Chryse at the time. We put in here.
It had been a long weary voyage. When we
    beached   (275)
I rested in the rocks and fell asleep.
They must have been delighted. Off they sailed.
And left me, with a few poor rags, some scraps
Of food—as you might throw them to a beggar.
I hope to god they get the same one day.   (280)
Can you imagine my awakening
To find them gone? Can you imagine, boy,
The way I wept, the anguish of my cries,
To find myself deserted, with no help,
No one to nurse my pain? I combed the island
                                            (285)
And nothing could I find but misery.
And that, boy, in abundance. Time moved on.
Day followed day, and weeks, and months, and
    years.
In this hovel I attended to my wants
As best I could. This bow was minister   (290)
To hunger. But this was not enough.
I never missed; but what my bow brought
    down
I had to hobble after to retrieve
In torment, dragging my infected foot
Behind me. Every time I needed water   (295)
Or firewood, when the frost was on the land,
It meant another journey, added pain.
I would have had no fire, except that I
Discovered how to make a flame the hard way
Rubbing two stones together. This kept me
    alive.   (300)
A place to live in, and a fire, I had
All I needed but a way to end this pain.
Now do you want to know about this island?
Only an accident can drive ships here.
It has no harbour. Nowhere for a man   (305)
To find a market or a friendly face.

DESIGNER: An island without a harbor suggests rocky cliffs dropping into the ocean, lack of sandy beaches, heavy spray, and dampness in stormy weather. The mention of clothing left by visitors may suggest some elements of diverse clothing which he might wear (line 278).

No mariner who knew what he was doing
Would come to Lemnos. Every now and then
A ship would come without intending to.
Life is long, and accidents will happen.   (310)
And when such visitors arrived, they would be
Ample in their sympathy, and leave me
Some charitable offering—provisions,
A suit of clothes; but when I asked them for
A passage home, no, anything but that.   (315)
It is ten years now. Ten bitter, famished years
To feed this glutton, pain. And this is what
The sons of Atreus and Odysseus' hand
Have done to me. May all the gods in heaven
Give them the suffering they gave to me.   (320)

CHORUS: We too are moved to pity, son of Poeas
Like all those who have passed this way
before.

NEOPTOLEMOS: And I can testify that everything
You say is true. I learned the hard way
From the sons of Atreus, and Odysseus' hand
(325)

PHILOCTETES: You mean you have some grudge
against the sons
Of Atreus, damn them! Have they hurt you,
too?

NEOPTOLEMOS: They have. And some day they
will pay for it.
Mycenae shall find out, and Sparta too,
That sons of Skyros can defend themselves.
(330)

PHILOCTETES: Bravo, boy! Tell me, what did they
do?
Why do you rage when you speak their names?

NEOPTOLEMOS: I'll tell you, son of Poeas, though
the words come hard.
I came to Troy, and they made me a laughing
stock.
When Achilles' life reached its appointed end
—   (335)

PHILOCTETES: Wait for a moment. First, I must
know
More about this. Is brave Achilles dead?

DIRECTOR: Line 321—the chorus is moved to sympathy, and from what we have seen of them it is probably real. Remember that they were not listening to the conversation of Odysseus and Neoptolemos. But Neoptolemos is involved in deceiving the man. He picks up immediately on Philoctetes' hatred of Odysseus and talks of his own grudges against that man and Menelaus and Agamemnon. One wonders at the effect of Philoctetes' very real grief at Achilles' death on his son's attitude toward the task he has been given by Odysseus. There is a double irony in all this: First, the audience is aware of the duplicity being practiced, but, second, they watch the young man's reaction to Philoctetes' concern. It is one thing to think of the man as an obstacle to be overcome, another to see him as an old friend of one's father and a suffering human being.

NEOPTOLEMOS: Dead. But it was god's work, none
  of man's.
They say it was Apollo's arrow killed him.

PHILOCTETES: He died, then, by a hand that
  matched his own.   (340)
I do not know which first to do, my son —
To ask your sorrow, or to mourn for his.

NEOPTOLEMOS: You have no call to shed your
  tears for others.

PHILOCTETES: That's true enough. Well, go on
  with your story.
Tell me again. How did the kings insult you?
                                             (345)

NEOPTOLEMOS: They came to fetch me in their
  flagship, godly
Odysseus and my father's tutor, Phoenix.
It may have been true; it may have been a lie;
But they said that now my father was no more
Troy would not fall to anyone but me.   (350)
These were their words, my friend. With all
  due speed
I set swift sail for Troy. What moved me most
Was longing to look once upon the father
In death, whom I have never seen alive,
Before they buried him. And then there was
                                             (355)
Their golden promise, that the walls of Troy
Would topple at my coming. Two days out,
With oars to help the wind, we reached
  Sigeum,
Of bitter memory. I disembarked
Amid the plaudits of the army. "It's Achilles."
                                             (360)

CHORUS: O mother Earth! O goddess of
The hills, the golden mountain!
Mother of Zeus! I prayed to you that day
When the sons of Atreus spat upon
Our King, and dressed Odysseus   (365)
In the armour of Achilles.
O blessed one, before whose name
The wild beasts bow, deliver us!

PHILOCTETES: My sailor friends, your grief is
  evident

DIRECTOR: Lines 361–368—
the members of the chorus
speak the truth as they understand it. They would be,
of course, fiercely partisan,
but they don't have a democratic say in intertribal affairs.
More news of what has happened in the past ten years.
Philoctetes' concern and his
very human reactions to the
deaths of friends further hu-
manize him. Neoptolemos'
deceitfulness is almost overdone in his comment about
Odysseus.

And of a piece with mine. Your tale   (370)
Has struck a chord. I recognize the hand
Of the sons of Atreus and Odysseus here.
I know him through and through. His tongue is
     apt
For any falsehood, any perfidy,
To gain his end, as long as it's dishonest. (375)
No, this does not surprise me. But it does
If Ajax knew of it, and let it pass.

NEOPTOLEMOS: He died before it happened. They
     would never
Have dared to insult me if Ajax were alive.

PHILOCTETES: What! First Achilles, and then Ajax
     too —   (380)

NEOPTOLEMOS: Yes. Number him no more among
     the living.

PHILOCTETES: The more's the pity. What of
     Diomedes?
And that misbegotten prodigy Odysseus?
Are they dead too? They should never have
     been born.

NOEPTOLEMOS: Dead? Far from it. Very much
     alive.   (385)
The war has been too good to both of them.

PHILOCTETES: And what about my good old friend
     from Pylos,
Nestor? Is he still living? He always talked
Good sense, he would have stopped their
     tricks.

NEOPTOLEMOS: Yes, still alive. But not the man
     he was.   (390)
He lost his son. Antilochus is dead.

PHILOCTETES: Of all the names you could have
     said, those two
Are the last whose deaths I would have wished
     to hear.
What can we look to, when the likes of these
Must die and leave Odysseus still alive?   (395)
We should be talking of his death, not theirs.

NEOPTOLEMOS: He's quick on his toes. But it's
     men like him
Who know all the tricks, who trip over
     themselves.

PHILOCTETES: In the name of heaven, tell me
    what happened
  To Patroclus, whom your father loved above all
    others.   (400)

NEOPTOLEMOS: It won't take many words to tell
    you that he's
  Dead with the rest. War always takes the good
    men.
  It never takes the bad unless it has to.

PHILOCTETES: My feelings exactly. And that
    reminds me.
  You remember that good-for-nothing blabber-
    mouth   (405)
  Who was always arguing? What became of
    him?

NEOPTOLEMOS: Odysseus, you mean. It's a perfect
    description.
  He was always talking. Nobody listened
  But that didn't stop him. Is he still alive?

PHILOCTETES: No, Thersites.   (410)

NEOPTOLEMOS: I didn't see him. Someone said he
    was.

PHILOCTETES: He would be. Evil always
    flourishes.
  It has a dispensation from above
  That keeps the mean and vicious of this world
  Clear of the jaws of death, and hurries on
  The virtuous and honest to destruction.   (415)
  Where is the sense of it? Why should we have
  Religion, when we see the gods are false?

NEOPTOLEMOS: I can tell you one thing,
    Philoctetes,
  You'll never catch me going anywhere
  Near Troy again. Or the sons of Atreus either.
                                     (420)
  I could never love those who rank the better
    man
  Below the worse, or let honest merit
  Go empty-handed, while the coward takes the
    prize.
  No. For the future, I have no desire
  Except to live in Skyros and be happy.   (425)
  I must go back on board now, son of Poeas.
  I leave you my blessing. May the powers above

DIRECTOR: Lines 407–409—
Neoptolemos' misunderstanding of Philoctetes' reference
to Thersites, a loud-mouthed
noncom, is almost overdone
in his downgrading of Odysseus. Most of the incidents
and deaths mentioned here
and on the previous page are
described in Homer's *Iliad*.

DESIGNER: Should the wind
freshen during this scene, reminding us of the boat rest-
ing in the water beside the
island?

Answer your prayers, and send you remedy.
Now, let us go. As soon as heaven sends
A favorable wind, we raise our anchor.   (430)

PHILOCTETES: Are you leaving so soon?

NEOPTOLEMOS: We have to take
    The weather when it comes. We should be
        ready.

PHILOCTETES: I beg you, by your father, by your
        mother,
    By all your fondest memories of home.
    I go down on my knees to you and pray;   (435)
    You've heard my story, seen my desolation;
    Don't leave me. You have many things to think
        of,
    But spare a thought for me. I know I'm not
    An easy freight. Bear with me, all the same.
    A noble heart despises what is mean   (440)
    And knows that virtue is its own reward.
    If you refuse me, it will be a blemish
    On an honorable name. But if you do it,
    If I get back home alive, the world will sing
    Your praises. Come. It isn't much to ask.   (445)
    Less than a day. You can afford it. Stow me
    Anywhere you like: the hold, the prow, the
        stern,
    Wherever I'll be least offensive to
    Your shipmates. Listen to me, in the name
    Of Zeus the all-compassionate. Say yes.   (450)
    I am a poor thing to be asking favors,
    A man much victimized, a cripple. Still
    You must not leave me here, a castaway.
    Rescue me and take me home with you,
    Or to Euboea: that's Chalcedon's country.
                                                 (455)

    It's an easy crossing to Oeta, and the ridge
    Of Trachis, where the broad Spercheios flows.
    Deliver me to my beloved father.
    And yet the fear has haunted me for years
    That he is dead, or the men, more likely,   (460)
    Who promised to tell him, forgot their errand
    In half an hour, and went their own way home.
    I turn to you now. Be my messenger
    And escort, both. Protect me. Pity me.
    Life is a dangerous adventure, full   (465)

DIRECTOR: Line 433—the important passage is Philoctetes' request that Neoptolemos take him with them. His line, "A noble heart despises what is mean/ And knows that virtue is its own reward," is not only a very ordinary sentiment, but also is strongly ironic in this context. Avoid letting Philoctetes whine or seem too self-pitying. We are still concerned with developing sympathy for him.
There is desperation in this man. He does *beg* to be taken away from the island and returned to his homeland and father. The chorus' reaction is very human. They have no idea of the ruse being perpetrated.

Of chances—up one minute, down the next,
When things are going well, look out for
    trouble.
When life is smooth and easy, that's the time
Destruction may be waiting round the corner.

CHORUS: Pity him, lord. It breaks my heart   (470)
    To hear his long, sad story.
God keep such things from any friend of mine!
Now you have set the kings against you
You should make your loss his gain.
There's a wind, and the ship is waiting;   (475)
Take him home, where he longs to be,
And keep your peace with the powers above.

NEOPTOLEMOS: It's easy to be sympathetic now.
    But once on board, with his stink in your
        nostrils,
    You'll soon have enough, and sing another
        tune.   (480)

CHORUS: That's the last thing in the world I'd do.
    You'll never have cause to accuse me of that.

NEOPTOLEMOS: And I shall never let you find me
        wanting
    To help a friend in need. It's settled then,
    Raise anchor and we'll sail. His wish is
        granted.   (485)
    Our ship will find room for him somewhere.
    May the gods
    Watch over us. Grant us a safe departure
    And happy landfall where we long to be.

PHILOCTETES: O joyous day! Kind sailors, dearest
        friend,
    What can I do to show my gratitude?   (490)
    Come, my young friend. Let's bid a fond
        farewell
    To my old home—if you can call it home.
    See for yourself. It took a lot of courage
    To live this way. The very sight of it
    I think would frighten any other man.   (495)
    I learned the hard way to love misery.

CHORUS: Wait! What's happening? Two men are
        coming,
    One of our shipmates and a stranger.
    Wait a moment, and hear what they have to
        say.

DIRECTOR: Line 470—apparently, Philoctetes has turned away during the chorus' speech on the previous page. He is out of earshot as Neoptolemos chides the sailors. How will they act when Philoctetes is on the boat with them and they smell the wound? Without saying it out loud, he is reminding us of the earlier crew who left the poor man on this island because they could no longer stand his screams of pain or the odor of the wound. It is decided, however, that they will take him with them, and they will leave now.

DESIGNER: Line 475—could there be something on stage which moves with the wind? They have posted a guard during this interlude with Philoctetes. He should probably be on a high point of ground. And there should be two different approaches to this place: one from the place where boats land, unseen from the high point, and another from the island in general, where Philoctetes entered.

DIRECTOR: Events begin to happen very rapidly. It appears that the boy is complying with the older man's wishes when the merchant arrives. The merchant is probably Odysseus in disguise and he has returned in order to find out what has transpired. Perhaps he wears a broad-brimmed hat and stays below Philoctetes, so that his face cannot be seen. He is deathly afraid of the man's bow and deadly arrows, but he still reminds us

MERCHANT: Son of Achilles, I found this sailor
(500)
  Guarding your ship with two of his mates
  And asked where you were. I never expected
  To run into you here. It was a lucky wind
  That brought us both to Lemnos.
  I'm a merchant shipper, on a light run home
(505)
  From Troy to Peparethus, where the vineyards
    grow.
  When I heard these sailors were part of your
    crew,
  I couldn't continue my voyage without
  Offering you some information, in the way
  Of honest trade. The Greeks have new designs
    on you. (505)
  You didn't know that, did you? And it's not
  Just talk. Things are moving already. It won't
  Be long before you find out what they are.

NEOPTOLEMOS: I don't know who you are, but it
    was kind of you
  To think of me. As I'm an honest man, (515)
  I won't be ungrateful. Tell me your news.
  What do the Greeks have in mind for me now?

MERCHANT: They're after you. Their ships have
    left already.
  The old man Phoenix, and the sons of
    Theseus—

NEOPTOLEMOS: To argue with me, or take me
    back by force? (520)

MERCHANT: Who knows? I can only tell you what
    I heard.

NEOPTOLEMOS: And why should Phoenix and his
    shipmates be
  In such a hurry? Is it a royal command?

MERCHANT: They're not wasting any time, you
    can be sure.

NEOPTOLEMOS: Where was Odysseus? What
    prevented him (525)
  From running his own errands? Was he scared
    of me?

MERCHANT: No. He was after someone else. I saw
  him

of the fact that, as the *Odyssey* says, Odysseus is "skilled in all ways of contending." In this interpretation, it must be assumed that Neoptolemos recognizes Odysseus. But he is probably puzzled by Odysseus' strategy and doesn't know how to communicate to him what he has accomplished, if indeed he wants to.

DIRECTOR: Line 520—the audience should also be confused by Odysseus' strategy.

DESIGNER: There is a very clear need to maintain spatial levels of separation. In this case, Odysseus wishes to be overheard, but he can't be seen by Philoctetes, who is looking down on the crown of his hat.

DIRECTOR: Deception is apparent again. What does he have in mind? Note the way Odysseus talks against himself. Later, however, he will identify Odysseus as "mighty Odysseus." The man has gall, if nothing else.

Setting out with Diomedes when I left.

NEOPTOLEMOS: After someone else? Do you know
    who it was?

MERCHANT: It was a boy! You have to tell me
    something first.   (530)
    Who's he? Be careful he doesn't hear us.

NEOPTOLEMOS: That's Philoctetes. You must have
    heard of him.

MERCHANT: Don't say another word! Get on your
    ship,
    And sail away as quickly as you can!

PHILOCTETES: What's he saying, boy? What sort of
    deal   (535)
    Is he making with you behind my back?

NEOPTOLEMOS: I don't know yet. Whatever it is,
    He can say it openly, before us all.

MERCHANT: I shouldn't do it. If they ever catch
    you,
    Don't give me away. I have to make a living.
                                                                                   (540)
    I work for them and they've been kind to me.

NEOPTOLEMOS: I have no love for the sons of
    Atreus.
    That is the bond between this man and me.
    You came with good intentions. You must not
    Refuse me now. I must know everything you
    heard.   (545)

MERCHANT: Watch out for yourself.

NEOPTOLEMOS: I'm used to doing that.

MERCHANT: On your own head be it.

NEOPTOLEMOS: Anything you say.

MERCHANT: Then listen. This is the man they're
    after—
    Diomedes, I mean, and the mighty Odysseus.
    They took an oath that if their arguments (550)
    Had no effect, they'd bring him back by force.
    Odysseus went 'round bragging to the army.
    It's public knowledge now. He never lacked
    For confidence. The other's not so sure.

NEOPTOLEMOS: What could have possessed the
    sons of Atreus   (555)
    To take an interest after all this while,

DIRECTOR: Line 542—it would appear that the chief intention of Odysseus' ruse is to help Neoptolemos get Philoctetes on board the ship. Odysseus did not know what the boy had accomplished, but his strategy would fit almost any device the boy might invent. It is tempting to think that Odysseus probably never trusted the boy's ability to persuade the man to come on board ship. There is nice irony in Philoctetes' lines about Odysseus (592–595): "but that man would say anything, venture any risk. . . . Let's go, my boy, and put a few sea-miles between ourselves and Odysseus' ship. . . ." Then when he slept, they could overpower him. Odysseus would come out of hiding and they would have their prize. In critical discussions of this drama there is often argument about this point. It represents a mis-

In a man they had abandoned years ago?
What urgency? Or did they have no choice?
Did heaven intervene to right a wrong?

MERCHANT: I'll tell you how it came about.
Perhaps you never heard that Priam had a son (560)
Whose name was Helenus. He had the power
To look into the future. Well, one night,
Odysseus—every filthy name you know
Fits him—went sneaking through the lines
    alone (565)
And captured him. He brought him back in
    chains
And paraded his distinguished prize
Before the whole Greek army. Helenus
Made many prophecies, but most important
Was what he had to say concerning Troy. (570)
He said its walls would never yield to them
Unless they persuaded this man, Philoctetes,
To leave his island and rejoin the army.
That was the prophecy. The minute that
Odysseus heard it, he undertook to bring (575)
Philoctetes back—by persuasion if he could,
By force if he had to. If he failed,
He pledged his head as forfeit. Now, my boy,
You know it all. My best advice to you
And anyone you care about, is hurry. (580)

PHILOCTETES: So he swore, did he, that devil
    incarnate,
To talk me into rejoining the Greeks?
If he died he could charm me back from Hades
After I'm dead, the way his father came.

MERCHANT: I wouldn't know. It's time I was
    getting back (585)
To my ship again. And god help both of you.

PHILOCTETES: This is madness! Does Odysseus
    really think
That he can wheedle me on board his ship,
And take me back to show off to the Greeks?
I'd sooner listen to my deadliest enemy, (590)
The viper that did this mischief to my foot.
But that man would say anything. He'd
    venture

understanding by Odysseus of the oracle. Philoctetes had to come willingly. If we take it as dramatic license at this point, there is no interruption of the causal connection. In regard to the dramaturgy to this point: We have been introduced to the major characters, been shown their relationships to one another and the major conflict. We have been given ample exposition, and are now deeply involved in a series of actions that are leading to a conclusion unless a "complication" occurs. One possible complication has been foreshadowed. The boy might be softening toward Philoctetes. An important moment is about to arrive.

Any risk. He'll be here soon, I know.
Let's go, my boy, and put a few sea-miles
Between ourselves and Odysseus' ship.   (595)
A little haste now when haste is called for
And we'll sleep in peace when the labor's done.

NEOPTOLEMOS: We can't sail yet. We don't have a chance
Till the head wind drops. It's dead against us.

PHILOCTETES: When you're running for safety, any weather's good.   (600)

NEOPTOLEMOS: At least the wind's against Odysseus too.

PHILOCTETES: Pirates don't care if it's blowing a gale
When there are men to rob and ships to plunder.

NEOPTOLEMOS: All right, let's go. If there's anything you need,
Any special treasure, bring it along.   (605)

PHILOCTETES: A couple of things. There's not much choice.

NEOPTOLEMOS: Is it something I couldn't supply on board?

PHILOCTETES: There's an herb I have. It makes a good poultice
To dress my sore. It helps to ease the pain.

NEOPTOLEMOS: Bring it, by all means. Anything else?   (610)

PHILOCTETES: There may be some arrows lying around.
I shouldn't leave them for anyone to find.

NEOPTOLEMOS: Is that the bow that everybody talks about?

PHILOCTETES: The very same. This bow here in my hands.

NEOPTOLEMOS: I wonder—could I look at it more closely,   (615)
And hold, and adore it as a god?

PHILOCTETES: This bow, my boy, and anything I own
Is yours to hold if it will give you pleasure.

DIRECTOR: Line 599—the indication is that the wind is blowing against them if they wish to sail to Philoctetes' home, away from the direction of Troy. It doesn't sound as though these are ships capable of beating upwind. Is it deception on Neoptolemos' part? Will he steer to Troy with the wind behind him when he gets the man on board?

Philoctetes begins to gather his few possessions. The boy's attention is on the bow, now that the task of getting Philoctetes on shipboard is accomplished. Perhaps the audience will think it means he will take the bow away from him, but this doesn't fit with the notion of bringing the man along with them to Troy. Or does it? Will they immobilize him and carry him on the ship? In any event, it is a powerful moment when the poor man, so much the victim, hands over the only possession which stands between him and total vulnerability. And the terms by which he does it, the words he speaks, as well as the act of submission itself, speak powerfully to the relationship that he feels growing between himself and the young man. This is an excellent example of an action being stronger than narration. The bow passes from hand to hand. Either a bond has been formed or a terrible violation prepared for.

NEOPTOLEMOS: Please. I have an urgency, a
>   yearning—if
>   It is permitted. If not, forget I spoke.   (620)

PHILOCTETES: Reverently said. It is permitted.
>   For you and you alone restored to me
>   The gift of light, to see my land of Oeta,
>   My father in his age, my friends. When I
>   Was stricken by my enemies, you raised me.
>   (625)
>   Take heart. It shall be given you to hold
>   And give back whence it came. Be ever mindful
>   That for your virtue it was given you
>   To handle this, and to no man besides.
>   It was thus I had it, for a kindness done.   (630)

NEOPTOLEMOS: This I never shall regret: that I
>   have come
>   To know you as my friend. To help somebody
>   And then be done by as you did to me
>   Is treasure beyond price.
>   Will you go in now? Let me lead the way. (635)

PHILOCTETES: My malady craves company. Stay
>   near me.

CHORUS: I have heard the ancient story
>   Of the ravisher who lusted
>   For the wife of Zeus:
>   How the Father Almighty   (640)
>   Bound him for his sins
>   To a wheel ever turning.
>   But in all the world I never
>   Saw or heard the like of this.
>   He was guileless, a man   (645)
>   Of peace; in esteem
>   He yielded to none.
>   What crime had he done
>   That he should suffer so?
>   No sound to be heard   (650)
>   But the surf on the shore.
>   How could he endure
>   Those desolate days?

>   He was crippled, with no neighbor,
>   No companion in distress,   (655)
>   No sympathetic ear

DESIGNER: Line 620—the entrance to the shelter is nearby. Could the interior be open enough to allow scenes such as those that follow to be played as interior scenes? Can it be handled realistically? Perhaps he has removable roofing pieces which allow him to leave the cavern open in the daylight on clear days.

DIRECTOR: It seems very certain that the boy has been deeply moved by the action. And part of the proof is the fact that he does not seize the bow and carry it away, or give orders to the sailors to bind Philoctetes. The departure is delayed by the older man's presentiment that one of his seizures is coming on him. Neoptolemos offers to stay with him during it. Remember, the sailors who abandoned him on the island had been unable to bear his seizures. Can Neoptolemos? What is the depth of the relationship being formed between the two men? How will this bear on the purpose of Odysseus?
The chorus reminds us of the larger perspective. Philoctetes has suffered alone for years.

To receive his cry of anguish
For the pain that sucked his blood,
Or wipe the venomous
Pus from his foot   (660)
And assuage the fire
With a dressing of herbs
Plucked from the meadows.
When the spasm shook him,
When the fever abated   (665)
And left him a respite
To look to his wants,
He would stumble and crawl
Like a child that has tottered
Away from his mother.   (670)
He could not live by honest sweat
Like other men, or till the fields
To find god's bounty. Only his bow,
His flying arrows, to fill his belly.
His life was blighted: for ten long years   (675)
No delight of wine, but water lapped
From any puddle he could find.

And now the release, the happy ending:
A savior born of heroes, come
In fullness of time, to bear him home   (680)
To Malea, where nymphs dwell, where
     Spercheois rolls
Between its banks; and Oeta, where
A mighty warrior was wrapped in flame
And men and deity were one.

NEOPTOLEMOS: Here, aren't you coming? Is
     something wrong?   (685)
  Why don't you move? Have you been struck
     dumb?

PHILOCTETES: Ah. Ah.

NEOPTOLEMOS: What is it?

PHILOCTETES: It's nothing.
  Go ahead.

NEOPTOLEMOS: Is it your old wound troubling you
     again?

PHILOCTETES: No. No. I think it's better now.
  Oh, gods in heaven!   (690)

NEOPTOLEMOS: Why do you cry so loudly to the
    gods?

PHILOCTETES: For help. For comfort. For a gentle
    hand.
    Ah. Ah.

NEOPTOLEMOS: What is it? Tell me! Won't you
    speak to me?
    I can see you're in pain.   (695)

PHILOCTETES: I'm done for, boy. I have to admit
    it.
    The pain's going through me like a knife.
    Ah, how it hurts. This is the end.
    For the love of god, boy, if you have a sword,
    Draw it, cut off my foot.   (700)
    Now! This minute! Cut off my foot!
    I don't care if you kill me!

NEOPTOLEMOS: What's happened to you all at
    once?
    What makes you scream and cry?

PHILOCTETES: You know!

NEOPTOLEMOS: What is it?   (705)

PHILOCTETES: You know!

NEOPTOLEMOS: What's happened to you?

PHILOCTETES: You must know! Aaah!

NEOPTOLEMOS: Another attack. It must be torture.

PHILOCTETES: Torture! I can't tell you—pity me!

NEOPTOLEMOS: What shall I do?

PHILOCTETES: Don't be frightened away. (710)
    It comes on me like this, from time to time
    When it thinks it's left me alone too long.

NEOPTOLEMOS: Poor devil. Poor, poor devil.
    Everything bad happens to you.
    Come. Let me help you. Take my hand.   (715)

PHILOCTETES: No. But do one thing for me.
    Take the bow
    I let you hold a minute ago.
    Keep it for me till the crisis passes.
    Let no one touch it. Every time
    The fever goes, there comes a sleep, a
      weakness.   (720)
    That's how it always leaves me. Let me sleep.

DIRECTOR: Line 704—Philoctetes repeats "you know" when the boy asks him what is happening. But of course Neoptolemos doesn't know, any more than the audience does in the safety of its seats, and then the suffering man cries out, "Take my hand," (line 715) and Neoptolemos crosses the gap between them. He has made contact.

Then there is our reaction to Philoctetes' request that the boy take his bow. We know that it is safe with him, unless Odysseus should return. In a brief span of time, we have seen the relationship change and grow. There is also something strange, perhaps mystical about Philoctetes' punishment and his isolation from other men. There could be another meaning to the plan which has been ignored in our concern with the issue of whether or not Odysseus and Neoptolemos could trick him into returning with them. Philoctetes' agony is more than a man should have to bear, but he may also be an instrument of the gods.

Figure 7-2. (A) Poseidon or Zeus. (Courtesy Greek National Tourist Organization, Chicago.)

(B) Reputed to be Philip II, Alexander's father. (Courtesy Greek National Tourist Organization, Chicago.)

(C) Drawing from bust of Pericles.

Don't try to wake me. If anybody comes
While I'm asleep—now listen to me, boy—
Whatever happens, whatever tricks they try,
Don't give them the bow, or let them take it
    from you.   (725)
If you do, you'll be the death of both of us.
I count on you. My life is in your hands.

NEOPTOLEMOS: Rest easy. I'll take care. No one
    shall have it
But you and me. Give it here, with your bles-
    sing.

PHILOCTETES: There it is, boy. Take it. Reverently,
    now   (730)
Or the gods will be jealous. I wouldn't wish
On you the suffering it has brought on me
Or the man who had it before I did.

NEOPTOLEMOS: God grant his prayer and mine,
    and send
A wind to fill our sails, so we may go   (735)
With godspeed to our journey's end.

PHILOCTETES: I fear your prayer is doomed to go
    unanswered.
The dark blood is still welling from the vein.
There's something else to come.
Aaaah!
It comes—it comes—it's here!   (740)
See how it is with me! Don't go!
Odysseus, if this stabbing pain
Were only in your heart. You generals.
Agamemnon, yes, and Menelaus both,
If you could have been in my place all these
    years!   (745)
If you could know what it is to feel this pain!
Death, oh, Death, I call upon you daily
And still you never come.
There's a volcano on the island, boy.
A fire that lights up Lemnos. Take me there
                                                                      (750)
And throw me in the flames. I had to do
The same for Heracles, and won the bow
That you are holding now.
Well?
Say something, boy.   (755)

DESIGNER: Perhaps a literal treatment of the wound as revealed by the darkening flush of blood?

DIRECTOR: The full fury of the spasm strikes him. It is inhuman pain, not the over-acting of a coward who craves sympathy. There is pathos in Philoctetes' requests that the boy stay and obvious surprise when he does. The rough sailors on the ship, his own friends, could not stand this, but the well-born youth *does* remain. Is there mysticism in the event? Do the lights begin to dim? Philoctetes begins to hallucinate. The pain is making him delirious. But there seems to be a connection between Heracles' fiery death and Philoctetes' agony.

Say something! I can't hear you! Where have
  you gone?

NEOPTOLEMOS: What is there left for me to do but
  weep?

PHILOCTETES: Take courage, boy. The fit will pass
  from me
  As quickly as it came. I only ask you
  To stay here at my side.   (760)

NEOPTOLEMOS: I'll stay, don't worry.

PHILOCTETES: You will?

NEOPTOLEMOS: I promise.

PHILOCTETES: You swear it? No, I have no right to
  ask.

NEOPTOLEMOS: I don't need to swear. I couldn't
  leave you now.

PHILOCTETES: Give me your hand on it.

NEOPTOLEMOS: Here. I'll stay.

PHILOCTETES: Take me! Take me!

NEOPTOLEMOS: Take you where?

PHILOCTETES: Up there.   (765)

NEOPTOLEMOS: Up where? In the sky? You're
  losing your mind.

PHILOCTETES: Let me go! Let me go!

NEOPTOLEMOS: What for?

PHILOCTETES: Let me go!

NEOPTOLEMOS: I have to keep hold of you.

PHILOCTETES: No! You're killing me!

NEOPTOLEMOS: See. There you are. Are you better
  now?

PHILOCTETES: Earth, open to me. Let this be my
  death.   (770)
  The pain's too great for me. I cannot bear it.

NEOPTOLEMOS: It won't be long now. Sleep will
  fall
  Upon him soon, his head's already nodding,
  His body's streaming with sweat, and the
  blood
  Is pouring in a dark stream from his heel.
                                               (775)
  Don't disturb him, friends. He's falling asleep.

DESIGNER: Could there be an abstract pattern of light behind this action that further extends the emotional meaning of the scene?

DIRECTOR: The climax of the pain is reached and the blood flows from the heel. Does it sound like an invented ailment, made up to represent what the gods can do to man, or does it sound like epilepsy or leprosy? After all, in primitive and not so primitive times epileptics were looked on as having special powers of communication with the gods. There

CHORUS: Come, gentle sleep, our nurse, our balm,
  To breathe your benison upon
  His eyes, and draw a veil across
  The sun. Come, kindly healer, come.   (780)
  Master, what should the next step be?
  Where would you have us turn our hand?
  Look at him now. The time has come
  To act without delay.
  Opportunity never comes but once.
  It shows the way. So take it while you can.
                                        (785)

NEOPTOLEMOS: He is deaf to the world. But it
    would do little good
  To take his bow and arrows and leave him
    here.
  God has given him the glory. We must take
    him too.
  We could not face our comrades with our work
    half done.
CHORUS: God will take care of his own, my son.
                                        (790)
  But softly, softly when you speak.
  The sick sleep fitfully. A word
  May stir his scattered senses.
  Careful now, whatever you do.
  Take it from him before he wakes.   (795)
  But if you mean what I think you mean,
  If you have other plans for him,
  Take care. There are pitfalls lying ahead,
  As any sensible man can see.

  The wind is blowing our way now.   (800)
  The man has no resource. The night
  Is thick upon him, his eyes are blind.
  Happy the man who sleeps in the sun.
  His hands, his feet do not obey,
  He lies as one dead. Consider, my lord,   (805)
  If what you suggest is wise.
  Better, I have always thought,
  To do the work without the risk.
NEOPTOLEMOS: Quiet! Keep your wits about you
    now.
  He's sitting up and opening his eyes.   (810)

is a problem in that the chorus does speak as a conspirator at this moment. Perhaps we could have that part of the speech spoken by a sailor who accompanied the merchant to the spot or change the earlier interpretation. But that would change the personality of the chorus, make it manipulative. I'd prefer the former.
Neoptolemos knows that Philoctetes must accompany the bow to Troy.
The moment is hushed, still. The tormented man sleeps. There is a strange sort of union between the victim and the hunters. Is something moving in the silence? Destiny? When he slept like this before, his friends on the ship put him ashore and abandoned him. There is the danger that Neoptolemos will act as Odysseus would, but the moment passes as Philoctetes awakens. Neoptolemos has not committed himself one way or the other. Philoctetes tells the boy what we have already thought. The boy's reaction was different. And Neoptolemos' words to the man are those of deep respect and kindness. Neoptolemos *seems* to be growing up. He is going through an enormous change.
We begin to guess what he will say to Odysseus in the obligatory scene which is coming. (There will have to be a showdown.)

PHILOCTETES: The light again. I am awake.
    And what I never
Dreamt to see, my friends around me,
    watching—
This is more than I could ever hope.
That you could have compassion on me, hear
My sufferings, and stay here at my side.   (815)
The sons of Atreus could not do as much.
The great commanders found it more than they
    could bear
But you inherit the nobility,
That was your father's. When the cries of pain
And smell of sickness were inflicted on you,
                                      (820)
You took them in your stride. And now the
    pain
Is but a memory, I have a space to breathe:
Boy, put your arms around me. Lift me up.
When this weakness has departed from me,
We'll sail from here with all the speed we may.
                                        (825)

NEOPTOLEMOS: This is unlooked for joy, to see
    you alive
And breathing still, delivered from your pain.
When the sickness came upon you, all the signs
Proclaimed you dead. Come then. Get on your
    feet,
Or if you'd rather, my men will carry you (830)
And never flinch. Whatever you decide.

PHILOCTETES: Thank you, my boy: but let me lean
    on you.
Spare them the trouble. I would not wish
This smell of pestilence upon them yet
Before I must. They'll find it hard enough (835)
To live in the same ship with me.

NEOPTOLEMOS: As you wish. Stand up, put your
    arm 'round my shoulders.

PHILOCTETES: See. It's not too bad. My legs
    remember.

NEOPTOLEMOS: Oh, what am I going to do?

PHILOCTETES: What is it, boy? What are you
    talking about?   (840)

NEOPTOLEMOS: How can I tell you? I can't find
the words—

PHILOCTETES: The words for what? You mustn't
talk like this.

NEOPTOLEMOS: Now things have gone this far. I
have no choice.

PHILOCTETES: Don't tell me. My disease has
sickened you.
You've changed your mind. You don't want me
on board.   (845)

NEOPTOLEMOS: Everything is sickening, when a
man
Must be false to himself, and act against his
nature.

PHILOCTETES: But everything you've said and
done has shown
Your father's image. You have shown true
merit —

NEOPTOLEMOS: And now I shall disgrace him.
(850)
This has grieved me from the start.

PHILOCTETES: You have not disgraced him so far.
But you talk as though you may.

NEOPTOLEMOS: Zeus, what shall I do? Tell
another lie?
Speak with a forked tongue, hide the truth
from him?

PHILOCTETES: He's going to leave me. That's what
he means.   (855)
Leave me and sail away from here without me.

NEOPTOLEMOS: Leave you? No, it might be better
for you
If I did. That's what has grieved me from the
start.

PHILOCTETES: What do you mean, boy? I don't
understand you.

NEOPTOLEMOS: I'll tell the whole truth. You have
to go to Troy.   (860)
Go back to the Greeks, and the sons of Atreus.

PHILOCTETES: What?

NEOPTOLEMOS: Save your tears, there's more
to come.

DIRECTOR: As the boy sup-
ports the man, not heeding
the smell of his wound, he
feels the need to unburden
himself. This is a clear sign of
the maturity he has achieved
in just this short time. He has
reflected on his promise to
Odysseus, knows now that
he has made a terrible mistake and wants to tell all.
Ironically, Philoctetes misun-
derstands his desire to
speak, imagines that it will
have to do with his wound.
As Neoptolemos says, he
now realizes that what he
was doing was against his
nature.
Note the irony of Line 859:
"What do you mean, boy?" It
is time to tell all; and this will
undoubtedly lead to the next
complication.
Neoptolemos takes the hard
line: he admits to his deceit
and tells Philoctetes that he
must come with them to Troy.
This is a surprise.

PHILOCTETES: More? What do you intend to do
    with me?

NEOPTOLEMOS: Save you from your recent plight,
    and then
    Go to Troy with you, and take it with your aid.
                                                    (865)

PHILOCTETES: You really mean to do this?

NEOPTOLEMOS: Yes, I have
    No other choice. Do not be angry with me.

PHILOCTETES: This is the end for me; I am
    betrayed.
    What have you done to me! Give me back my
    bow.

NEOPTOLEMOS: It is not in my power. I must do
    what is right   (870)
    And what is best for me. I have my orders.

PHILOCTETES: Scourge, fiend incarnate, villainy
    personified,
    Vile, loathesome! Do you see what you have
    done?
    How you have cheated me? Have you no
    shame
    To look me in the face? I turned to you   (875)
    For succor, and you took my bow, my life.
    Give it back to me, boy; give it back, I beg you.
    By the gods of your fathers, do not take my
    life.
    I waste my time. He will not condescend
    To speak, or look at me; he will not give them
    back.   (880)
    Beaches and headlands, wild beasts of the hills
    That kept me company, you rugged rocks.
    Familiar presences, it is to you
    That I must cry, for no one else will hear me.
    See what Achilles' son has done? He swore
                                                    (885)
    To take me home, but takes me now to Troy.
    He offered me his hand, and took the bow
    That Zeus and Heracles have sanctified,
    To show it as a trophy to the Greeks!
    He takes me by force—as if it needed force
                                                    (890)
    To master me! Does he not understand
    That his opponent is already dead,

DIRECTOR: Neoptolemos has his orders. But there is no question in our minds that he hates himself for what he has had to do. Imagine Philoctetes' feelings. The boy was the first person to show him real kindness in ten years, and it turns out that he is prepared to do him the greatest ill anyone has since he was first left there. The despair he feels, his anger knows no bounds. There was no harm left which could be done to him, and yet this boy under the guise of friendship has done him the worst possible harm. Philoctetes cannot even imagine going with them. He will stay here, die without his bow.

An insubstantial shadow? If I had
My strength, he'd not have taken me—or even
  now,
Unless by treachery. I am lost, betrayed.   (895)
What can I do? Be your old self again.
Give me my bow. No word? Then I am
  finished.
I must return to you again, my cave,
My burrow in the rock, stripped of my arms,
My means of feeding; in my lonely dell   (900)
I shall be doomed to wither away and die.
No flying bird, no wild beast of the hill
Shall fall to my bow again. I fed on them;
It will be their turn, soon, to feed on me.
When I am dead. The hunter shall be hunted
                                          (905)

And I shall pay for their blood with my own
Because I thought I saw an honest face!
Die!—But not yet, not till I know
If you've changed your mind; if not, die and be
  damned.

CHORUS: What shall we do? It's your decision,
  master.   (910)
Do we sail? Or shall we listen to his prayers?

NEOPTOLEMOS: My heart is struck with pity for
  the man
As I have pitied him this long, long while.

PHILOCTETES: Mercy, for the love of god!
  Remember
What the world will say, if you do this to me.
                                          (915)

NEOPTOLEMOS: What can I do? I wish I had never
  gone
Away from Skyros. The world is too much with
  me.

PHILOCTETES: You are honest at heart. But you
  have been schooled
To evil by bad masters. Leave such things
Where they belong. Give back my bow and
  sail.   (920)

NEOPTOLEMOS: Men, what shall I do?

ODYSSEUS: You fool! You traitor!
  Let go of the bow, and give it to me!

DIRECTOR: The chorus is anxious to go, but Neop-tolemos pauses, and surpris-ingly (and most painfully for Neoptolemos), Philoctetes shows pity for the boy's di-lemma. He turns to ask the sailors, young men like him-self, what to do. At that mo-ment Odysseus appears, probably from close at hand where he has been hiding, waiting. The ultimate confron-tation has come, but the boy is changing.
The confrontation, however, first seems to be between Odysseus and Philoctetes, two old enemies. The boy stands by with the bow in his hand.

PHILOCTETES: Who was that? It sounded like
   Odysseus.

ODYSSEUS: You're right. It is Odysseus, here in
   person.

PHILOCTETES: So. I am bought and paid for.
   I am finished.   (925)
   It was his doing. He robbed me of my bow.

ODYSSEUS: My own unaided work. I don't deny it.

PHILOCTETES: The bow, boy! Give me the bow!

ODYSSEUS: He won't,
   However much he'd like to. Now you have to
   Come with us. Or else these men will make
   you.   (930)

PHILOCTETES: You devil, won't you stop at
   anything?
   Make me?

ODYSSEUS: Yes, if you don't come quietly.

PHILOCTETES: Do you see this, Lemnos? Do you
   see,
   You fiery mountain that Hephaestus wrought?
   Will you allow this? Will you let them take
   me?   (935)

ODYSSEUS: All things must bow before the will of
   Zeus.
   And I am Zeus' minister on Lemnos.

PHILOCTETES: Why, what abominable tale is that?
   You hide behind the gods and make them liars!

ODYSSEUS: No lie, but truth. We must be on our
   way.   (940)

PHILOCTETES: No!

ODYSSEUS: Yes. You have to learn obedience.

PHILOCTETES: It was for this my mother bore me,
   then,
   To have no liberty. To be a slave.

ODYSSEUS: No! To be ranked equal with the
   highest
   To stand beside them, help them conquer Troy!
                                               (945)

PHILOCTETES: Never. Let them do their worst.
   Not while I have this precipice to help me!

ODYSSEUS: What are you doing?

DIRECTOR: Philoctetes' fury is followed by a manic desire to kill himself, but the sailors intercede and he is held, helpless. It is a pathetic moment. It does seem that Odysseus has gone too far in his claim that he is on the gods' side, though as far as he is concerned, if he is winning then they must agree (and if he were losing it would be up to him to find a way out). It seems like the classic confrontation of "doers" and "noble fumblers." Philoctetes turns to the boy. He absolves him of guilt. This is nothing as simple as self-pity. Rather, it is the humiliation of a proud man.

PHILOCTETES: I'm going to jump.
  Leave my bleeding body on the rocks below.
ODYSSEUS: Hold him, men! Don't let him get
      away!   (950)
PHILOCTETES: Oh, hands, what can you do
      without my bow,
  My treasure! You are a prisoner now. He holds
      you.
  This is the second time your filthy plots
  Have caught me unawares. You hid behind
  This boy, this stranger! We are kindred spirits,
                                                     (955)

  He and I; he is too good for you.
  He carried out his orders. That was all.
  Look at his face. See how ashamed he is
  Of his mistake. Of what he made me suffer.
  It was your devious and furtive mind   (960)
  That warped his innocence, perverting him
  Against his will, and schooling him in evil.
  And now you mean to take me, bound in
      chains,
  From this same desert island, where you once
  Abandoned me to die a living death.   (965)
  May you perish! How many times that prayer
      has been
  On my lips: but the gods withheld their favor.
  It is yours to live and flourish, mine to grieve
  That I must live, beset by misery,
  A laughing stock for you and those you serve,
                                                     (970)
  The two set in authority, the sons of Atreus.
  Why did you mourn their cause? Because they
      made you.
  They tricked you into it. But I—unhappy day—
  I volunteered, and took them seven ships.
  Then they stripped me of my rights and honors
                                                     (975)
  And threw me out. At least, you say they did.
  They told me it was you.
  Now where are you taking me? And why?
  I am of no account. I have been dead to you
  For years. You devil, am I not the maimed
                                                     (980)

DIRECTOR: Even before the
war, as Philoctetes points
out, he was the sort of man
who volunteered to fight for
the cause, while Odysseus
had to be tricked into it.
Odysseus answers him in a
by now familiar fashion: winning, he says, is what matters. "I am the sort of man I
have to be." In some ways,
at this point, the play has
become a vivid, dramatized
discussion of the two ways to
raise a child: either train him
to be noble, fair to others,
and ethical or teach him to
prevail in all situations.
Should he be trained to be
like the famous but dead
Achilles or a living
Odysseus?
The chorus has now landed
squarely on the side of expediency. Odysseus is talking,
the wind is blowing to Troy,
it's time to be gone and stop

And stinking wretch I was? If I sail with you,
What happens to your prayers and sacrifices?
This was your pretext, everyone of you, who
   did
Philoctetes wrong. If the gods are just, you will
   perish:
And now I know they must be. You would
   never   (985)
Have sailed to rescue this poor derelict
Without the stimulus of heaven. You needed
   me,
Land of my fathers, gods that watch our lives.
Bring down retribution on their heads
Late though it be, if you have compassion.
                               (990)

It is my pain, my need that asks, if I
Could see them dead, I would be whole again.
CHORUS: Bitter as ever. These are the words of
   one
Who will not admit that he is beaten.
ODYSSEUS: There are many ways that I could
   answer you   (995)
If time permitted. One must suffice.
I am the sort of man I have to be.
In a fair fight between honest men,
You'd find me a model of propriety.
I only want to win. I don't care how.   (1000)
You've beaten me, for once. Have it your own
   way.
Stand easy, men. Let the prisoner go.
He can stay on the island. We don't need him;
We have his weapons. When we get to Troy,
Teucer will be there. He understands such
   things   (1005)
And I consider myself as good a shot
As you are, any day. You are expendable.
I leave you to your island. It is yours
To walk about in and enjoy yourself.
So, let us go. This honour could have been
                               (1010)
Yours for the asking. I shall have it now.
PHILOCTETES: What shall I do? Will you display
   yourself

arguing. Also, nothing magical happened when Philoctetes was seized. He seems to be only a man after all. However, there are problems here. Is this another trick? Or does Odysseus misunderstand the oracle? Odysseus gives commands. They must leave, taking with them the bow but not the man. Is this also a trick?

Among the Greeks in weapons that are mine?

ODYSSEUS: I am going now. I have no time to
argue.

PHILOCTETES: Son of Achilles, shall I never hear (1015)
Your voice again? Will you desert me too?

ODYSSEUS: Come, Neoptolemos. You're too kind-
hearted.
Don't look back at him. Leave well enough
alone.

PHILOCTETES: And you, my friends. Will you
abandon me?
Is there no pity in your hearts? (1020)

CHORUS: The boy is our commander. Ask him.
Whatever he says, we say.

NEOPTOLEMOS: Odysseus will call me a soft-
hearted fool,
I know. But if this is what he wants,
Stay awhile longer. We have to stow our gear
And offer a prayer before we sail. (1025)
Perhaps he'll be more favorably disposed
Towards us. Odysseus, it's time to start.
Men, come running when you hear the order.

PHILOCTETES: This is the destiny that I
Must live with, this is my lot; (1030)
Never to see a human face again,
To live here till I die. I have no way
To feed myself, no longer shall
My flying arrows find their mark,
For I have been deceived, betrayed (1035)
By fictions woven in a cunning mind.
If I could only see the man
Who brought these things to pass, endure
My agony, and for as long!

CHORUS: It is the will of Providence (1040)
That you should suffer. It was not
By treachery of ours.
So do not in the bitterness of anger
Call down your curse on me. I want
What I always wanted. To be your friend.

PHILOCTETES: And while I suffer, he (1045)
Sits laughing by the margin of the seas.

DIRECTOR: So this was his plan? To work on the man's vanity? Philoctetes turns to the sailors, and they refer the matter to Neoptolemos. It is finally time for him to speak. The youth compromises. He will stay a little longer while the ship is being readied. Neoptolemos seems to mean a god, perhaps Poseidon, when he says "perhaps he'll be more favourably disposed towards us."

It seems to me that there has been pressure on the whole play, a clock ticking. What happened to Philoctetes could happen to anyone. The gods have contempt for humankind and use their power accordingly.

Philoctetes is a man who has crossed an unseen barrier between men and gods. His suffering and friendship with Heracles set him apart. Matters are coming to a close and must be resolved.

Holding in his hands my bow,
My means of feeding, that has never lain
In any other hands but mine.
My bow, my treasure, ravished from   (1050)
My tender grasp: do you know, I wonder,
That you have lost your master, that the friend
Of Heracles possesses you no more!
You are another's now. You will be wielded by
A master of deceit. What guile,   (1055)
What wickedness it will be yours to see
From one who knows no shame, who brought
Uncounted agonies on me.

CHORUS: A man must speak as he thinks right.
    But there are limits. Keep your tongue   (1060)
    From slandering a man who did
    No more than he was told, who was
    Selected by his fellows. All he did
    Was for the common good.

PHILOCTETES: You flying birds, you beasts   (1065)
    That stalk with gleaming eyes upon
    The hills of Lemnos, you are safe
    Within your lairs, you need not run away:
    For I am empty-handed now.
    The bow that made me terrible has gone.
                 (1070)

What use is Philoctetes now?
Roam at your pleasure, for the woods and hills
Can hold no terrors for you any more.
I am fair game now. Take blood for blood
And feed upon this rotting flesh,   (1075)
At will, for I shall soon be dead.
How can I live? I cannot feed
On air, or force the earth to nourish me.

CHORUS: You still have a friend, in heaven's
    name.
    Go gently to him, as he comes to you.   (1080)
    It is up to you to cast
    The devil out of you that feeds
    Upon your flesh, that does not come alone
    But brings you pain two thousand fold.

PHILOCTETES: Of all that ever visited me here
                 (1085)
    You have been kindest. Must you resurrect

DIRECTOR: This seems to be temporizing. The chorus tells him that what Odysseus did, he did under orders and for the common good. The moment is very much like the earlier interlude when he slept while the chorus spoke. There is a lull in the action here.

These torments from the past? The memory
Is torture. Why do you do this to me?

CHORUS: What do you mean?

PHILOCTETES: Your hope
To take me to the hated land of Troy.   (1090)

CHORUS: It is best for you.

PHILOCTETES: Leave me alone!

CHORUS: With pleasure. I have no urge to stay.
The ship is waiting. Let us go.

PHILOCTETES: No! As you are god-fearing men,
I beg you, don't leave me.

CHORUS: We've heard enough.   (1095)

PHILOCTETES: Stay friends, for the love of God!

CHORUS: What now?

PHILOCTETES: Oh, oh.
I am cursed, cursed!
My foot, what shall I do with you
From now until I die?   (1100)
Friends, come back. Come back to me.

CHORUS: You told us to go. Have you changed
your mind?

PHILOCTETES: Do not be angry. I have not
deserved it.
Adrift in my pain, I do not know
What I do or what I say.   (1105)

CHORUS: Take our advice, and come with us.

PHILOCTETES: Never! Not if Zeus in majesty
Reached down to blast me with his
thunderbolt!
My curse on Troy, and all who fight in her,
Who threw me out with this poor crippled foot.
                                    (1110)
Grant me this prayer. It is all I ask.

CHORUS: What do you want?

PHILOCTETES: If someone has
A sword, an axe, any weapon at all —

CHORUS: Are you going to do some violence to
yourself?

PHILOCTETES: Cut the flesh from my bones.
Sever limb from limb.   (1115)
I want to kill myself. To kill myself.

DIRECTOR: The chorus very clearly wants to be done with arguments and return to the ship. The members of the chorus are impatient with Philoctetes. His reaction to their impatience is to lose his control for a moment and seem to plead. The men, of course, turn away from such unmanliness.

CHORUS: But why?

PHILOCTETES: I have to go find my father.

CHORUS: Where is your father?

PHILOCTETES: In the underworld.
  Yes, I know that he is dead.
  My fatherland, my country,   (1120)
    If I could only see you once again,
  Before I died; I left your sacred waters
  To help the cursed Greeks, and now my life is
    ended.

CHORUS: We have spent too long. We should have
    been on board
  Long since. But look! I see Odysseus coming,
                                                (1125)

  And the son of Achilles at his side.

ODYSSEUS: Tell me what's the matter. Why the
    hurry?
  Why are you turning back in your tracks?

NEOPTOLEMOS: To right a wrong that I did before.

ODYSSEUS: You're up to something. What did you
    do?   (1130)

NEOPTOLEMOS: Listened to you, and the whole
    Greek army.

ODYSSEUS: What have you done that you need to
    be ashamed of?

NEOPTOLEMOS: I played a vile trick on a man. I
    lied.

ODYSSEUS: I hope you're not planning anything
    rash.

NEOPTOLEMOS: Just something I owe to the son of
    Poeas.   (1135)

ODYSSEUS: What do you mean? All at once, I'm
    scared —

NEOPTOLEMOS: To take the bow back where it
    came from.

ODYSSEUS: You can't mean to give it back to
    Philoctetes?

NEOPTOLEMOS: That's right. I came by it
    dishonestly.

ODYSSEUS: For god's sake tell me you're only
    joking.   (1140)

DIRECTOR: His resolve not to go with them to Troy is firm. They are at an impasse and then Odysseus and Neoptolemos return. The youth says he is going "To right a wrong that I did before," and Odysseus, probably very impatiently, says he hopes the boy isn't planning anything rash. The boy still has possession of the bow. It must be remembered that the boy has changed. He is not the vulnerable, trusting youth he was at the play's beginning, and the bow is deadly. He presents a very real danger to Odysseus and the sailors at this moment. He repeats his newly rediscovered belief in honesty and fairness towards others. Did Philoctetes go into his cave when the two men appeared?

NEOPTOLEMOS: If you think it's a joke to tell the
    truth.

ODYSSEUS: Son of Achilles, what have you just
    said?

NEOPTOLEMOS: How many more times do I have
    to tell you?

ODYSSEUS: I wish I'd never had to hear it once.

NEOPTOLEMOS: Then take it to heart. I've nothing
    more to say.   (1145)

ODYSSEUS: They'll stop you. You'll never get
    away with it.

NEOPTOLEMOS: And who will stop me? I'd like to
    know.

ODYSSEUS: The entire Greek army. Me included.

NEOPTOLEMOS: You talk a lot of nonsense for a
    clever man.

ODYSSEUS: Everything you say and do is
    nonsense.   (1150)

NEOPTOLEMOS: Honesty is better, as a last resort.

ODYSSEUS: Honesty! If it hadn't been for me
    You wouldn't have the bow to give.

NEOPTOLEMOS: I acted wrongly. I must try to put
    it right.

ODYSSEUS: Aren't you afraid of what the Greeks
    will say?   (1155)

NEOPTOLEMOS: If my conscience is clear, I'm
    afraid of nothing.

ODYSSEUS: If you won't listen to reason, I must
    make you.

NEOPTOLEMOS: Make me? I'd like to see you try.

ODYSSEUS: Do I have to fight you, instead of the
    Trojans?

NEOPTOLEMOS: If that's how it has to be.

ODYSSEUS: On guard!   (1160)

NEOPTOLEMOS: On guard. Come on; I'm ready for
    you.

ODYSSEUS: No. I won't touch you. I'll report this
    to the army.
    They'll know how to deal with you.

NEOPTOLEMOS: That's healthy. And if you want to
stay that way,
Keep out of trouble. Philoctetes!   (1165)
Son of Poeas! Can you hear me?
Come out of your cave.

PHILOCTETES: Who's shouting there?
Why are you calling me? What do you want?
Oh, this means trouble. Have you come to
bring   (1170)
New sorrow to me? You have brought enough
already.

NEOPTOLEMOS: Don't worry. Listen to what I have
to say.

PHILOCTETES: No. I'm afraid. I listened to you
before.
And nothing came of it but trouble.

NEOPTOLEMOS: I know, but if I admitted I was
wrong?   (1175)

PHILOCTETES: That's how you talked before.
And then you stole
My bow. I trusted you, and you deceived me.

NEOPTOLEMOS: But not this time. Come. Answer
me one question.
Are you determined to remain, or would you
rather
Sail with us?

PHILOCTETES: Stop! You can save your
breath.   (1180)
I don't want to listen to any more.

NEOPTOLEMOS: You've made up your mind?

PHILOCTETES: That's putting it mildly.

NEOPTOLEMOS: I had a proposition. It's a pity.
You wouldn't listen. If I'm speaking out of turn
I'll say no more.

PHILOCTETES: It's useless, do you hear? (1185)
I feel nothing but contempt for you.
You cheated me. You robbed me of my bow.
And back you came to give me more advice—
You, who have disgraced your father's name.
May you perish, all of you. The sons of Atreus,
                                                   (1190)
Odysseus, and you.

DIRECTOR: Odysseus re-
treats, the sailors move away,
perhaps stand beyond the
brow of the hill, partly visible.
The final encounter of Philoctetes and Neoptolemos be-
gins. In a way they are now
equals. The boy has chal-
lenged Odysseus and held
his own. He wants to correct
the wrong he did. And Philoctetes has lost part of his
stature. He came close to
begging the sailors to help
him off the island, to return
him to his homeland.

DIRECTOR: Philoctetes ac-
cuses the youth of deceiving
him, which he didn't do before. Neoptolemos pleads
with Philoctetes to come to
Troy. In one way, Odysseus'
estimate of the situation and
choice of means is being vin-
dicated. Philoctetes will not
budge, and matters of honor
are taking precedence over
matters of war and destiny,
involving whole populations.
They have arrived at an impasse, and the boy does the
only thing he feels he can do.
He returns the bow to the
man.

NEOPTOLEMOS: Before you go further,
You see this bow I am holding? Take it.

PHILOCTETES: What do you mean? Is this another
trick?

NEOPTOLEMOS: I swear it's not, by the power of
Zeus Almighty.   (1195)

PHILOCTETES: This is joy to my ears—if it's really
true.

NEOPTOLEMOS: See for yourself. Put out your
hand.
Here is the bow. It is yours to have and hold.

ODYSSEUS: As heaven is my witness, in the name
Of the sons of Atreus and the army. I forbid it.
                                                        (1200)

PHILOCTETES: We'll see about that, if my arrow
flies true!

NEOPTOLEMOS: Don't shoot! By all the gods, don't
shoot!

PHILOCTETES: By all the gods, let go my hand.

NEOPTOLEMOS: Never.

PHILOCTETES: But this is the man I hate,
My enemy. Why did you have to stop me?
                                                        (1205)

NEOPTOLEMOS: It would have been unworthy, of
yourself and me.

PHILOCTETES: Now you can see what cowards
they all are.
These officers, these ambassadors with their
lies.
They talk, but have no stomach for the fight.

NEOPTOLEMOS: The bow is yours. You have no
reason   (1210)
To be angry with me now. Do you forgive me?
It will be yours to write the final chapter
In the sad, eventful history of Troy.

PHILOCTETES: Oh life, why do you torture me so
long
When you could send me to the dark below?
                                                        (1215)
What shall I do? Can I refuse a man
Whose every word is spoken for my good?

DIRECTOR: Let's guess that Odysseus leaped out of a hiding place, and then a very significant thing happened: Philoctetes hesitated before firing an arrow at his enemy, and Odysseus ducked away. The boy has had an important influence upon the man. Their relationship has been resolved.
But Neoptolemos has the last word. It is a sad one. Because the bow and the man will not return to Troy, the war will be lost. All of the suffering will be in vain, including the death of the boy's father, Achilles.
The dilemma is stated. The speech of Philoctetes is a summing up of all he and the boy have learned through this encounter and a reiteration of his resolve not to go but to demand that the boy fulfill his pledge to him.

Must I surrender, then? How can I bare
My misery to the daylight? Who will speak to
   me?
Can these my eyes, that saw my whole sad
   story,   (1220)
See me consorting with the sons of Atreus,
My murderers, or with that fiend Odysseus?
But this is of the past. My heart is rent
By fear for what I still must undergo
At these men's hands. For when an evil mind
                       (1225)

Has hatched one crime, its other thoughts are
   kin,
And this is what I wonder at in you.
You never should have gone to Troy yourself,
Much less take me. Those men insulted you;
They stole your father's armor. Even Ajax
                       (1230)

Was thought unworthy. They awarded it
To Odysseus! And these are the men
You go to fight for. And you ask me to go with
   you?
No, boy, not I. You swore a solemn oath
To take me home. Then do it. Stay in Skyros
                       (1235)

And leave them to the fate that they deserve,
Then I shall have things to thank you for.
So will my father. If you help these villains,
The world will think that you are one of them.

NEOPTOLEMOS: I could not expect you to say
   otherwise.   (1240)
   But put your trust in heaven, and with me
   You have a friend now.

PHILOCTETES: You mean to Troy? To meet one of
   those cursed
   Sons of Atreus? With this crippled foot?

NEOPTOLEMOS: To find those who will cure you,
   who will end
   This agony and make you walk again.   (1245)

PHILOCTETES: You tell me this! I thought you
   were my friend —

NEOPTOLEMOS: I speak as I see best. For both of
   us.

DIRECTOR: Neoptolemos is no longer a boy. He has come of age. "I could not expect you to say otherwise," he says, and then promises to carry out the request. I think we have to understand his plan to take Philoctetes to the physicians in Troy is not a further trick. Haven't we evidence enough now that he will stake his life on protecting the man against others? The physicians are in Troy, with the army, not in the homeland. It is Philoctetes who shows a lack of character in arguing with this solution. There is no human means left to resolve the problem. And history tells us that Philoctetes returned to Troy and the battle was won by the Greeks. This is another lull before a storm. We know that this is not the proper resolution. Matters cannot rest at this point. The audience must be made to feel the irony of this scene. Philoctetes and Neoptolemos cannot prevail against the Greeks or history or even their own moral choices. While Odysseus seemed to exemplify one strategy of human affairs carried to the extreme, here we see Philoctetes' moral right taken to extremes.

PHILOCTETES: You say that! You, a god-fearing
man!

NEOPTOLEMOS: The gods love those who help
their friends.

PHILOCTETES: Are you helping me, or the sons of
Atreus?   (1250)

NEOPTOLEMOS: You. I told you. You are my
friend.

PHILOCTETES: By handing me over to my
enemies?

NEOPTOLEMOS: After all you have suffered, you
still hold back.

PHILOCTETES: It will mean my death, if I listen to
you.

NEOPTOLEMOS: No. I tell you. You don't
understand.   (1255)

PHILOCTETES: I know the sons of Atreus cast me
out.

NEOPTOLEMOS: They did, and now they bring you
back to life.

PHILOCTETES: Not if I have to go to Troy again.

NEOPTOLEMOS: What am I to do with you?
Nothing I say
Has any effect. I might as well be silent. (1260)
And you must go on living as you are.
There is no way of saving you.

PHILOCTETES: Leave me to suffer what I have to
suffer
But remember you gave me your solemn
promise
To take me home. You must keep it, boy.
(1265)
Do it at once. And never talk to me
Of Troy again. It has cost me tears enough.

NEOPTOLEMOS: Very well, then. Let us go.

PHILOCTETES: That is nobly spoken, boy.

NEOPTOLEMOS: You must walk. Step boldly now.

PHILOCTETES: I shall do the best I can.

NEOPTOLEMOS: I'll be punished by the Greeks.

PHILOCTETES: Don't let that worry you. (1270)

NEOPTOLEMOS: What if they attack my land?

PHILOCTETES: I shall be there at your side.

NEOPTOLEMOS: How can you assist me then?

PHILOCTETES: With the bow of Heracles.

NEOPTOLEMOS: Yes, the bow.

PHILOCTETES: I'll keep them off.

NEOPTOLEMOS: Make your last farewell,
    and go.   (1275)

HERACLES: Wait, son of Poeas. There is something
    more
    That you must hear, and I must say.
    Know then, it is the voice of Heracles
    That speaks to you, his shape you see.
    From the high abode of heaven I have come
                    (1280)
    To tell the will of Zeus: this journey
    Is not for you to take. Hear me,
    And I will tell you.
    First, listen to the story of my life.
    Behold. This glorious immortality
    Is mine through long and weary labors done.
                    (1285)
    And so it is ordained for you
    To pass through pain and suffering to glory
    Here on earth. Go with this man to Troy.
    There your sickness shall be taken from you.
    You shall be chosen champion of the Greeks,
                    (1290)
    And with the bow that once was mine you
       shall
    Kill Paris, who first brought this suffering
    Upon the earth. You shall sack Troy, and carry
       home
    Its spoils, the army's tribute to your valor,
    To your father Poeas in the land of Oeta. (1295)
    Take but a tithe to decorate my shrine
    In memory of what my bow has wrought.
    And now, Achilles' son, I speak to you.
    Without him you will never conquer Troy
    Nor he without you. You must hunt together
                    (1300)
    Like lions in the field. And I will send
    Asklepios to Troy, to heal you. So
    It is ordained: that for the second time

DESIGNER: What happens visually when a god appears to mortals? Is it a disembodied voice? Light? A shape? Does the god only speak to them and not to any of the sailors who might still be hiding nearby? It would seem best if whatever is done could have "roots" deep in the play and be prepared for during earlier action. For example, in those prior "lulls" in the action, a phrase of music, use of lights, or some other device could make the eventual appearance of the god appropriate at this moment.

DIRECTOR: Line 1276—this is a "deus ex machina" and has the usual associated problems unless it's carefully handled. It could seem too pat, too easy. Just as the effect of the god's appearance should be prepared for, so the meaning of his appearance must be underlined. For one thing, the play never was about a conflict among men on a deserted island. It was part of a much larger drama, and also symbolically represented many aspects of all human struggles. The will of the gods, the force of history, as well as the dilemma of people who seek to do what is right were all part of the drama. Also, there is the point made by the god Heracles that his own power was born out of suffering, as Philoctetes' will be. There is no doubt that when the god has spoken, Philoctetes will obey.

Its walls shall fall before my arrows.
Remember: when you seek the city, pay (1305)
Due honor to the gods that dwell therein.
This is the first command of Zeus the Father.
For piety does not die when men die.
Come life, come death, it lives forever.

PHILOCTETES: Oh, voice that I have longed to
    hear. (1310)
Oh, lord, to see your face again
After so many years.
I hear, and will obey.

NEOPTOLEMOS: I cry amen.

HERACLES: Then lose no time. The hour
    Has come. The wind
    Is in your quarter now.

PHILOCTETES: And so I make my last farewell
    To Lemnos. To the cave (1315)
That shared my vigil; to the nymphs
Of streams and meadows, to the thunder
Of waves on rock, whose spray these many
    times
Has fallen on my head within my cavern.
And many times has Hermes sent my voice
    (1320)
Back from the mountain, as I cried aloud
Above the storm. Farewell, you waters.
And Lycian stream, farewell. I leave you now
At last; this is the day I never
Thought to see. Farewell to you, (1325)
My island home of Lemnos. Speed me on
My voyage with your blessing, for I go
Obedient to my destiny, my friends,
And the great arbiter who governs all.

CHORUS: Come all; and let us pray to
    The Nymphs that rule the sea (1330)
    To grant good sailing, and a safe return.

DESIGNER: All that should remain at the play's end is the rocky island, sky, and water. If there were such a place, it might look the same today. The lights fade, the drama and the day end.

DIRECTOR: Philoctetes' final speech reminds us of the poem by Byron, "The Prisoner of Chillon," in which the old man, imprisoned for so many years in the dungeon, finds it difficult to leave his cell. It is human to form ties with our homes, no matter how unpleasant. Curtain calls are a problem. Should they be used? Also, the play is short. Should there be an afterpiece?

Section II: Arnott Interview

What follows is an interview with Peter Arnott, the translator of *Philoctetes*. Peter Arnott is unusual in that he combines the skills of a theatre person and a classical scholar. He is the author of a number of books, a Professor of

Theatre at Tufts University, and an actor/director/puppeteer. The insights he will share with us are the kind you would ordinarily have to research in a library, using the types of texts listed in our bibliographies. Peter Arnott, in fact, is one of those sources. For your first attempt at gaining insight into various aspects of a play, I thought it would be more interesting (and encouraging) to do this interview.

WOODS: Can you tell us something about your interest in the classics and theatre?

ARNOTT: I was trained as a classicist. As I was educated in England, I was introduced to classical languages at a very early age and read Latin at eleven, Greek at the age of thirteen. By the time I entered university I was already well acquainted with Greek drama in the original, and I was very moved and excited by it. I still remember, when I must have been a 15-year-old boy, sitting alone in a dusty classroom on a summer's afternoon reading Sophocles' *Ajax* for the first time and crying. It had a tremendous emotional effect on me. I became more and more concerned with the problems of presenting these plays to audiences and trying to lead others to feel the same affection for them that I did, trying to convey to others the power they had for me. I found myself rather frustrated by traditional scholarly explications of the plays which always seemed to miss the point and concerned themselves with matters of grammar, matters of archeology, matters of textual studies which never seemed to be truly relevant to the play as play, and so finally I left Classics for the theatre, where, happily, I have been ever since.

I have difficulty thinking of myself as a professor. I'd much rather be thought of as a performer who talks to others about what he has performed. You have to know the works on the stage. You have to know them from the inside as an actor and as a director before you can venture to comment on them. And I have a rigid rule now, that I will not write about or lecture on any play that I have not performed or directed. I know how very little I know about any play when I have not had that practical stage experience of it.

WOODS: The students reading this interview will have just finished *Philoctetes.* Let me ask some of the questions that most often come up when I've taught this play. First, what is Sophocles' language like in the original and how does it compare to that of Aeschylus and Euripides?

ARNOTT: Sophocles, as in so many other ways, holds the middle position here between Aeschylus and Euripides. The language of Aeschylus is rich, highly ornamented, allusive, often deliberately ambiguous, dense, often to the point of impenetrability. The language of Euripides verges on the colloquial. He goes out of his way to use a more common vocabulary and to break up the rhythms of Greek verse in a way which much more approximates the random pattern of everyday discourse. Sophocles, as I say, stands in the middle. His Greek is conspicuously devoid of figures of speech. He is very sparing in his use of metaphor and simile. At the same time, he does not go anywhere near as far as Euripides in attempting to put ordinary conversational Greek into verse, and so one of the hardest problems for the translator of Sophocles is to find an English idiom which is simple but still dignified. It must work on a level that ordinary speakers can use and comprehend but at the same time must not descend too far into the vernacular.

WOODS: Did his style change during his career?

ARNOTT: I don't think that there is much stylistic variation among the plays of Sophocles so far as the language is concerned. The kind of language I just described is the kind of language he uses in all his work. He always seems to have this characteristic of speaking very simply, very clearly in a way that audiences could immediately understand. When Sophocles entered the tragic contest for the first time in 468 B.C., he was competing against Aeschylus, the recognized master of that time, and Sophocles won. Some critics have found this to be a matter for wonder that a neophyte and a very young playwright could compete with the master and win. I don't find this strange at all. I think that Sophocles had a much more straightforward approach which endeared itself to audiences.

WOODS: One concept which often gives students difficulty is that these writers were borrowing and adapting from what was in many cases an oral tradition; that they were, indeed, the myth-makers or fabricators whose versions were then passed on to us.

ARNOTT: Yes, in a very real sense all the Greek tragedians were myth-makers. We often talk loosely about Greek tragedy as being derived from myth, but in most cases it would be more accurate to say that tragedy is a creative contribution to the evolving myth. In so many cases we know the stories in the way that we do simply because the tragedians chose to make a play out of them and the version that has been handed down as the canonical version is the one that the dramatist wrote. So, in this sense, we know the historical outcome of Sophocles' *Philoctetes* because the historical outcome is largely what Sophocles chose to construct. Of course, he is leaning on stories which were known before his time. Philoctetes and his bow were involved in the Trojan War saga long before Sophocles came on the scene, but Sophocles does introduce some variations in his treatment of it just as he does in his treatment of Oedipus. For example, there are things in *Oedipus Rex* which were probably never widely known to audiences before Sophocles wrote his play.

WOODS: Let me ask some questions about the three major characters in this play. First, how close does Neoptolemos come to epitomizing the Greek ideal of nobility?

ARNOTT: In many ways in his plays Sophocles harks back to an earlier concept of nobility. He is very Homeric sometimes in establishing the guidelines by which some of his characters choose to operate. I think you see this very clearly in a play which comes very early in his career. That is *Ajax*, which he probably wrote about 441 B.C. In *Ajax* you have a character whose life is motivated by very simple considerations. The hero has a responsibility largely to himself. He must not give way to cowardice. He must not, above all, lose face. Of course, Ajax does lose face and is humiliated in the eyes of his fellow Greeks. The only way out for him is to commit suicide. I once saw a production of Sophocles' *Ajax* which was realized in terms of the heroic legends of the American Indian. The director felt that the characteristics of Homeric nobility, and the way Sophocles uses them, could best be conveyed to a modern American audience in terms of the past of this continent. Similarly, in *Philoctetes*, Neoptolemos is represented as a young boy who still clings to a certain heroic ideal which, for many of his fellow warriors, his older companions, had now been invalidated, outdated. He still clings to really a rather romanticized vision of what a hero should be. One gets the feeling that in the play he is constantly shocked by Odysseus and shocked by Philoctetes to some extent. These are aspects of life that he has not yet learned to deal with, and his code of honor is likely to be shattered by these unexpected encounters. He obviously believes that lying is wrong and now he is placed in a situation where he is asked to lie for what are explained to him as the best possible reasons. And it's this attempt to make some sort of compromise between the standards he has been used to living by and the standards which are now imposed upon him which gives the play a lot of its interest. The play is called *Philoctetes* but in a very real sense it is also about Neoptolemos growing up. Incidentally, one example of the way in which the tragedians felt free to handle myth can be seen in Neoptolemos. Neoptolemos had another name. He is also known as Pyrrhus. And it's Pyrrhus who at the end of the Trojan War, when the city was sacked by the Greeks, mercilessly killed Priam at the altar of his gods.

WOODS: What of that same audience's feelings about Odysseus and how he is portrayed in this play?

ARNOTT: Odysseus is a character who changes markedly according to the changing nature and needs and expectations of the society. In the *Iliad*, Odysseus is a warrior among others and he's just as skillful, just as venturesome as they are. He is a brave archer. He is ranked among the best when it comes to leading his men into battle. The only thing that sets him apart from the other Homeric warriors, like Ajax and Achilles, is that he is a skilled talker. Whenever any tricky diplomatic negotiation is to be done, it is Odysseus who is called upon to do it. Now in *The Odyssey*, Odysseus figures much more largely as a man who uses his wits rather than his physical prowess when the occasion demands it. He is placed in situation after situation where he has to extricate himself from the hands of his enemies, be they divine or mortal. More often than not he does this by manipulation of the situation, by trickery, by deceit. And so we are already shifting to a different kind of Odysseus here. Some of the things that Odysseus does in *The Odyssey* are morally abhorrent, and this is the aspect of the man that's largely taken up by the tragedians. In Sophocles, he figures for the first time in *Ajax*, that early play of which I spoke, and the characterization of him is largely as a schemer and a man who prefers to avoid physical confrontation. The hero warrior of *The Illiad* has largely vanished by this time. Euripides, in fact, prefers to treat him as a symbol of the mode of thought of the time. Philosophical thought in the later 5th century in Athens was largely dominated by the school of philosophy whose practitioners were known as the Sophists. They were concerned with situational ethics rather than with metaphysics, and taught men how to conduct themselves in human situations. They placed a very heavy premium on the art of speech and the formal art of rhetoric as a way of getting ahead, as a way of making friends and influencing people. At the extreme, they were prepared to dismiss any absolute standards of justice and morality and argue that all things were dictated by expediency. And that's the kind of man that Odysseus is portrayed as in Euripides: as the villain, the man who is devoid of any moral scruple, who is prepared to do anything, even lie, cheat, or steal if it will serve his immediate ends. In *Philoctetes*, we have an Odysseus who is very much like this. Odysseus here appears rather late in Sophocles' life and Sophocles is obviously rather strongly influenced by Euripides' treatment of the man. So, the Odysseus of *Philoctetes* exemplifies a particular contemporary point of view for Sophocles' audience. And Neoptolemos, as I said earlier, exemplifies an earlier point of view. You have a clash between modern expediency and traditional ideals of duty. You can see the same confrontation in other writings, not necessarily dramatic writings, which appear at this time. You can see it, for example, in Thucydides' *History of the Peloponnesian War*. In the early books of the history, in the beginning of the war, the Athenians are still very concerned with traditional notions of right and justice, and they make speeches invoking these ideals. By the time you get to the later stages of the war, you are shown the Athenians behaving like a crowd of Odysseus's. They argue that might is right and that they are going to do whatever needs to be done in the light of the current situation. And this I think has made Odysseus, as a dramatic character, very appealing to our times. He appears, really, as the Greek prototype of our shifty politician. In a way, we enjoy his stage villainy, the same way that we enjoy the manipulations of Shakespeare's Richard III.

WOODS: Is Philoctetes at fault for having been bitten by the sacred snake, for not controlling himself on shipboard, for behaving as he does toward those who put him on the island, using the boy as he does? Again, I imagine I'm really asking about the 5th century ethic regarding a warrior's behavior and general notions of manliness.

ARNOTT: I don't think we need go that far back to earlier actions to justify anything that happens in the play. Sophocles often begins a play with a certain given set of data without which the play cannot proceed. It's the same with *Oedipus*. It has sometimes been suggested that the chain of errors in the plot begins far before the play opens, with Laius and Jocasta. If Laius had not fathered a son in defiance of the oracle's predictions all of this would never have happened. That's a critical error, I think. Sophocles gives us a certain set of facts with which his play begins and we are asked to take them for granted. It's like the eternal question about *King Lear*. Why does King Lear divide his kingdom in the first place? Why does he perform the act which initiates this chain of disasters? I don't think Shakespeare meant to have us ask that question either. Given that that is so, what happens next? And so what really interests us in *Philoctetes* is what happens to him once he's on the island. What happens to the other people who want to get him off it? We are not interested in why he was there in the first place or whether or not he should have trodden on the sacred snake.

WOODS: How would you interpret the appearance of Heracles at the play's end? How would you integrate this appearance with the rest of the play?

ARNOTT: Don't let the whole play depend on the last scene. Don't start from the god and work backward. You have here a script in which several human beings are involved in a very human dilemma. Let them work out their own destiny and let the treatment of the god follow from this. What is the god, after all? In one interpretation of the play, the god can be the real god who does come down from heaven and issues a divine commandment. In another interpretation, you could see the god as the voice of Philoctetes' conscience. In yet another interpretation of the play you could see Heracles as Odysseus in disguise. That would be a very cynical interpretation of the play, but it is possible. But start with the play and let the ending follow from that.

WOODS: One last question relating to the characters, though I suspect this also relates to Greek stage conventions. Is it Odysseus who returns as the Trader?

ARNOTT: That's an often-asked question and one which, in dramatic terms, has rather less meaning than scholarly critics would try to attribute to it. If you accept, as I do, that this play was performed with a cast of three actors, doubling roles where necessary, then obviously Actor One plays Odysseus, Actor Two plays Neoptolemos, and Actor Three plays Philoctetes, and when Odysseus has left the stage, that same actor must return as the Trader. So, it can be ironic. Whether or not this is what Sophocles intended, there is no way of telling, but you can make enormous practical advantage out of this theatrical convention.

WOODS: To get back to more question about the art of the translator. How complete and accurate is the manuscript that you must work from for this play?

ARNOTT: It is quite clean. The manuscripts of Sophocles usually are. This is another aspect of the comparative ease of Sophocles' language to which I referred earlier. Manuscript corruption often comes about because the author is using words which the copyist does not recognize or easily understand, and so the natural tendency is for the copyist to assume that when he does not understand a word, it is because there has been a miscopying somewhere earlier along the line. That is, he thinks the word he can't understand is a mistake, and so he changes the word for one that is similar but one which he can understand and makes sense in the context. And so you have errors gradually creeping in, because copyists don't recognize sometimes their own limitations.

WOODS: How do you approach the translation of a play?

ARNOTT: It depends a great deal on the author and on the context in which the translation is going to appear. I think there are certain basic qualities in any author which the translator has an obligation to convey to his audience. In the case of Sophocles, it's that simple clarity which I have talked about already. Many people, I think, have the mistaken idea that Sophocles' Greek is much more complex than it actually is. My translation of *Antigone* was once performed at the University of Virginia and the reviewer for the production disapproved of my translation for being so simple and said that ideally Sophocles ought to be translated by somebody like Christopher Fry. Now I really didn't mind his objecting to my translation. He has a perfect right to do that, but if he thinks that the way Christopher Fry writes, which is in a very Renaissance manner, is appropriate for Sophocles, then he ought to go back to the Greek again. The two are poles apart. So, yes, with Sophocles what I first try to do is to match in English the clarity of his Greek. Cultural equivalents vary according to circumstances. There are some concepts, some Greek terms which you cannot easily and simply render into English. You always have to find a paraphrase for them. And this makes clumsiness often inevitable. There were not many such problems in *Philoctetes*, but as a translator primarily for the stage I always tend to search for an equivalent which will make sense to a modern audience, in terms of what they know even at the risk of an anachronism so far as the Greek is concerned. I'd much rather say something which is meaningful than be pendantically or historically accurate.

WOODS: What is the verse like in the Greek?

ARNOTT: Sophocles uses iambic trimeter for his actors' speeches. This was the standard verse form of the time and standard English practice has usually been to translate this into the English iambic pentameter hallowed by Shakespeare. This is an obvious verse form to use, and I think the right one. Most of us do it. The only problem is that Greek is a much more succinct language than English. You find that where Greek takes two lines

to say something, you need three lines in English. There's a real danger that you may expand the play to a point that it becomes unwieldy in trying to recapture every nuance of what the Greek says. And so here, as in so many other ways, the translator has to make up his mind what he is willing to lose and what he wants to keep. You can't do it all. No translation can reproduce every aspect of the original.

WOODS: How good were the translations of the past?

ARNOTT: There was a long period of time when translation as an art was hardly practiced at all. The sole function of translation where Greek plays were concerned was simply as an aid to the understanding of the Greek text, designed by scholars for budding scholars or for schoolboys. There was no pretense at literary merit. Quite the opposite in fact. It's incredible to me that some of these translations are still on the market. I think these translations give many people a bad taste of Greek drama in their early years.

Then you have a phase when the plays did start to receive serious attention from a literary point of view. It began to be recognized that everyone couldn't read Greek anymore, and so you got a number of very good English translations, from the literary point of view. The problem with many of these is that they were never intended for use in acting. That leads us into phase three, or the recognition that Greek plays are still a lively part of the modern repertory and that a translation which is superb when it is read may be very fallible when it is acted on the stage. This is the sort of thing that governs my own approach to translating Greek drama. Of course, my own experiences as a performer have enabled me to avoid most of the obvious pitfalls, but I still find myself writing things which other actors cannot say with ease. My invariable practice here is to change the lines. If the actor cannot say the lines, then they are bad lines. It's as simple as that.

WOODS: As my next to last question, may I ask what you would say to young actors and directors approaching Greek drama?

ARNOTT: I think perhaps the most important thing to tell actors and directors, and what I always tell actors in dealing with works like this is simply to forget that this is a Greek play. Greek plays have come down to us so wrapped in clouds of glory, so hallowed by centuries of tradition that the tendency is to look on them almost as sacred writ and not as scripts for acting. Perhaps the greatest damage that has ever been done to the modern comprehension of Greek drama is the one indisputable fact that everyone knows about Greek tragedy, namely that the plays were performed as part of a religious festival. This, of course, is perfectly true. The trouble is that we tend to interpret it in the light of our own notions that a religious festival should include a priest, rabbi, or whatever and a largely passive congregation with the emphasis on a spiritual message. Now the Greek religious festivals were nothing like this. The Greeks could worship their gods in any number of ways: by boxing matches, by chariot races, by other kinds of athletic contests, by displays of humor and proficiency of which plays were simply a part. We always, very mistakenly I think, tend to think of Greek tragedy in terms of preaching a religious message, when often it does nothing of the kind. Yes, the plays were part of the religious festival, but in many of the plays we have there is no religious message in the way that we would now understand such a thing.

WOODS: And for my last question, would you recommend some commentaries on Greek plays?

ARNOTT: I think that one of the most useful works and one which is often disregarded by classical scholars is a work by an Australian scholar, Waldock, called *Sophocles, the Dramatist,*[1] which is a very refreshing study of the plays purely from the point of view of their dramatic structure. In fact, he tries to present the plays in the same way that they would have appeared to an audience seeing them for the first time.

Another valuable work is Cedric Whitman's *Study in Heroic Humanism.*[2] Of the older studies, H. D. F. Kitto's books on Greek tragedy are always eminently sensible and practical. Kitto has the great advantage of having worked with these plays in stage performance. And so I recommend them as reading to anyone who is engaged in the same discipline.

Section III: Images from the Time of the Trojan War

The accompanying illustrations (Figures 7-3 through 7-5) are taken from J. L. Benson's *Horse, Bird, and Man: the Origins of Greek Painting,*[3] a text which explores connections between Mycenaean and Egyptian and Early Archaic Greek art. Included is an Egyptian funerary painting of a battle scene, but the rest are drawings done from Mycenaean vases. They give a firsthand view of what warriors, weapons, boats, and perhaps even sea battles looked like at the time of Achilles and Odysseus. Also included is a series of bird drawings which show how these early artists stylized nature.

The first illustration is an Egyptian depiction of a naval and land battle that occurred at the same time as the Trojan War. It is difficult to establish the exact influence of the most important culture in the region on its neighbors, but it seems reasonable that the weapons, boats, style of battle, and

[1]A. J. A. Waldock, *Sophocles, the Dramatist.* Cambridge University Press, 1951.
[2]Cedric H. Whitman, *Sophocles: A Study of Heroic Humanism.* Cambridge, Mass.: Harvard University Press, 1951.
[3]Drawings reprinted from *Horse, Bird, and Man: The Origins of Greek Painting,* by J. L. Benson, copyright © 1970 by the University of Massachusetts Press. (Plates XXXVIII, XXVII, XXXIX, XXXVII, and XXIV.)

Figure 7-3.

ways of depicting death and triumph give us clues about similar scenes in the
Trojan War.

Next, a series of pictures from vases ranging from a typical warrior, to a
helmsman, oarsmen straining on their benches, two young men meeting, and
two archers, one with a simple bow and another with a composite bow.

The last drawings show waterfowl and land birds. Notice how the artists have learned to simplify shapes to suggest flight and swimming, and how
they use various patterns for feathers.

Section IV: Pincher Martin *by William Golding*

William Golding is the author of many well-known novels. Perhaps his most
famous is *Lord of the Flies*, but the list includes four of my favorites: *The Spire*,
The Inheritors, *The Pyramid*, and *Pincher Martin*. In the following excerpts
from the last, the central character imagines he has come ashore on a rocky
and deserted island.[4]

[4]William Golding, *Pincher Martin*. (New York: Capricorn Books, 1965), pp. 60, 62–63.

Figure 7-4.

190

The place in which he had found water was like a little cave. The floor of the trench sloped down gently under water so that this end of the pool was shallow. There was room for him to lie with his elbows spread apart for the slab had smashed down the wall on the right-hand side. The roof stone lay across at an angle and the farther end of the cave was not entirely stopped up. There was a small hole high up by the roof, full of daylight and a patch of sky. The light from the sky was reflected in and from the water so that faint lines quivered over the stone roof. The water was drinkable but there was no pleasure in the taste. It tasted of things that were vaguely unpleasant though the tastes were not individually identifiable. The water did not satisfy thirst so much as allay it. There seemed to be plenty of the stuff, for the pool was yards long before him and the farther end looked deep. He lowered his head and sucked again. Now that his one and a half eyes were adjusted to the light he could see there was a deposit under the water, reddish and slimy. The deposit was not hard but easily

Figure 7-5.

disturbed so that where he had drunk, the slime was coiling up, drifting about, hanging, settling. He watched dully.

Presently he began to mutter.

"Rescue. See about rescue." . . .

He ignored his eye and tried to think.

"Food?"

He got to his feet and climbed down over the trenches. At the lower end were cliffs a few feet high and beyond them separate rocks broke the surface. He ignored these for the moment because they were inaccessible. The cliffs were very rough. They were covered with a crust of tiny barnacles that had welded their limy secretions into an extended colony that dipped down in the water as deep as his better eye could see. There were yellowish limpets and coloured sea-snails drying and drawn in against the rock. Each limpet sat in the hollow its foot had worn. There were clusters of blue mussels too, with green webs of weed caught over them. He looked back up the side of the rock—under the water-hole for he could see the roof slab projecting like a diving-board—and saw how the mussels had triumphed over the whole wall. Beneath a defined line the rock was blue with them. He lowered himself carefully and inspected the cliff. Under water the harvest of food was even thicker for the mussels were bigger down there and water-snails were crawling over them. And among the limpets, the mussels, the snails and barnacles, dotted like sucked sweets, were the red blobs of jelly, the anemones. Under water they opened their mouths in a circle of petals but up by his face, waiting for the increase of the tide they were pursed up and slumped like breasts when the milk has been drawn from them.

Questions for *Philoctetes*

1. What is the theme of the play?
2. Describe the main action.
3. What was your emotional reaction to the play?
4. Could you picture or sense the space in which the play took place? For example, was it cramped and small, claustrophobic? Was it open to the sky and surrounded by the flat seas? What sorts of marks had Philoctetes made on his surroundings?
5. What do you have in mind for the costumes, the weapons, the pots and storage vessels around the cave?
6. If there was sound, what was it? Is it natural? Wind, surf, seagulls? Or is it music, either played by the sailors or unmotivated, background music?
7. Can you relate to Neoptolemos' feelings? What about his surprise when he discovers that the older man's affliction doesn't offend him the way it did Odysseus and his sailors? What are your reactions to the pressures brought to bear on him by both Odysseus and Philoctetes? Is he wrong to do what he finally decides? What of his responsibility to the Greeks and the fate of Troy? Can you excuse Philoctetes' unwillingness to return to Troy? What are the consequences of any of these actions, including Odysseus' manipulation of the situation, if they are carried to their logical end?
8. A crucial problem in producing this play lies in how one handles the appearance of Heracles at the end. It may seem silly and arbitrary to your audience if you haven't prepared for it. How can this be accomplished? If you use foreshadowing,

what form will it take? What would equivalents for the literal appearance of the god be in a realistic version of the play?

9. How will you seat your audience? Why? What sort of stage will you use?

10. How will you handle the chorus in your production? Will you try to individualize them or will you attempt to preserve the original convention? Why?

11. What do you want your audience to carry away from your production?

12. Now, plan your production using the other steps and the sequence suggested in the chapter on directing. In particular, pay attention to IMAGERY.

Vase painting, Crete, seventh century B.C.
(Heraklimeion Museum.)

8
De Musset:
No Trifling
with Love

Heard melodies are sweet, but those unheard
      Are sweeter; therefore, ye soft pipes, play on;
Not to the sensual ear, but, more endear'd,
      Pipe to the spirit ditties of no tone:
Fair youth, beneath the trees, thou canst not leave
      Thy song, nor ever can those trees be bare;
          Bold Lover, never, never canst thou kiss,
Though winning near the goal —yet, do not grieve;
          She cannot fade, though thou has not thy bliss,
      For ever wilt thou love, and she be fair!

                        Keats, "Ode on a Grecian Urn"

The *Philoctetes* is a classic Greek drama. This next play for consideration is an anomaly. It is both comic and tragic, but is neither romantic nor realistic; it has some of each of these elements. It was probably written to be read, not produced, and seems to be a parody or satire of popular pastoral plays. But it also has serious elements that cannot be taken lightly. The use of the quotation from John Keats given above is meant ironically, but it is also mentioned to remind you of the pastoral world, a world which, even when it exists in action and not in the frozen moment of the relief figures trapped on the urn, has values that are contradicted by many of the facts of the real world. Lovers do grow old, fools can hurt us, and class differences may result in privileges for the rich but cause cruelty to be perpetrated on the poor. In his plays, Alfred de Musset wanted to fuse romanticism and classicism. He was also protesting against the dryness and lack of sensibility of the well-made play. While his attitude may frequently be satiric, it is rarely heavy-handed. So you should take these subtleties into account in your realization of this play for the stage. This will be made particularly difficult by the strangeness of Musset's world to most modern audiences. Some works and authors that might be helpful in this regard are Alexander Pope's *Rape of the Lock,* a satire of classical mythology and social class, and Lord Byron's *Don Juan,* which takes on the parallel conventions of the epic. Many of Giraudoux's plays are modern reworkings of myth and fantasy, as are certain plays of Jean Anouihl and the German playwright Heinrich von Kleist.

    Alfred de Musset was a contemporary of George Sand, and in fact was her lover for a time. He began his career as a dramatist, but turned away from it after a series of controversies with critics and producers of the time. The plays he wrote after this period, including *No Trifling with Love,* he protested were meant to be read, not produced. However, since his death, several of his plays have found audiences and have gained strong reputations as theatrical pieces.

    As twentieth century Americans, you will have to start afresh with this play, not only to recreate the world the playwright had in mind, but to find equivalents for your own time. You should listen to the music of the period, read about the dance, furnishings, painting, and the manners of the elegant and not so elegant people of the period. *No Trifling*, as you may have gathered, is a very special reflection of a particular time and place. Its parallels to our culture might be seen in the problems people will have in two hundred years with a rock-opera like *Tommy* or with the meaning of *All in the Family*, or the plays of John Guare. One fascinating feature of Musset's technique is his tendency to parody his grandfather's France while satirizing the well-made play and the attitudes of the bourgeois society of his time. The play is rewarding, I believe, but nothing in it will be simple or easily available.

No Trifling with Love

ALFRED DE MUSSET

(Translated by Porter Woods)

CAST OF CHARACTERS

The BARON
PERDICAN, his son.
BLAZIUS, his tutor.
BRIDAINE, curé to the Baron.

CAMILLE, niece to the Baron.
DAME PLUCHE, her governess.
ROSETTE, Camille's stepsister.
CHORUS, villagers.

ACT ONE

Scene One

CHORUS: Gently rocking on his lively mule, Father Blazius advances through the blue corn-flowers, his clothes new, a writing case at his side. Like a baby on a pillow, his head rolls on his round belly, and, his eyelids half open, he mumbles a Pater Noster into his double chins. (*Softly.*) Hail, Father Blazius, you have arrived at grape harvest like an ancient and commodious jug.

BLAZIUS (*waking up and noting them*): If you want to hear really important news, bring me a glass of cool wine.

CHORUS: Here is our biggest pitcher. Drink, Father Blazius. The wine is good, eh? You can talk later.

BLAZIUS (*after taking the edge off his thirst*): As you know, my children, young

Perdican, the son of your Baron, has reached his majority and has received his doctor's degree in Paris. He returns today to the chateau, his mouth full of phrases so flowery and complicated, that one doesn't know how to answer him three-quarters of the time. This splendid young man is like a book of gold. He has but to see a blade of grass and he'll tell you what it's called in Latin, and if the wind blows or it rains, he can clearly tell you why. Your eyes will open as wide as the castle gates over there, when he unrolls one of the parchments which he has covered with every color, with his own hands, and without help from anyone. He's a real gem from head to toe, and that's what I've come to tell the Baron. You realize this does me some honor, seeing that I have been his tutor since he was four. Now, my dear friends, give me a hand down, so that I won't break my neck getting off this beast; the animal is a bit stubborn; and I wouldn't mind another swallow before I go.

CHORUS: Drink, Father Blazius, and refresh your spirits. We have all known Perdican since he was a child and it was not necessary for you to go on and on about him. Let us hope that we find that child again in the heart of the man.

BLAZIUS: Heavens, the pitcher's empty. Where did it go? Well, goodbye. I have prepared, during my canter here, two or three unpretentious phrases which should be pleasing to the Baron. I'll go ring the bell. (*He exits.*)

CHORUS: Roughly jolting on a breathless ass, Dame Pluche struggles up the hill. Her groom cudgels the poor beast with all his strength, the ass shakes his head, a thistle in his mouth. Her long, thin legs tremble with rage, while her bony hands claw at her rosary. Good day, Dame Pluche. You come like the fever with the winds that turn the leaves yellow.

PLUCHE: A glass of water, scoundrels, a glass of water with a little vinegar.

CHORUS: Where do you come from, Pluche, old dear. Your wig is covered with dust, and awry, and your chaste gown has climbed up almost to your garters.

PLUCHE: Know, peasants, that the lovely Camille, the niece of your master, arrives today at the chateau. She has left the convent, on the express orders of the Baron, to come in proper time and place, as well she should, to receive the inheritance she has from her mother. Her education, praise be to God, is finished, and all who see her have the joy of sniffing a glorious flower compounded of wisdom and devotion. Never has there been anyone so pure, so like an angel, so like a lamb or a dove, as this dear novice, may the Lord God watch over her. (*Back to her earlier manner.*) So be it! Out of the way, scum! I think my legs are swollen.

CHORUS: Don't get ruffled, honest Pluche. And when you pray to God, ask for rain. The fields are as dry as your shins.

PLUCHE: You have brought me water in a pitcher that smells of garlic; give me a hand down, you dumb clucks. (*She exits.*)

CHORUS: Put on your Sunday best, and wait for the Baron to summon us. Unless I'm mistaken, there's going to be a real celebration today. (*They exit.*)

Scene Two

BARON: Father Bridaine, my friend, let me present you to Father Blazius, tutor to my son. Yesterday, at eight minutes past noon, my son reached his majority. He is now truly twenty-one years old. And he has graduated with honors from the University. Father Blazius, may I present Father Bridaine, the priest of this parish and my dear friend.

BLAZIUS (*bowing*): Your son had four "firsts," sir. In Literature, Botany, Roman Law and Canon Law.

BARON: Go along to your room, dear Blazius. My son will soon be here. So freshen up and come down when you hear the bell. (BLAZIUS *exits.*)

BRIDAINE: Forgive me, but your son's tutor reeks of wine.

BARON: It's impossible.

BRIDAINE: I'd swear to it. He stood very close to me just now, and the smell was frightening.

BARON: Enough, I repeat. It is not possible. (*Enter* PLUCHE.) Hail, Dame Pluche, my niece is, of course, with you.

PLUCHE: She follows me, monsieur, by several steps.

BARON: Father Bridaine, my friend, may I present Dame Pluche, tutor to my niece. Yesterday evening at seven o'clock my niece reached the age of eighteen; she has just left the best convent finishing school in France. Dame Pluche, may I present Father Bridaine, the priest of this parish and my good friend.

PLUCHE (*bowing*): Yes, the best convent in all France, and I might add, she was the best Christian there.

BARON: Go and freshen up, Dame Pluche; my niece will soon be here, I hope, so please make yourself ready for dinner. (*She exits.*)

BRIDAINE: The old girl seems a model of propriety.

BARON: Of propriety and piety, Father Bridaine. Her virtue is unassailable.

BRIDAINE: But the other one smelled of wine. I'm positive.

BARON: Father Bridaine, there are moments when I doubt your friendship. Are you trying to contradict me? Not another word! I plan to marry my son to my niece. They are a perfect match. And their education, alone, has cost me six thousand crowns.

BRIDAINE: But you will need a papal dispensation because of their relationship.

BARON: I have it, Bridaine, on the table in my study. Oh, my friend, how happy I am! You know what a profound horror I have of solitude. However, my position demands that I be at the chateau three months in the winter and three months in the summer. It's impossible to please people in general and tenants in particular, without commanding one's valet to enforce absolute privacy on occasion. How austere and difficult the life of a statesman! So, imagine the pleasure I will find in tempering, by the presence of my two united children, the heavy melancholy which has held me since the king named me his representative here.

BRIDAINE: Will the marriage be here or in Paris?

BARON: I was waiting for that question, Bridaine. Well, my friend, what would you say if these hands (*holding* BRIDAINE's *hands*), yes, Bridaine, these very hands, don't look at them so piteously, were destined to give the solemn blessing to the happy confirmation of my dearest dreams? Eh?

BRIDAINE: I'm silent. Gratitude seals my lips.

BARON: Look through that window. Do you see my tenants crowding the gate? My two children have arrived at the same time. What luck! I have planned everything. My niece will be brought through the left gate, and my son through the right gate. What do you say to that? I can't wait to see them greet one another. What they will say. How they'll behave. Six thousand crowns is no trifle, there must be no mistakes. Besides, these children have loved each other tenderly from the cradle. Bridaine, I have an idea.

BRIDAINE: What is that?

BARON: During dinner, without appearing to stress it—you understand, my friend—while toasting, perhaps—you understand Latin, Bridaine?

BRIDAINE: "Omnia Gallia," do I understand Latin!

BARON: I should be very pleased if you could discreetly dispute with the boy, in front of his cousin. This would produce a good effect. Prod him into speaking a little Latin, perhaps not precisely during dinner, that would be gauche, and I don't understand a word of it, but during dessert, you understand?

BRIDAINE: If you don't understand a word, Baron, it's possible your niece doesn't either.

BARON: All the more reason. You don't expect a woman to admire something she understands, do you? Where's your sense, Bridaine? That's foolish.

BRIDAINE: Well, I'm no judge of women, but it seems far-fetched to me that anyone could appreciate something they don't understand.

BARON: Well, I do know them, Bridaine. Oh, how well I know those charming, subtle creatures. Take it from me, they love to have dust thrown in their eyes, and the more you throw, the wider they open them, so the more you can throw. (PERDICAN *enters from his side,* CAMILLE *from hers.*) Good morning, my children. My dear Camille, my dear Perdican! Embrace me, and then give one another a kiss . . . a hug?

PERDICAN: Father! My dearest sister! What joy . . . I'm so happy.

CAMILLE: My uncle, cousin, I greet you.

PERDICAN: How tall you are, Camille, and lovely as the day is long.

BARON: When did you leave Paris, Perdican?

PERDICAN: Wednesday, I think, or Tuesday. You've changed into a woman! And I'm a man. It seems only yesterday when you were no taller than that!

BARON (*speaking to fill the pause*): You must be tired. It's a long trip and it's hot . . . .

PERDICAN: Oh, heavens, no. Look, father, how pretty Camille is.

BARON: Come, Camille, give your cousin a hug.

CAMILLE: Excuse me.

BARON: A compliment deserves a kiss; embrace her, Perdican.

PERDICAN: If my cousin turns away when I hold out my hand, I would say it's my turn to say "excuse me" . . . I forgot that love can steal a kiss but friendship cannot.

CAMILLE: Neither love nor friendship should take what they cannot return.

BARON (*to* BRIDAINE): That's a rotten beginning.

BRIDAINE: Too much modesty is undoubtedly a defect, but marriage can remove many scruples.

BARON (*to* BRIDAINE): I'm shocked by your comment. Excuse me. Did you see her cross herself? Come here so I can speak to you. This is extremely painful to me. This meeting was to be so sweet and it's completely spoiled. I'm vexed. Piqued. Devil take it, this is terrible!

BRIDAINE: Speak to them, they're turning their backs on one another.

BARON: Well, children, what are you thinking about? Camille, what are you doing with that locket?

CAMILLE: It's a miniature, uncle, of our great aunt.

BARON: Oh, yes, my child, it is your great grandmother, or rather the sister of your great grandmother, for the dear lady never contributed—other than by her prayers—to the increase of our family. She was, indeed, a saintly woman.

CAMILLE: Oh, yes, a saint. My Grand Aunt Isabelle. How well the nun's habit suits her.

BARON: And you, Perdican, what are you doing with that flower?

PERDICAN: A charming flower, father. It's called a heliotrope.

BARON: Are you joking? It's no bigger than a fly, and a name like that?

PERDICAN: It may be no bigger than a fly, but it has its value.

BRIDAINE (*feeling his chance for a grand wedding slipping away*): Of course, the doctor is right. Ask him its sex, its classification, from what elements it is composed, from whence comes its sap and color. He will transport you with ecstasy as he details the phenomenology of this blade of grass, from root to blossom.

PERDICAN (*subdued*): As much as that, curé? I only know it smells sweet.

Scene Three

CHORUS: There are a number of things that divert me and excite my curiosity. Come, my friends, and let's sit down on this grassy knoll. Think on it. At this moment, up at the chateau, two formidable trenchermen have begun mortal combat. Father Bridaine and Father Blazius. Have you ever noticed that when two men are almost identical, equally fat, equally foolish, sharing the same vices and the same passions, and they happen to chance to meet, it always happens that they will either love or despise one another. Perhaps it's for the same reason that opposites attract one another: a tall, skinny man will like a short, fat man, a blond finds brunettes agreeable, and the reverse. In this case, I foresee a secret struggle between our priest and the tutor. Both are well-armed with impudence, both have beer bellies, neither is solely a glutton, but also fancies himself a gourmet, and during dinner both will dispute both quantity and quality. But, if the fish is small, what will they do? And what if they can't share a carp's tongue because it only has one. Likewise, both are talkers, but perhaps it is possible that both can gossip while neither listens? Listen. Father Bridaine is attempting to catch young Perdican with pedantic questions, while his tutor sits frowning. He doesn't like it when anyone puts his pupil to the test. Item. They are both ignorant. Item. Both are priests. Item. One brags about his parish and the other about his student. Blazius is confessor to the son; Bridaine confessor to the father. Already I can see them, elbows on the table, their cheeks enflamed, their eyes bulging, hatred rattling their double chins. They look each other up and down. This is the preliminary skirmish, soon war will be declared; tautological arguments of all sorts will be thrust and parried and for heaping measure of misfortune, Dame Pluche will flutter between these two drunkards, repulsing first one and then the other with her well-honed elbows. Ah, now the dinner is finished and the chateau's gates are being opened. Here comes the dinner party, taking their postprandial stroll. Let's draw aside.

BARON: Dame Pluche, I am pained.

PLUCHE: Is it possible, Baron?

BARON: Yes, Pluche, it is possible. For a long time I have been noting in my journal that today was to be the happiest of all my days. Yes, my good woman, the happiest. You are not unaware that from the outset it was my intention to marry my son to my niece. That was long ago resolved, settled. But now, see. My children speak coldly to each other; or they don't speak at all.

PLUCHE: Here they come, Baron. Are they aware of your plans?

BARON: I have said a few words to them in private. I believe it would be wise, since they are together over there, for us to sit down in that shady place and leave them alone for a few minutes. (*They exit as* CAMILLE *and* PER-DICAN *enter.*)

PERDICAN: Camille, it was cruel of you to refuse me a kiss.

CAMILLE: I am like that. It is my manner.

PERDICAN: Would you take my arm for a tour of the village?

CAMILLE: No, I'm weary.

PERDICAN: Wouldn't you like to see our meadow again? Do you remember our games in the boat? Come, let's go down by the mill. I'll take the oars and you can steer.

CAMILLE: I have no desire to.

PERDICAN: You break my heart. What, no memories, Camille? Not a beat of your heart for our childhood? For all that dear, departed past, so sweet, so full of delicious silliness? Wouldn't you like to see the path we used to follow to the farm?

CAMILLE: No, not this evening.

PERDICAN: Not this evening? Then when! All our life is there!

CAMILLE: I am not young enough to play with dolls, nor old enough to love the past.

PERDICAN: What do you mean?

CAMILLE: I mean that childhood memories are not to my taste.

PERDICAN: They bore you.

CAMILLE: Yes, they bore me.

PERDICAN: Poor child, I sincerely pity you. (*They exit in opposite directions.*)

BARON (*reentering with* DAME PLUCHE): You saw that? Did you hear, my dear Pluche? I was expecting sweet harmony and instead I seem to be at a concert where the violin is playing Mozart while the horn plays a drinking song. Think of the appalling discord such a duet would produce. Yet that's what's going on in my heart.

PLUCHE: I agree, but I find it impossible to blame Camille, since nothing is in worse taste, to my mind, than boating parties.

BARON: Are you serious?

PLUCHE: Baron, a self-respecting young woman cannot trust herself on ponds.

BARON: But Dame Pluche, her cousin wishes to marry her, and besides . . .

PLUCHE: Decency forbids one to hold a tiller, and it is in bad taste to allow your feet to leave dry ground with a young man.

BARON: But I repeat . . . I tell you . . .

PLUCHE: That is my opinion on the matter.

BARON: Are you mad? In truth, you'll make me say . . . There are certain expressions that I don't wish to use . . . which are repugnant to me . . . but you make me want to . . . Truly, if I don't restrain myself . . . You are an idiot! Pluche, I don't know what to make of you.

Scene Four

PERDICAN: Good day, my friends, don't you recognize me?

CHORUS: Sir, you do resemble a child we once loved very much.

PERDICAN: Wasn't it you who used to carry me on your back to cross the streams in the meadows, who made me bounce on your knees, who let me ride behind you, hanging onto your waist, when you were mounted on your sturdy horse, and who used to push over and make room for me at supper on your farm?

CHORUS: We remember, young sir. You were by far the worst young scamp and the best young man for miles around.

PERDICAN: Then why not embrace me as a friend, rather than bow to me as a stranger?

CHORUS: God bless you, young man. There isn't a one of us who doesn't want to give you a hug and a pinch, but we're old now and you're a man.

PERDICAN: True. It's been ten years since I last saw you, and in a single day everything can change. I've stretched up a bit, and you have bent slightly toward the grave. Your heads are grey and your steps are slower, and I don't suppose you could toss me up in the air as you did when I was a child. Now I shall have to look after you, as you once did me.

CHORUS: But your return is a happier time for us than your birth. After all, it's sweeter to meet an old friend than to kiss a new baby.

PERDICAN: So here is my dear valley. The walnut trees, the green paths, the tiny spring. Here are all my bygone days, still so full of life. Here is the mysterious world of my childhood dreams. My home! What an incomprehensible word! Can it be that a man is meant to be born and build his nest and live his day in one small corner of the earth?

CHORUS: We've been told you're a learned man, young sir.

PERDICAN: Yes, I've been told that, too. And science is a fine thing, my friends, but these trees and fields teach the strongest lessons, how to forget all that one has learned.

CHORUS: There have been many changes since you left. Girls have married and boys have gone to the army.

PERDICAN: You must tell me everything. I want all the news. But not yet. See how small the fountain is. It used to be so big. I have carried an ocean and a forest in my head, and I return to discover a puddle and a clump of grass. Who is that girl singing in her window behind those trees?

CHORUS: It is Rosette, Camille's foster sister.

PERDICAN: Quick, Rosette, come down and join us.

ROSETTE (*entering*): Yes, my lord.

PERDICAN: Are you married, little one? I was told you were.

ROSETTE: Oh, no!

PERDICAN: But why not? There's no prettier girl in the village. We must find you a husband, child.

CHORUS: Young sir, perhaps she wishes to die a maiden?

PERDICAN: Is that true, Rosette?

ROSETTE: Oh, no, sir! (*She blushes when she realizes what she has said.*)

PERDICAN: Your sister, Camille, has arrived. Have you seen her?

ROSETTE: No, she hasn't been here.

PERDICAN (*impetuously*): Quickly, go put on your best dress and come to supper with me at the chateau.

Scene Five

BLAZIUS (*to the* BARON): Baron, a word with you? The parish priest is a drunkard.

BARON: For shame. That's not possible.

BLAZIUS: I'm certain. He drank three bottles of wine at dinner.

BARON: You exaggerate!

BLAZIUS: And on leaving the dinner table, he trampled the flowerbeds.

BARON: The flowerbeds? I'm confounded! That's too strange. To drink three bottles of wine at dinner and then march through the flowerbeds. Incomprehensible! And why didn't he use the path?

BLAZIUS: Because he was moving slant-wise. (*Demonstrating and then leaning triumphantly into the* BARON.)

BARON (*aside*): I have to believe what Bridaine was saying this morning. This Blazius stinks of wine.

BLAZIUS: Furthermore, he made a pig of himself at dinner and his speech was fuzzy. (*Imitating.*)

BARON: It's true. I noticed it, too.

BLAZIUS: He let drop a few phrases in Latin, mostly ungrammatical. Baron, the man is depraved.

BARON (*aside*): Eh! I can't bear his breath. (*Back to* BLAZIUS.) However, Mister

Tutor, I have better things to do than concern myself with what people drink and eat. What do you think I am, the majordomo?

BLAZIUS: As God's witness, I didn't mean to displease you, Baron, just inform you. And your wine's very good.

BARON: My good wine is still in my cellars.

BRIDAINE (*enters*): Baron, your son's in the village square, talking with every rogue in the valley.

BARON: Impossible.

BRIDAINE: I saw him with these very eyes. He's skipping stones on the pond.

BARON: Skipping stones? My head's spinning. Confusion. What you're saying can't be true. Bridaine, who ever heard of a Doctor of Botany, of Roman Law, much less Canon Law playing ducks and drakes?

BRIDAINE: Look, see him with your own eyes.

BARON (*aside, watching* BRIDAINE *move*): Heavens! Blazius was right. Bridaine moves slant-wise. (*Repeating movement.*)

BRIDAINE: Look, Baron, there he is. Down by the fountain, with his arm around a peasant girl.

BARON: A peasant? A girl? My son has come home to debauch my tenants? His arm around her? And surrounded by the villagers? I'm going crazy.

BRIDAINE: This calls for a firm hand!

BARON: All is lost! Hopeless! I am lost. Bridaine walks slant-wise, Blazius stinks of wine, and my son is seducing all the virgins in the village while playing ducks and drakes!

END NOTES FOR ACT I

Scene 1. The chorus is probably made up of several men and women. Should they speak in unison? Probably not, and pains should be taken to try to develop them as individuals. This opening scene is extremely theatrical. Note the comic turns; for example, the way the chorus introduces each new character.

In terms of design, pay attention to the clues given, particularly the references to the village and the chateau. There seems to be some edginess in Dame Pluche's "Know, peasants" line, suggestive of her own struggle for social status. The scene, overall, is bright, sunny, and comic.

Scene 2. Notice that we have moved immediately into complications and what could be the major problem: difficulties with the hoped for marriage of Camille and Perdican. It is apparent that Bridaine and Blazius will vie with one another throughout the play, and we should begin to wonder how seriously to take the Baron. The mood of the play is still comic and bright.

What would the Baron's home be like? How much is 6,000 crowns, and did he really spend it? If the play is broad comedy, we will need one kind of lighting and costuming, if it's drama, another. Should the lighting, settings, and perhaps musical backgrounds change with the locales of the action?

The tension builds as we wait for the young people. The Baron seems a pleasant fool and the characters around him, with the exception of the chorus, farcical. The chorus knows much more than it says. Then we have the entrance of Perdican and Camille from separate entrances and the failed moment of reunion. Camille: "My uncle, cousin, I greet you." She is cool and restrained and the moment is an embarrassment. If we have been thinking farce, physical comedy, or even a light amusement, we would seem to have been mistaken. She goes on, "Neither love nor friendship should take what they cannot return." This is a very pompous young lady.

This scene has been a surprise. Are we being advised of future surprises? The designer must be concerned about the shifting moods one senses in all this. What will be appropriate to the range of the entire play? Should the settings be specific or should the action take place in a neutral space?

Scene 3. Meanwhile, back at the farce . . . How can we make such shifts in acting style? Should Camille's monumental self-absorption be done humorously, a little bigger than life?

Perdican meets with Camille and it appears that he wants to mend fences. But what are his intentions? Is it marriage, courtesy, or what people of the time called dalliance? Is this a special place where they meet? Perdican has probably changed his clothing. He is now the country squire, the young man who grew up with these simple people.

All of this is rather standard stuff: the awkward linking of village and chateau, peasants and aristocracy, and the romantic notion of the pastoral.

After the interlude between the young people, we return to Pluche and the Baron. It's quite clear that neither of them would have the wit to correct any drift of the action into muddy waters.

Scene 4. A delightful scene, truly pastoral. Both Perdican and the chorus seem to be speaking from their hearts, but now we are ready for the introduction of the next complication, and a very predictable one: Rosette.

Have we decided where such scenes as these take place? Mention is made of "trees and fields" and a girl (Rosette) singing in a window behind the trees. Remember that the best satires are those which not only imitate the thing they are criticizing, but can capture the essential flavor of the original. Musset does this here.

Would Rosette wear a dress like those of other village girls or does her costume show her position relative to the two worlds?

Scene 5. Farce again. The Baron is upset by Perdican's refusal to behave like a proper young lord. Now there is another young lady! and the two priests are behaving like idiots! But this seems to be a simple case of fulmination. He will not take charge.

Some other thoughts might be forming. Go back to the frozen figures on Keats' Grecian urn. So far in this play, we have been taking a slice of pastoral life and setting it in motion and examining it. We have had a lovers' quarrel. The local beauty has become part of a love triangle. And a small army of clowns has begun doing turns and pratfalls all over the landscape. But there is a marked drift, not only in the mood but also in the technique of the author, toward something dark and uncontrollable.

What is the chateau like? Is it zany and cluttered like the Baron?

The act ends with the ineffectual Baron crying out, for dramatic effect to be sure, that all is lost! It may be.

ACT TWO

Scene One

BLAZIUS: Sir, your father despairs.

PERDICAN: Why is that?

BLAZIUS: You are not unaware that he had in mind your marriage to your cousin, Camille?

PERDICAN: Oh? I'd like nothing better myself.

BLAZIUS: However, the Baron noted that your personalities don't seem to match.

PERDICAN: That's too bad, but I can't remake mine.

BLAZIUS: Would you make this marriage impossible?

PERDICAN: I repeat. I would like nothing better than to marry Camille. Go find the Baron and tell him that.

BLAZIUS: Sir, I'll leave you. Here comes your cousin. (*He exits.*)

PERDICAN (*to* CAMILLE *as she enters*): Already up, Camille? I still believe what I told you yesterday. You're as lovely as the day is long.

CAMILLE: Let's talk seriously, Perdican. Your father wishes us to marry. I don't know what you really think of all this, but I believe I should warn you that so far as I'm concerned, it's decided.

PERDICAN: All the worse for me if I displease you.

CAMILLE: No more than any other man. I simply do not wish to marry, and there's nothing in my decision that should be a blow to your pride.

PERDICAN: Pride is not one of my concerns. I care nothing for its joys or pains.

CAMILLE: I came here to receive my mother's inheritance. Tomorrow I return to the convent.

PERDICAN: Thank you for your frankness. Give me your hand and let's be friends.

CAMILLE: I don't like touching.

PERDICAN: Give me your hand, Camille, I insist. Are you afraid of me? You don't wish us to marry. Ah, well, we won't marry. Is that reason enough for us to hate one another? Are we not like brother and sister? When your mother ordained this marriage in her will, she wished our friendship might be eternal, and that is all she wished. Why should we marry? Here is your hand and here is mine, and we don't need a priest, do we, to keep them united until our last breath? All we need is God's blessing.

CAMILLE: I'm so glad you don't seem to mind my refusal.

PERDICAN: But I do mind it, Camille. Your love would have given me life, but your friendship will console me. Don't leave the chateau tomorrow. Yesterday you refused to walk with me in the garden, because you saw in me a husband you did not want. Stay a few days. Allow me to hope that our past is not entirely dead in your heart.

CAMILLE: I must go.

PERDICAN: Why?

CAMILLE: It is my secret.

PERDICAN: You love someone else.

CAMILLE: No. But I must go.

PERDICAN: Irrevocably?

CAMILLE: Yes, irrevocably.

PERDICAN: Very well, goodbye. I should have liked to sit under the chestnut trees with you in the grove and talk as friends for an hour or two but if this displeases you, let's talk no more. Goodbye, child. (*He exits.*)

CAMILLE (*to* DAME PLUCHE, *who enters*): Dame Pluche, is everything ready? Can we leave tomorrow? My guardian has finished the accounts.

PLUCHE: Yes, my dear, spotless dove. The Baron called me an "idiot" last night and I'll be delighted to go.

CAMILLE: Wait. Here is a note that I want you to take to my cousin, Perdican, before dinner.

PLUCHE: Dear God, is it possible? You've written a billet-doux to a man?

CAMILLE: I'm to be his wife, aren't I? Surely, I can write a note to my fiancé.

PLUCHE: But Perdican just left you. Why must you write him? Your fiancé! God have mercy on you, surely you haven't forgotten Jesus?

CAMILLE (*sternly*): Do what I tell you. And then get everything ready for our departure. (*They exit arguing.*).

Scene Two

BRIDAINE (*entering*): Yes, it's certain. They'll give him the seat of honor again today. That chair on the Baron's right which I occupied for so long will be the tutor's prize. Oh, how unhappy I am! A numbskull. A shameless drunkard has relegated me to the end of the table. The steward will favor him with the first glass of malaga, and by the time the platters reach me, they'll be half cold, and the choicest cuts already taken, and the sprouts, the carrots and the partridge. Oh, holy church. I understand why he should have had the best seat yesterday, he had just arrived, and it was after an absence of many years. And, *Mon Dieu,* how he ate! No, nothing will be left for me today but the chicken's bones and its feet. I cannot bear this insult. Adieu, old chair, where I have so often collapsed, gorged with succulent dishes. Farewell, vintage wines, and the odor of venison cooked to perfection. Adieu, splendid banquets and noble dining room where I will never more say the benediction. I return to my rectory and I will never again be seen mingling with the throngs of guests, for, like Caesar, I would rather be first in a village than second in Rome. (*Exits.*)

Scene Three

PERDICAN (*kissing* ROSETTE): Since your mother's not at home, come and take a walk with me.

ROSETTE: Do you think it's right to give me all these kisses?

PERDICAN: What harm is there in that? I'd kiss you in front of your mother. Aren't you Camille's sister? Aren't I your brother as much as hers?

ROSETTE: Words are words and kisses are kisses. I know as soon as I try to speak, that I'm not very witty. Fine ladies know what it means when someone kisses their right hand or their left; their fathers kiss them on the forehead, their brothers on the cheek, their lovers on the lips. But everyone kisses me on both cheeks, and it annoys me.

PERDICAN: How pretty you are, my child.

ROSETTE: You mustn't bother yourself with that. You seem sad this morning. Has your wedding been cancelled?

PERDICAN: The peasants in the village remember that they once loved me; the hogs in the barnyards and the trees in the forest remember me, too, but Camille remembers nothing. And you, Rosette, when will you marry?

ROSETTE: Don't talk of that, please. Talk about the weather, about those flowers over there, about your horses and my bonnets.

PERDICAN: We'll talk about anything you like. Anything that can cross those lips without removing that heavenly smile which I love more than anything else. (*He kisses her.*)

ROSETTE: You respect my smile, but you don't seem to respect my lips, so far as I can see. Why look, a drop of rain has fallen on my hand . . . and the sky is cloudless.

PERDICAN (*choking*): Forgive me.

ROSETTE: What have I done to make you cry? (*They exit.*)

Scene Four

BLAZIUS: Baron, I have something odd to tell you. Just now when I was in the pantry—I mean, in the art gallery—what would I be doing in the pantry? Well, I was in the gallery. I found by accident a bottle of—I mean a carafe of water—how could I have found a bottle of wine in the gallery? So, as I was drinking a glass of wine, I mean a tumbler of water, to pass the time, and stood gazing out of the window, looking out between two modern vases, but they were imitation Etruscan —

BARON: What an insupportable manner of speech you've adopted, Blazius! Your conversation is gibberish!

BLAZIUS: Listen to me, Baron. Just give me one moment of your attention. I was looking out the window — Don't be impatient, in the name of God, it has to do with the family's honor.

BARON: The family's honor? This is incomprehensible. Our family's honor, Blazius. Do you know that there are thirty-seven males and almost as many females living in both Paris and the provinces?

BLAZIUS: Allow me to continue. While I was drinking a glass of wine, I mean water, for my digestion. Can you guess? I saw Dame Pluche under the window. Out of breath.

BARON: Why out of breath, Blazius? This is bizarre.

BLAZIUS: Red with rage, and at her side, your niece Camille.

BARON: Who was red with rage, my niece or Dame Pluche?

BLAZIUS: Your niece, Baron.

BARON: Red with rage? Unheard of. And how do you know it was anger? She could have had high coloring for a thousand reasons . . . she was chasing butterflies in the garden.

BLAZIUS: I can't comment on that. It's possible. But she was shouting very loudly, "Go on. For the last time, find him. Do what you're told. You're a fool. I insist." And she was beating Dame Pluche on the neck with her fan, so that she leaped into the clover patch with each shout.

BARON: Into the clover patch? And how did the governess react to my niece's extravagant behavior?

BLAZIUS (*gesturing*): Into the clover patch . . .

BARON: Extravagant. That's the only way to describe it.

BLAZIUS: And she replied, "I won't go. I don't know where to find him. He's busy flirting with the village girls and the shepherdesses. Besides, I'm too old to begin carrying billet-doux. By the grace of God, I have kept these hands pure until now." And with that she crumpled a little paper, which had been folded in quarters.

BARON: I don't understand a word. My thoughts are completely confused.

What reason would Dame Pluche have to crumple a little paper and leap into the clover patch? I can't make heads nor tails of such grotesque carryings-on.

BLAZIUS: But, Baron, don't you really understand what it must signify?

BARON: No, truly, my friend, I understand nothing. It all seems to be unruly behavior, without rhyme or reason.

BLAZIUS: It must mean that your niece is carrying on a clandestine correspondence.

BARON: What are you saying? Do you know to whom you are speaking? Weigh your words carefully, Father Blazius.

BLAZIUS: If I were to weigh them in the heavenly balance that's to scale my soul at the Last Judgment, I should not find a single word that rings false. Your niece has a secret correspondent.

BARON: But think, my friend, that's impossible.

BLAZIUS: Then why should she give the governess a letter? Why would she cry, "Find him," while the other sulked and groused?

BARON: To whom was the letter addressed?

BLAZIUS: Ay, there's the "rub" precisely. To whom was the letter addressed? Well — to a man who flirts with shepherdesses. Now if a man is publicly known to pursue shepherdesses, he is perhaps to be strongly suspected of being born to look after sheep himself. However, it's impossible that your niece, with the education she's received, could be in love with such a man. That's how I see it, and that's why I cannot understand it any better than you—with all due respect.

BARON: Heavens! Only this morning my niece told me she was refusing her cousin, Perdican. She can't be in love with a shepherd? Come along to my study. Since yesterday I've suffered so many violent shocks that I can't collect my thoughts. (*They exit.*)

Scene Five

PERDICAN (*enters reading a note*): "Be at the little spring at noon." What can that mean? Her refusal was so positive, so cold, so cruel, proud and insensitive, and after all that a rendezvous? If she wants to talk business, why does she pick a spot like this? Is she being coquettish? This morning when I was walking with Rosette, I heard the bushes stirring, and I thought it was a doe . . . is it a plot of some kind?

CAMILLE (*entering*): Good day, cousin. I seemed to notice, rightly or wrongly, that you were sad when you left me this morning. You took my hand against my will, and now I ask that you give me yours. I refused to give you a kiss, and now . . . (*she kisses him*). And you told me we should be the best of friends, so let's sit down and talk.

PERDICAN: Was that a dream or is this?

CAMILLE: You found it strange to receive a note from me? I'm changeable. But this morning you said something to me that was very true: "As we part let us do so as friends." You don't know why I am leaving, so I have come to tell you. I'm going to take the veil.

PERDICAN: Is it possible? Is this really you, Camille, reflected in the fountain, seated on the daisies as in former days?

CAMILLE: Yes, Perdican, it is. I have come to relive fifteen minutes of our past life. I was brusque and haughty this morning. The explanation is simple. I have renounced the world. However, before I leave it, I should like to have your opinion. Do you think I'm right to become a nun?

PERDICAN: Don't ask me about that. I'll never become a monk.

CAMILLE: In the ten years we have lived apart, you have begun to learn about life. I know the sort of man you are, and with feelings and a spirit like yours you have probably learned a great deal in a short time. Tell me, have you had mistresses?

PERDICAN: Why do you ask?

CAMILLE: Answer me, please, and without false modesty or vanity.

PERDICAN: I have had mistresses.

CAMILLE: Did you love them all?

PERDICAN: What strange questions. What do you want me to say? I was neither their husband nor brother, and so they've gone where they wanted to go.

CAMILLE: There must have been one whom you preferred to all the others. How long did you love your favorite?

PERDICAN: You're an odd girl. Do you want to be my confessor?

CAMILLE: I'm asking you a favor — answer me honestly. You are certainly not a libertine, and you have an honest heart. You must have inspired love and you deserved it, and you wouldn't have given in to any passing fancy. Answer me, please.

PERDICAN: In faith, I don't remember.

CAMILLE: Have you ever known a man who only loved one woman?

PERDICAN: Certainly there are such people.

CAMILLE: But was he one of your friends? What's his name?

PERDICAN: I can't give you a name, but there must be men who are capable of loving only once in their lives.

CAMILLE: How often should a gentleman fall in love?

PERDICAN: Do you want me to recite a litany, or are you saying a catechism?

CAMILLE: I want to know if I'm right or wrong to become a nun. If I married you, wouldn't you have to answer all of my questions honestly? And bare your heart to me? I esteem you highly, and because of your education and breeding I believe you superior to other men. Well, I'm sorry you can't answer my questions. Perhaps if I knew you better, I would be bolder.

PERDICAN: Whatever you ask, I'll answer.

CAMILLE: Then answer my first question. Am I right to remain in the convent?

PERDICAN: No.

CAMILLE: I should marry you instead?

PERDICAN: Yes.

CAMILLE: If your parish priest breathed on a glass of water and announced that it was now wine, would you drink it as such?

PERDICAN: No.

CAMILLE: If that parish priest breathed on us and said we were married for life, should I believe him?

PERDICAN: Yes . . . and no.

CAMILLE: What would you advise me to do the day I discovered you no longer loved me?

PERDICAN: Take a lover.

CAMILLE: And what would I do the day I realized my lover no longer loved me?

PERDICAN: Take another.

CAMILLE: And how often would that be repeated?

PERDICAN: Until your hair was grey and mine white.

CAMILLE: Do you know what a cloister is, Perdican? Have you ever sat a whole day in a monastery pew?

PERDICAN: I have.

CAMILLE: I have a friend, a sister, who is only thirty years old, and who had an income of five hundred thousand livres at the age of fifteen. She is the loveliest and noblest creature who ever walked on the face of the earth. She was married to one of the most distinguished men in all France. She was the most cultured of all women, like a small tree whose branches are covered with buds of promise. Never had love and happiness placed their coronet on a lovelier brow. But her husband deceived her, then she found another man, and now she dies of despair.

PERDICAN: It can happen.

CAMILLE: We live in the same cell. And I have spent whole nights talking with her of her misfortunes. They have almost become mine. Strange, isn't it? I don't know how that happens. When she told me of her marriage, she drew a picture for me of the ecstasy of those first days, then the tranquillity of the ones that followed, and then how everything flew away. How she would sit by the fire and he by the window, without exchanging a single word. How their love languished, and how all their efforts to come together ended in quarrels. How bit by bit a strange face came to hover between them and glided above their sorrows. I felt what she had felt, as she talked. When she said, "Then I was happy," my heart leaped. And when she added, "Then I wept," my tears flowed. But imagine something even stranger. I ended by creating an imaginary life for myself which has lasted these past four years. It's useless to attempt to enumerate all the thoughts and meditations that caused this. What I wanted to tell you, as a curiosity, is that all of Louise's stories and all the fictions of my dreams bore your likeness.

PERDICAN: My likeness? Mine?

CAMILLE: Yes, and it's only natural. You were the only man I had ever known. Truly, I loved you, Perdican.

PERDICAN: How old are you, Camille?

CAMILLE: Eighteen.

PERDICAN: Go on. I'm listening.

CAMILLE: There are two hundred women in our convent, a few of these will never know life, all the others now wait for death. More than one of these left the convent, as I left it, pure and full of hope. They returned a little later, old and desolate. Every day another dies in the long dormitory, and every day a new one takes the place of a dead one on the horsehair mattress. Strangers who visit us admire the calm and order of our establishment; they note the whiteness of our veils, but they are puzzled why we wear them low over our eyes. What do you think of these women, Perdican? Are they right or wrong?

PERDICAN: I can't say.

CAMILLE: Many people have advised me to remain a virgin. I would value your opinion. Do you really think these women would have been better off to have taken a lover? Is that what you'd tell me to do?

PERDICAN: I can't say.

CAMILLE: You promised you'd answer.

PERDICAN: Naturally, I'm excused. I can't believe it's you speaking.

CAMILLE: That's possible. There must be things about my ideas which are ridiculous. Perhaps I've learned my lesson the way a parrot does. In the gallery there is a tiny picture of a monk bent over a missal; through the dark bars of his cell steals a feeble ray of sunlight. You can see an Italian inn, and next to it a goatherd is dancing. Which of these men do you admire?

PERDICAN: Neither one nor the other nor both. They're both flesh and blood. One reads and the other dances. I see nothing more. (*Exasperated.*) You'll make a good nun.

CAMILLE: Just now you told me I shouldn't.

PERDICAN: It's possible.

CAMILLE: Now this?

PERDICAN: Perhaps you should believe in nothing?

CAMILLE: Think again, Perdican. What kind of person believes in nothing? (*Pause.*)

PERDICAN: I am one! I don't believe in immortality. My dear sister, the nuns have taught you what they know, but believe me, it isn't what you would learn by experience. Could you die without loving?

CAMILLE: I want to love, but I don't want to suffer. I want an eternal love and vows which cannot be broken. Here is my lover. (*Shows him her crucifix.*)

PERDICAN: But that lover will allow you others.

CAMILLE: Not for me. Perdican, don't smile. It has been ten years since I last saw you. I leave tomorrow, perhaps in another ten years we will meet again and we can talk of this meeting. I didn't want to remain in your memory as a cold statue, because of how I acted here. Listen to me. Return to your life, so long as it can make you happy, and forget your sister Camille. But if you ever arrive at that point where you are forgotten by others, or forget yourself, if the angel of hope abandons you, then when you are alone with a hollowness in your heart, think of me, and I will pray for you.

PERDICAN: You're arrogant!

CAMILLE: Why?

PERDICAN: You're eighteen and you don't believe in love.

CAMILLE: But do you believe in it either? Here you kneel beside me on knees that have been worn out on the carpets of your mistresses, those ones whose names you can't remember. You've wept tears of joy and tears of despair, but you knew that spring water was more constant and that it would always be there to bathe your swollen eyelids. You acted as young men always do. You smile when you hear of desolated women. You can't believe that someone could die of love, you who live and have loved. Then what is the world about? It would seem to me that you should heartily despise the women who take you, just as you are, and chase away their last lover to entice you to their arms with another's kisses still on their lips. Just now I asked you if you had ever loved, you answered me like a traveller who, when asked if he has ever been in Italy or Germany answers, "Yes, I've been there." Then he thinks of Switzerland, or the first country that comes to mind. Your love is a coin which will pass from hand to hand until you die. No, it can't be like money. Because then the smallest gold piece is more valuable than you are, because it will keep its value no matter how many hands hold it.

PERDICAN: Camille, you're beautiful when your eyes are fiery.

CAMILLE: Yes, I'm beautiful. I know it. Compliments teach me nothing. The cold nun who will chop off my hair may grow pale at the mutilation she is doing, but my tresses will never be made into rings and chains to be hung about in boudoirs. Not a hair will be missing from my head when the scissors pass over it; one single snip of the scissors and when the priest blesses me and places the gold ring of my heavenly husband on my finger, the lock of hair I will give him could serve him as a mantle.

PERDICAN: You really are angry!

CAMILLE: I was wrong to speak. My whole life is on my lips. Oh, Perdican, don't tease me. It's all too sad.

PERDICAN: Poor child, I've let you speak, but now I should like to say a word in reply. You've told me of a nun who seems to have a morbid influence on you. You say she was deceived, then she herself deceived her husband, and now she despairs. Are you certain that if her husband or her lover returned and stretched his hand through the convent grill that she would not reach out to touch it?

CAMILLE: I don't understand.

PERDICAN: Are you positive that if her husband or her lover came back to tell her to suffer once more, that she would say "no"?

CAMILLE: I believe it.

PERDICAN: There are two hundred women in your convent, and most have deep wounds in their hearts; they have made you feel them, and they have colored your innocent thoughts with their blood. But they have lived, experienced! And they have shown you with horror the road they have travelled. You have crossed yourself at the sight of their scars as you would before the wounds of Christ. They have given you a place in their lugubrious parade and you squeeze up against their skinny bodies with religious terror when you see a man go by. Are you certain that, if the man who passes was the one who deceived them, who made them weep and suffer, who they are cursing as they pray to God, are you certain that at the sight of him they would not break their chains to run back to their past miseries and press themselves against the very dagger that stabbed them? Oh, child, imagine the dreams of these women who tell you not to dream. They sit beside you, pouring into your ear their withered old age, their heads shaking, sounding in the ruins of your youth the doomsday tolling of their despair, and making your bright blood slow with the chill of their tombs— do you know what they're doing?

CAMILLE: You frighten me. Now you're angry.

PERDICAN: Do you know what the nuns are doing, you unhappy girl? They have represented man's love to you as a lie. But do you know something far worse? The lie of divine love. Do they know the sin they commit when they whisper women's words into a virgin's ear? Ah, how well they've taught you. This is what I was afraid of from the first, when I saw you looking at your great aunt's portrait. You wanted to leave without touching my hand, you didn't want to see this forest or this poor, tiny fountain which sees us now and weeps. You were denying the days of your childhood, and that plaster mask the nuns have placed on your face refused me a brother's kiss. But your heart still beats. It had forgotten, but then you returned to sit beside me on the grass. Very well, Camille, the ladies have had their turn. They've put you on the "right" road. It will have cost me my happiness, but tell them for me, "Heaven is not for them."

(*Pause.*)

CAMILLE: Nor for me?

PERDICAN: Goodbye, Camille. Return to your convent, and when they recall those hideous tales which have poisoned your mind, agree with them: all men *are* liars, fickle, false, gossips, hypocrites, arrogant or cowardly, contemptible and sensual; but women are perfidious, artificial, vain, inquisitive and depraved; the world is a bottomless sewer where shapeless creatures climb and squirm on mountains of muck; but if there is one holy and sublime thing which remains in this world it is the union of two of these imperfect and frightening creatures. We are often tricked by love, often blessed and often hurt, but we love, and when we are on the edge of the grave, turn around to look back and say, "*J'ai souffert souvent, je me suis trompé quelquefois, mais j'ai aimé. C'est moi qui ai vécu, et non pas un être factice créé par mon orgueil et mon ennui.*" . . . I have suffered often, have repeatedly been mistaken, but I have loved. And it is I who have lived this life and not some make-believe creature created from my pride and my despair. (*He exits.*)

END NOTES FOR ACT II

Scene 1. We are immediately taken back into the heart of the play. Blazius brings a message from the Baron and then leaves as Camille enters. Her first statement is "Let's talk seriously, Perdican . . . . I simply do not wish to marry . . ." Is she just a little disturbed when he takes her hand? We don't yet know Perdican's intentions. Will we ever? If you are known by the way you treat your servants, then Camille reveals herself somewhat. When she says, "I'm to be his wife," to Pluche it is nothing more than her withholding her true intentions from the woman.

Scene 2. Now, for contrast, in comes Bridaine. Be careful that you don't overdo this opportunity for comic relief. The play certainly doesn't seem headed in that direction any longer.

Scene 3. Watch out, Rosette, he's on the rebound. Rosette is a pleasant, simple, unpretentious girl, whose good sense has probably been destroyed by her partial acceptance in the chateau. The chorus members would never make this mistake.

Why did Perdican cry?

Scene 4. The clowns are struggling in increasingly unfunny ways to get things back to normal. The scene is in the chateau but without the usual zaniness and hustle-bustle.

The Baron says, "she was chasing butterflies in the garden," a line which shows how out of touch he is with what is really going on.

The letter is a very common device for plays such as this, as are assignations, and shepherds or shepherdesses hiding in bushes to overhear one another. Notice that the craziness between the Baron and the fathers is no longer humorous.

Scene 5. The mood is idyllic. Camille seems different. Is she reacting to Perdican's interest in Rosette? It should be played so that the audience has an ironic sense of Camille's own confusion about her emotions. Why is she so interested in his mistresses? Perdican is fatuous; Camille self-centered. I'm worried about Rosette.

These two spoiled youngsters are play-acting at being lovers in a pastoral. But the dialogue is increasingly psychological and realistic. Camille thinks she knows the truth about love and is ready to reveal it in the story of Sister Louise. Do we detect the playwright making the wry point that this naive girl is willing to turn away from life on the advice of women who at least experienced it before leaving it themselves? Yes, and he says so.

Be careful. This could become a very dull scene unless the audience feels it reveals more about the characters. For example, when she shows Perdican her crucifix, it should be a funny moment because we know it is a schoolgirl reaction to the shelter of the convent and the confusions of going out into the real world.

Perdican is equally fatuous: "You're arrogant . . . . You're eighteen and you don't believe in love." This scene has its gentle moments, if we can momentarily forget their treatment of Rosette. Be careful, though; the scene is long and must be kept alive.

As for design, note the description, "this poor, tiny fountain." Even the setting becomes melancholy, echoing their own self-pity. This is play-acting for them, but bear in mind that their "trifling" could have serious results for those not protected by social position.

ACT THREE

Scene One

BARON (*to* BLAZIUS): Apart from your drunkenness, you're a good for nothing, Father Blazius. My servants saw you sneak into the pantry, but when you're accused of having stolen my wine in this despicable manner, you try to justify yourself by accusing my niece of carrying on a secret correspondence.

BLAZIUS: But, Baron, please remember —

BARON: Get out, Father Blazius, and never let me see you again. It is insupportable to behave as you have, and my position makes it impossible for me to ever forgive you. (*He exits, then* BLAZIUS *follows.*)

PERDICAN (*enters*): I would like very much to know if I'm in love. On the one hand, her manner of asking questions is a bit cavalier for a girl of eighteen, and the ideas which the nuns have planted in her head will be difficult to root out. What's more, she leaves today. Devil take it! I love her. That's certain. After all, who knows? Perhaps she was only repeating a lesson, and besides . . . it's clear she doesn't care for me. As for her being pretty, that doesn't prevent her from being much too decided in her ways and a bit too brusque. I should put her out of my mind. It's obvious she doesn't love me. But she's so pretty. Why can't I put yesterday's conversation out of my head? I've been babbling on like this all night. Now where was I going? Oh, yes to the village. (*He exits.*)

Scene Two

BRIDAINE: What are they doing now? Alas, it's noon. They have just sat down for dinner. What are they eating? What aren't they eating, I mean. I saw the cook cross the village square carrying an enormous turkey. The maid was carrying truffles and a basket of grapes.

BLAZIUS: (*entering. They don't see one another*): Banished! What an unforeseen disgrace, to be thrown out of the chateau and, of course, the dining room. I shall never again sip wine from that pantry.

BRIDAINE: I will never again smell those platters; I will never again warm my well-filled stomach before a fire in that noble hearth.

BLAZIUS: What fatal curiosity made me listen to that conversation between Dame Pluche and the Baron's niece? And why did I report to him everything I saw?

BRIDAINE: Why did arrogant pride pull me away from that honorable table, at which I was so well received? What did it matter if I was on the Baron's right or left? .

BLAZIUS: Ah me, I was drunk, I must admit it, when I committed this folly.

BRIDAINE: Ah me, the wine went to my head when I acted so impudently.

BLAZIUS: Is that the village priest over there?

BRIDAINE: It's the tutor, in person.

BLAZIUS: Ah, Father Bridaine, what are you doing here?

BRIDAINE: I'm on my way to dinner, aren't you?

BLAZIUS: Not today. . . . Alas, Bridaine, intercede on my behalf. The Baron has turned me out. I falsely accused Mademoiselle Camille of having a secret correspondence; but as God is my witness, I did think I saw Dame Pluche in the alfalfa! I'm ruined, my dear Father.

BRIDAINE: What are you saying?

BLAZIUS: Alas, the truth! I am in disgrace for having snitched a bottle of wine.

BRIDAINE: What are you talking about, sir? Stolen bottles? Something about alfalfa . . .

BLAZIUS: I meant to say clover. . . .

BRIDAINE: And a secret correspondence?

BLAZIUS: I beg of you. Plead my cause. I'm really an honest man, Father Bridaine. Oh, honorable Bridaine, I am your servant!

BRIDAINE (*aside*): What luck! Is it a dream? Will I be seated on you again, happy chair?

BLAZIUS: If you'd only listen to my side of it, I'd be so grateful, my dear sir.

BRIDAINE: But it's impossible. It's noon and I'm on my way to dinner. If the Baron has complaints about you, that's your affair. Should I act as intermediary for a drunk? (*Aside.*) Quick, let's hurry to the gate, and you, dear stomach, stretch! (*He leaves at a trot.*)

BLAZIUS (*alone*): Miserable Pluche! You will pay for this. Yes, it is you who have caused my downfall, you shameless woman, procuress, it's you who have ruined me. Oh, blessed University of Paris, I've been treated like a drunkard. I'm lost if I can't seize a letter and prove to the Baron that his niece has a secret correspondent. I saw her writing at her desk this morning. Patience, here she is again. (DAME PLUCHE *crosses.*) Pluche, give me that letter.

PLUCHE: What does this mean? It is a letter from my mistress which I am to post in the village.

BLAZIUS: Give it to me, or I'll tear you limb from limb!

PLUCHE: Help, help, Mary, Jesus!

BLAZIUS: Yes, I'll kill you, Pluche. Give me that letter! (*They battle.* PERDICAN *enters.*)

PERDICAN: What's going on, Blazius? Why are you struggling with this woman?

PLUCHE: Give me that letter. He seized it from me, sir. I demand justice.

BLAZIUS: She's a go-between, young sir. It's a love letter.

PLUCHE: It's a letter from Camille, young sir, from your betrothed.

BLAZIUS: It's a love note to a shepherd.

PLUCHE: You lie, Father. You can take that from me.

PERDICAN: Give me the letter. I understand nothing of your argument, but since I'm to marry Camille, I have the right to read it. (*Reading aloud.*) To Sister Louise, at the convent of . . ." (*Aside.*) What dreadful curiosity seizes me in spite of myself. My heart beats in my ears and I have an odd feeling . . . You may go, Dame Pluche. You're a respectable woman and Blazius is a sot. Go along to dinner. I'll see to it that the letter is posted. (*They leave.*)

PERDICAN (*alone*): I know only too well that it's a crime to open letters. But what could Camille be saying to this sister? Can I be in love? What hold can this singular girl have over me that the three words of this address make my hand tremble? Odd. Look, in his struggle with Dame Pluche, Blazius has broken the seal. Can it be wrong to unfold the paper? After all, it will change nothing. (*He opens the letter and reads.*) "I leave today, my dear, and everything has happened as I expected. It is a terrible thing, for this young man is heartbroken. He will never be consoled at losing me. But I have done everything to make him hate me. God forgive me for having reduced him to despair with my refusal. Alas, my dear sister, what could I do? Pray for me. We shall see each other tomorrow and forever. My dearest love to you — Camille." Is it possible? Camille wrote that? It's me she's talking about. I'm supposed to be in despair at her refusal. My God, we'll see if that's true. What is there to be ashamed of in being in love? She's done everything in the world to make me hate her, she says, and I am heartbroken. What purpose can she have in inventing such a story? So it's true what I thought last night. Women! Poor Camille may be very pious. With the greatest joy she gives herself to God, but then she resolves and decrees to leave me in despair. This was settled between these two great friends even before she left the convent. It was decided that Camille would see her cousin, her family would try to make her marry him, she would refuse, and the poor cousin would be desolated. This is very interesting. A young woman sacrifices her cousin's happiness. No, no, Camille. I don't love you. I'm not in despair. I am not heartbroken. And I'll prove it to you. Yes, you'll know before you leave here, that I love another. Hey there, fellow. (*A peasant enters.*) Go to the chateau (*writing a note*) and tell them in the kitchen to take this note to Camille.

PEASANT: Yes, my lord. (*He exits.*)

PERDICAN: Now, for the other. So, I'm in despair. Hello, Rosette. Rosette!

ROSETTE: It's you, my lord. Come in, my mother's here.

PERDICAN: Put on your best bonnet, Rosette, and come with me.

ROSETTE: But where to?

PERDICAN: Later. Ask your mother's permission, but hurry.

ROSETTE: Yes, my lord. (*She exits.*)

PERDICAN: I've asked Camille for another rendezvous, and I know she'll come, but, by heavens, she won't find what she expects to find. I'm going to court Rosette in front of Camille. (*He exits.*)

Scene Three

PEASANT: Mademoiselle, I'm going to the chateau with a letter for you; should I give it to you now, or leave it in the kitchen, like Monsieur Perdican told me?

CAMILLE: Give it to me.

PEASANT: But if you'd rather I took it to the chateau, it's no trouble.

CAMILLE: I said, give it to me.

PEASANT: As you wish. (*Gives her the letter.*)

CAMILLE: Here's something for your pains.

PEASANT: Many thanks, I should go, should I?

CAMILLE: As you wish.

PEASANT: I'll go. I'll go. (*He exits.*)

CAMILLE (*reading*): Perdican asks me to say goodbye to him, before I leave, at the little spring where I made him come yesterday. What does he have to say to me? But there's the spring, and here I am. Is it right to give him this second rendezvous? Ah! (*She hides behind a tree.*) Here comes Perdican with Rosette, my stepsister. I suppose he'll leave her. Now he'll say goodbye to her. I'm glad I won't seem to be the first here. (ROSETTE *and* PERDICAN *enter and sit down.*)

CAMILLE: What does that mean? He has her sit down beside him. Did he arrange a rendezvous with me, to share it with someone else? But I'm curious to know what he'll say to her.

PERDICAN (*loud enough to be overheard*): I love you, Rosette. You of all the world have not forgotten those lovely bygone days. Share part of my new life; give me your love, dear child. Here is a pledge of my love. (*He places a chain around her neck.*)

ROSETTE: You're giving me your gold chain?

PERDICAN: Look at this ring. See our reflections in the water, leaning on one another. See your lovely eyes, your hand in mine? See it all disappear. (*He throws his ring in the water.*) Our image has disappeared, but now it will reappear, bit by bit. The troubled water regains its composure; it still trembles; great black circles rise to the surface. Patience, we will reappear. Already I can make out again your arms around me. One more minute and not a wrinkle on your pretty face . . . . Look! It was a ring Camille gave me.

CAMILLE: He threw my ring in the water.

PERDICAN: Do you know what love is, Rosette? Listen. The wind is hushed. The morning rain rolls in pearls off the dry leaves that the sun reanimates. By the light of the skies, by the sun up there, I love you! You wish me well, don't you? No one has blighted your youth; no one has mixed your bright blood with watery blood? You don't want to be a nun, do you? You are young and lovely, and in the arms of a young man. Oh, Rosette, Rosette, do you know what love is?

ROSETTE: Ah, Professor, I'll love you as best I can.

PERDICAN: Yes, as best you can. And you will love me best, the doctor and the peasant girl, better than these pale statues made by nuns who have brains in place of hearts, who leave their cloisters to spread through life the contagion of their humid cells; you have no learning, you can't read the prayer your mother taught you, as her mother taught her. You don't understand the words you repeat when you kneel at the foot of your bed, but you know you're praying, and that is all God requires.

ROSETTE: How you speak to me, my Lord!

PERDICAN: You can't read. But you know what the woods and the meadows are saying, these gentle streams, these lovely fields rich with harvest, all of nature splendid with youth. You have thousands of sun-browned brothers, and I am one of them. Get up. You will be my wife, and we will take root together in the heart of the primal world. (*He leaves with* ROSETTE, *having forgotten* CAMILLE.)

Scene Four

CHORUS: Something strange is happening at the chateau. Camille has refused to marry Perdican. She should return today to her convent. And I believe her noble cousin has been consoling himself with Rosette. Alas, I don't believe the poor girl knows what disaster she courts listening to the speeches of a young and gallant cavalier.

DAME PLUCHE (*entering*): Quick, quick, saddle my mule!

CHORUS: Will you pass like a fickle dream, venerable dame? Why do you go so soon to straddle once more this poor beast who is made so sad carrying you?

PLUCHE: Praise be to God, dear rabble, that I won't die here.

CHORUS: Die far away, then, Pluche, my dear. Die unknown in a sickly cell. We will offer up prayers for your resurrection.

PLUCHE: Here comes my mistress. Dear Camille, all is ready for our departure. The Baron has completed his accounts, and my mule is saddled.

CAMILLE: Go to hell, you and your mule. I'm not going today.

CHORUS: What? Dame Pluche is pale with terror. Her wig tries to stand on end, her breath comes in gasps, and her fingers stretch and claw.

PLUCHE: Lord Jesus! Camille swore! (*She exits.*)

Scene Five

BRIDAINE: Sir, it's necessary that I speak to you of an important matter. Your son is making love to a girl in the village.

BARON: That's absurd, my friend.

BRIDAINE: I distinctly saw him walking in the grove with her, arm in arm. He was leaning into her ear and promising to marry her.

BARON: This is monstrous.

BRIDAINE: Be certain of it. He even gave her a considerable gift, which she has shown to her mother.

BARON: Heavens, considerable, Bridaine? How considerable?

BRIDAINE: For value and sentiment. It's his gold chain.

BARON: Come along to my study. I don't know what to think.

Scene Six

CAMILLE: He took my letter?

PLUCHE: Yes, my child, but he said he'd mail it.

CAMILLE: Go to the livingroom, Pluche, and please ask Perdican to come here. (*She exits.*) He has read my letter, that is certain. The scene in the grove was revenge, like his love for Rosette. He wanted to prove that he loved someone else, and pretend indifference in spite of his anger. Could he be in love with me? Is that you, Rosette?

ROSETTE: Yes, may I enter?

CAMILLE: Listen to me, my child. Perdican has made love to you, hasn't he?

ROSETTE: Yes, he has.

CAMILLE: What do you think of what he said this morning?

ROSETTE: This morning? Where?

CAMILLE: Don't play the hypocrite. This morning by the fountain, in the grove.

ROSETTE: You saw me?

CAMILLE: Poor innocent. No, I didn't see you. He made beautiful speeches, didn't he? Pledges that he would marry you?

ROSETTE: How do you know that?

CAMILLE: What does it matter how I know? Did you believe his promises, Rosette?

ROSETTE: Why shouldn't I? Would he trick me? Why would he do that?

CAMILLE: Perdican won't marry you, my child.

ROSETTE: What do you mean?

CAMILLE: You love him, poor child. He will not marry you. And, as for proof, I'll show you. Hide behind the drapes. You have only to listen and then come out when I call. (ROSETTE *exits.*)

CAMILLE (*alone*): I thought to act in revenge, but will I be doing an act of kindness? The poor girl is in love with him. (*Enter* PERDICAN.) Good day, cousin.

PERDICAN: What a lovely dress, Camille. Who is it for?

CAMILLE: For you, perhaps. I'm sorry that I missed our rendezvous. You had something to say to me?

PERDICAN (*aside*): Upon my life, that's a pretty big lie for a spotless lamb. I saw her listening behind a tree. (*Aloud.*) I have nothing more to say to you, Camille, than goodbye. I understand you're leaving. However, your horse is in the stable, and you don't seem to be in traveling clothes. (*Pause.*)

CAMILLE: I like an argument. I am not certain but that I'd like to quarrel with you again.

PERDICAN: But what's the point of quarreling when you can't make up? The pleasure in disputing is in the peacemaking.

CAMILLE: Are you convinced I don't want to make peace?

PERDICAN: Don't joke. I'm not up to answering you.

CAMILLE: I would like to be made love to. I don't know if it's because I'm dressed up, but I want to enjoy myself. You proposed that we go to the village. Let's go. I should like to. Let's take the boat. I would enjoy eating under the trees, or taking a walk in the forest. Will there be moonlight tonight? That's strange. You're not wearing the ring I gave you.

PERDICAN: I lost it.

CAMILLE: Then I found it. Behold, Perdican, it's here.

PERDICAN: Is it possible? Where did you find it?

CAMILLE: A girl could spoil her dress, reaching into fountains! So put this on your finger.

PERDICAN: You retrieved this ring from the water, Camille, at the risk of falling in? Is this a dream? You're here. It is you who placed it on my finger. Ah, Camille, why do you give me back this sad pledge of happiness which is no longer? Say something? Are you going? Why do you remain? Why do you change appearance and color from one hour to the next like the stone in this ring in the sunlight?

CAMILLE: Do you really know women's love, Perdican? Are you so certain of their constancy? Do you really know that they change their ideas when they change their language? There are some who say they don't. Without doubt, we often must play a role, often lie. You see I'm being frank. But are you certain that everything in a woman lies when her tongue lies? Have you reflected on the nature of this feeble and violent being, how rigorously she is judged, the rules imposed on her? And who knows if, forced into deception by the world, this little, brainless creature can't take pleasure in sobbing and many times lying for amusement as she lies for necessity?

PERDICAN: I understand nothing of this. I never lie. I love you, Camille, that's all I know.

CAMILLE: You say you love me. And you never lie.

PERDICAN: Never.

CAMILLE: But here is someone who can attest that it happens to you some-times. (CAMILLE *opens the drape to reveal* ROSETTE, *who has fainted.*) How will you answer this child, Perdican, when she demands that you account for your words? If you never lie, then why did she faint when she heard you say you loved me? I leave her with you. Try to revive her.

PERDICAN: One moment, Camille, listen to me.

CAMILLE: What can you have to say to me? It's Rosette you must speak to. I don't love you. I didn't take this poor child out of her thatched cottage to make bait out of her, a plaything. I didn't repeat to her imprudently the passionate speeches addressed to another. I didn't pretend to throw away for her sake the souvenir of a cherished friendship. I didn't put my gold chain around her neck, and I didn't tell her I'd marry her.

PERDICAN: Listen! Listen!

CAMILLE: You smiled just now, didn't you, when I said I couldn't go to the fountain? Very well. Yes, I was there. And I heard everything. But God is my witness, I couldn't have spoken as you did. What will you do with this girl, now, when she will come to you with your ardent kisses on her lips, in tears, to show you how you've wounded her? You wanted to avenge your-self on me, didn't you. And punish me for the letter I wrote to the convent. You wished to strike me at any price and you counted it nothing if the poisoned arrow traveled through this girl provided it struck me, standing behind her. I prided myself I'd inspired some love in you, and I would leave you with some regret. And that injured your noble pride? Very well. Let me tell you, you love me. Do you hear? But you will marry this girl, or you're a coward!

PERDICAN: Yes, I will marry her.

CAMILLE: You must.

PERDICAN: Very well, and better than marrying you. Why are you so heated? This child has fainted. We must revive her. To do that we need a vial of vinegar. You wished to prove that I had lied once in my life. It's possible, but I find it impudent of you to decide when. Come, help me with Rosette. (*They exit.*)

Scene Seven

BARON: If that happens, I shall go out of my mind.

CAMILLE: Use your authority.

BARON: Out of my mind and refuse my consent. And that is definite.

CAMILLE: You must talk to him and make him listen to reason.

BARON: This will throw me into despair for the whole season. I won't be able to appear once at court. It's an ungainly marriage. No one has ever heard of marrying the stepsister of one's cousin. It's against nature.

CAMILLE: Call him in, tell him clearly that you deplore this marriage. Believe me, it's a folly on his part and he won't resist you.

BARON: I shall wear black this winter. You can be certain of that.

CAMILLE: But speak to him, in the name of heaven! It was impulse! Perhaps it's already too late. If he says he'll do it, he'll do it.

BARON: I'll shut myself up and abandon myself to my grief. Tell him, if he asks, that I am shut away and that I grieve to see him marry a nameless girl. (*He exits.*)

CAMILLE: Will I never find a courageous man? Truly, when you search for one it's terrible how alone you are. (PERDICAN *enters.*) Well, cousin, when is the wedding?

PERDICAN: The sooner the better. I have already spoken to the notary, the priest, and the villagers.

CAMILLE: You have definitely decided then to marry Rosette?

PERDICAN: Definitely.

CAMILLE: What will your father say?

PERDICAN: Whatever he wishes, I want to marry this girl. It is an idea that you gave me and I'm holding to it. Must I repeat to you the common bonds that tie her birthright to mine? She is young and pretty, and she loves me. That is more than we need to be three times happy. Whether she's intelligent or not, I could have done worse. Let people complain and laugh. I wash my hands of it.

CAMILLE: There's nothing to laugh at. You do well to marry her. But there is one thing that makes me sorry for you: that people will say you did it out of spite.

PERDICAN: You are sorry for that? But you aren't.

CAMILLE: Yes, I am really sorry for you. It's wrong for a young man to be spiteful.

PERDICAN: Then be sorry. So far as I'm concerned, it's all the same.

CAMILLE: But you haven't thought. She's a nobody.

PERDICAN: She'll be somebody when she's my wife.

CAMILLE: She will bore you before the notary has put on his new suit and shoes to come here. Your love will die at the wedding when you realize she smells of stew, like a servant.

PERDICAN: You'll see I shan't. You don't know me. When a woman is sweet and sensitive, blooming and good and lovely, I am capable of being content with that, yes, truly, to the point that it doesn't matter to me if she can't speak Latin.

CAMILLE: It's too bad so much money was spent teaching it to you. It's three thousand crowns lost.

PERDICAN: Yes, it could have been given to the poor.

CAMILLE: You'll be doing that, at least to the poor in spirit.

PERDICAN: And they will give me in exchange the Kingdom of Heaven, for it is theirs.

CAMILLE: How long will this joke last?

PERDICAN: What joke?

CAMILLE: I can't wait to dance at your wedding.

PERDICAN: Listen, Camille, your bantering tone is inappropriate.

CAMILLE: It pleases me too much to stop.

PERDICAN: I'll leave you, then. I've had enough.

CAMILLE: Are you going to your fiancée's house?

PERDICAN: Yes, this minute.

CAMILLE: Give me your arm, then. I'll go, too. (ROSETTE *enters.*)

PERDICAN: There you are, my child. Come with me. I want you to meet my father.

ROSETTE: Sir, I come to ask you a favor. Everyone in the village has been telling me this morning that you love your cousin and that you only make love to me to amuse you both. They mock me when I pass by, and I will never be able to find a husband in this village after being the laughing-stock of everyone. Allow me to give you back the chain you gave me, and let me live in peace in my mother's home.

CAMILLE: You are a good girl, Rosette. Keep the chain, I give it to you, and my cousin will take mine in its place. And don't be embarrassed about finding a husband. I will find you one.

PERDICAN: That's certainly not difficult. Come, Rosette, let's go and meet my father.

CAMILLE Why? What's the point?

PERDICAN: Yes, you're right. My father will receive us badly. This first moment of surprise which he has experienced must be allowed to pass. Come with me. We will go down to the village. I find it amusing that they say I don't love you, when I plan to marry you. By God, we'll make them shut up! (*He leaves with* ROSETTE.)

CAMILLE: What's happening inside me? He took her away so calmly. How strange: my head's spinning. Does he truly mean to marry her? Hello, Dame Pluche! Is there no one here? (*Enter valet.*) Run after Seigneur Perdican. Tell him to come back. I have to speak to him. (*The valet exits.*) But what is all this? I'm exhausted. My feet refuse to support me.

PERDICAN: You sent for me, Camille?

CAMILLE: No, no.

PERDICAN: You're very pale, what do you have to tell me? You called me back to speak to me?

CAMILLE: No, no! — Oh, dear God! (*She exits.*)

Scene Eight

CAMILLE: Oh, God, have you abandoned me? When I came here, you know I promised to be faithful! When I refused to marry any but you, I thought I spoke sincerely, before you and my conscience. You know it, Father. Now don't you want me any more? Oh, why do you make truth itself lie? Why am I so weak? Oh, I can't pray anymore. (PERDICAN *enters.*)

PERDICAN: Why did pride have to come between this girl and me? There she is, pale and frightened. She could have loved me, we were born for each other, what did pride do to our lips when our hands were about to join?

CAMILLE: Who has followed me? Who is talking over there? Is it you, Perdican?

PERDICAN: What fools we are. We love each other. What dream did we fabricate, Camille? What vain words, what follies have passed like a fatal wind between us? Which of us wished to deceive the other? Life is such a painful dream. Why should we want to add ours to it? Oh, my God, happiness is such a rare pearl in this earthly ocean. But you gave it to us, this heavenly pearl, you plucked it out of the abyss, this inestimable joy, and we are such spoiled children, we made a plaything out of it. Of course, we had to do wrong, though, because we're human. What fools we are. We love each other! (*He takes her in his arms.*)

CAMILLE: Yes, we love one another, Perdican. We must admit it. God will not be offended, he wants me to love you. For fifteen years he has known it.

PERDICAN: Dear creature, you're mine. (*They embrace. A cry is heard from behind the altar.*)

CAMILLE: That is Rosette's voice.

PERDICAN: What is she doing here? I left her on the stairs when I came in here. She must have followed me.

CAMILLE: Come to the gallery. That's where the cry came from.

PERDICAN: I don't know what I feel. It seems that my hands are covered with blood.

CAMILLE: The poor child must have seen us. She probably fainted again. Come, let's help her. How cruel this all is.

PERDICAN: No, I won't go in there. I feel a mortal chill which paralyzes me. Go and revive her, Camille. (*She exits.*) I beseech you, dear God, don't make me a murderer. You see what is happening. We are two foolish children who have played with life and death. But our hearts are pure. Don't kill Rosette; God, I will find her a husband, I will make it up to her. She is young. She will be rich. She will be happy. Don't do this, dear Lord. You can still bless us. Well, Camille, what is the matter?

CAMILLE: She is dead! Goodbye, Perdican!

The End

END NOTES FOR ACT III

Scene 1. This appears to be a continuation of the last Blazius-Baron scene. It is significant that the comic world is also coming apart. The key moment belongs to Perdican. He tells us of his love for Camille and his decision to go to the village, probably to see Rosette.

Scene 2. Contrast this scene with Act I. Musset entangles the clowns in the world of the lovers in the incident of the letter.

Camille, in the full blush of her self-assurance, says, "this young man is heartbroken," and decides to help him. Then Rosette enters. Such fortunate or unfortunate entrances always happen in musical comedies, but here? It is important to handle this scene with care. The pastoral world is growing darker.

Scene 3. Camille snaps her order, "I said, give it to me," and the peasant does. She sounds like a no-nonsense Mother Superior, and Musset wants us to bear this in mind as we move toward the climax.

What follows is a very difficult scene. There is great pathos and truth in Rosette's line, "Professor, I'll love you as best I can."

Scene 4. Camille is really on the peck. "Go to hell, you and your mule [to Dame Pluche]. I'm not going today."

Scene 5. There is absolutely no way that these particular characters could alter what is about to happen.

Scene 6. Camille thinks she is being kind when she tells Rosette that Perdican will never marry her and then has her hide behind the drape. This arrogance follows naturally from everything we know about her. And Perdican accepts Camille's seeming change of heart, which agrees with everything we ever knew about him. "You retrieved this ring from the water, Camille, at the risk of falling in?" One is tempted to believe that people like Camille never drown and rarely even get wet. Rosette is revealed. She has fainted from shock and despair.

Scene 7. The Baron can do nothing. Everything has been set up for this moment. What we don't know is how the playwright will handle the details. Pluche, Blazius, and Bridaine are no longer factors in the story of the lovers. Someone might be hurt, but be careful not to be too hard-edged or chaotic here. Balance satire and truth with the play-acting atmosphere of the pastoral world.

When Rosette enters, should her face be swollen with crying? Probably not, but think about it. The entire play is a balancing act.

With Camille's speech, "What's happening inside me," we have the final irony. The trickster has been tricked. She has been trapped in her own game of love, not that she understands what love is or is about to sympathize with others who might have the same feelings.

Scene 8. It ends, and perhaps not as you expected. Rosette loses all, but what did Perdican and Camille lose? Try to remember your initial feelings about the ending. This will be one of the keys to your production.

Further Questions on *No Trifling with Love*

1. Where do the various scenes take place? We have purposefully omitted the locales given in the original text, but aren't they obvious? Do you see the setting as specific scenes in defined spaces or does the play happen in neutral spaces which become what you call them? What kind of a world, visually, could contain this play? Another way of asking the same question is: Considering the mix of the comic and tragic, dark and light, silly and serious, fanciful and real, how can you accommodate all of these tensions in a single scenic world?

2. What is the theme of the play? Don't use the title. We can all go that far. Go beyond it. Musset is certainly questioning not only the motives of the young people in the play but those of the poets and artists who have created pastoral fantasies for us through the ages. Would you say the play supports the notion that he is angered by this? What exactly is his attitude?

3. How could you introduce sympathetic elements in your treatment of Camille? If you don't, you could be stuck with the Wicked Witch of the fountain and several very long scenes. Should your sympathy be based on the ideal or the real? We began by asking about Perdican's motives (in the end notes for Act One). What did they turn out to be? Is he a cad? How would you make Rosette interesting? Does she make us feel uncomfortable and guilty as victims sometimes do, or does she touch us? Their love triangle is the core of the play. You might want to read Strindberg's *Dance of Death* for a more in-depth psychological study of the dynamics of such relationships.

4. Is it important to place this drama in a specific time and place? Will your audience understand what a pastoral is? If not, how can you help them? What about the village/chateau configuration? Perhaps it has some echoes in Old Manse and miscegenation, but that is really far-fetched. How will you teach your audience to understand the context of the play?

5. The playwright was intelligent, and the play by turns is amusing, witty, perceptive, and tragic. How can you make the death of Rosette at play's end meaningful and not throw out something that has gone before? Remember, Musset didn't have to kill Rosette and he was a skillful artist. Find his reasons and his aesthetic.

6. Now create your own production.

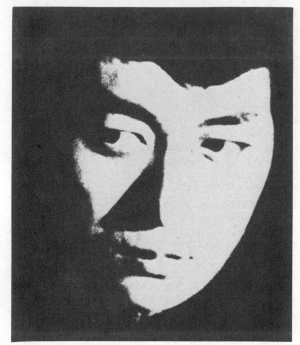

Shuji Terayama.

9

Terayama:
Directions
to Servants

Our final project deals with new forms of dramatic expression. While *Philoctetes* was a "closed," classical drama, and *No Trifling with Love* both a satire and echo of plays in the Romantic tradition, *Directions to Servants* is experimental. Our ground rules, as before, are to apply the understandings and skills we have developed, and to avoid discussing specific productions of this play. We understand that much of Terayama's material for this script grew out of the improvisations of a group of artists accustomed to working with one another. There are also cultural concerns that influenced their production. However, although there are facts you need to know about the playwright and his approach, the object of this final exercise is to give you the opportunity to create new solutions to theatrical problems.

Shuji Terayama was born in Japan in 1935 and was a published poet while still in his teens. In 1960, he wrote his first play, *Blood Sleeps Standing Up*, and became involved in founding an experimental theatre group. Through his work on movie scripts, articles, novels, plays, and poetry, he has become an internationally known artist. He visited America in 1970 and directed a production at the LaMama Theatre in New York City. His plays during this period drew considerable attention, some of it unwanted. In 1975, performances of his street theatre play, *Knock*, led to public controversy and the arrest of several company members. In 1978, his theatre company, Tenjosajiki, took its production of *Directions to Servants* to Europe and then on to the Spoleto Festival in Charleston, South Carolina, and a summer 1980 run at the LaMama.

Shuji Terayama is a prolific and versatile writer, interested in experimentation and the politics of change. His theory of drama[1] aims at the abolition of the play as the art form that is done in a theatre. He seeks to create a primary relationship between audience and performers in which they each can interact and influence one another. His actors are told to improvise and forget old solutions, and Terayama claims that there is no such thing as a theatrical space, that theatre can be done anywhere. His sense of the social implications of performance, of theatre's necessary impermanence, and the primacy of interaction between audience and performers are expressed in many aspects of the play to be studied here. For example, its dialogue is often fragmented and poetic, rather than specific; a number of the scenes are only guidelines for improvisation, and the final scenes of the play are titles for actions that must be created by the performers and that should break the sequence and logic of what has gone before. As Terayama comments, "the real play has not yet started." After its successful world tour, *Directions to Servants* is no longer performed in its original version but has since evolved into a new drama.

The script reproduced here is named after a satire by Jonathan Swift (1667–1745). Swift is cited as one of Terayama's inspirations for the play, but the purposes of the two works are by no means similar. The former's piece is

[1]Manifesto by Shuji Terayama, *The Drama Review*, Volume 19, Number 4 (T–68), December 1975.

a curmudgeonly itemization of the tricks that maids, groomsmen, cooks, and other servants play on their masters. It is by no means a denunciation of the institution which creates servants and masters; nor is it a condemnation of mankind's foibles of the sort we might expect from the author of *Gulliver's Travels.* Here he is seen as a put-upon master, commenting wryly on how difficult it is to find good servants. There is a terrible irony in this if you know that in his final illness, when he was unable to move or speak, Dean Swift's servants sold tickets to the curious and brought them in to gape at him.

Shuji Terayama's theme, on the other hand, asserts that it is human nature to invent masters even when there really are none. As he says in the preface to the English translation:

> What I hope to describe in this play is the present situation of the world, marked by the "absence of Master." Our revolt is not against this absent Master. "My enemy is myself." "Your enemy is yourself."
> "Everyone can be a Master for 15 minutes." But when Servants try to kill their absent Master, their venom and hatred create an image of Hell. The tragedy is not the absence of the Master—but the Servants' need for a Master.

Terayama is both an underground theatre leader and a left-wing intellectual, but he insists that politics and theatre don't mix. What is strongly evident in his play is his belief that modern Western ideals and capitalism are simply repeating the social patterns and values of feudal Japan. In the Japanese edition of *Directions to Servants*, the preface is a quotation from Kenji Miyasawa (1856–1925), a respected figure in the turn-of-the-century movement to accept Western ideas. In the passage quoted, Miyasawa says:

> I eat four cups of brown rice a day,
>   and bean paste, and a bit of vegetable.
> Whatever I do, I do for others.

Terayama apparently interprets this as shallow, self-serving humanism. In one scene of his play, the servants squat eating rice, a sign of their subservience, not their oneness with all mankind. The playwright comments, "Everyone who has to eat rice is a servant. Manservants and maids [those who wait on the master] eat rice with tears running down their cheeks." The play's repeated references to rice, to the Master's Farm, and the Master's Shoes all seem to be metaphoric extensions of this attack on both modern capitalism and earlier Japanese feudalism.

The Problem

How should we go about creating a production plan for this play? Clearly, the drama deals with issues that apply to all modern cultures, and if we are to believe the playwright, the burden of the play should not be its politics. If this is the case, then let's focus on the universality of its theme. Other concerns we must deal with are the need for improvisation and for new solutions to theatrical problems, the special relationship which Terayama wants between audience and performers, and his notions about theatre working in a variety of spaces. Furthermore, as you study the script you will find that it calls for unique makeup, costumes, machines, and set pieces. It must be admitted that the Tenjosajiki production relied heavily on music and special lighting, and the fact that the cultural flavor was strongly Japanese was surely a value for Western audiences. You might think in terms of cultural equivalents in dealing with this.

Follow the usual four steps with this piece: (1) read the play and respond to it, as you would to any script. As reproduced here, the play is relatively short, but it served as the basis for a full-length show, done without intermission. (2) Take the other steps you would normally in developing a production plan. (3) Deal with the problem of how you will work with the actors for this production. The play is meant to be improvised, but does this mean that it will have spontaneous moments during performance? How elaborate will your music and lighting be? If these are carefully worked out, won't they preclude the use of true improvisation in performance?

In regard to the third point, in the New York production of Genet's *The Blacks*, there was a moment when a character stepped into the audience, offering a ball of yarn to someone in the front row. This was a very threatening moment, particularly if you were in the front row, because the play dealt with the confrontation of black and white cultures. However, the moment was carefully rehearsed and the actors had anticipated a number of reactions and counterreactions.

(4) Perhaps you should write your own manifesto for this production, but in any case answer how you will treat your audience and say what you expect them to carry away from the performance. List what you imagine will be the major moments in your production. As we have noted, Terayama wants the four scenes at play's end, #16 *Anyone Can Be Master*, #17 *The Eve*, #18 *Shoot the Southern Cross*, and #19 *Absence*, to demolish the story line. What are your improvisations and dialogue for these scenes?

Several Suggestions

As noted in the chapter on directing, originality and creativity often seem to be a matter of linking ideas that don't normally go together or of drawing unusual analogies. In the case of *Directions to Servants*, it may be that the search for a unifying image will lead to a solution of how to manage the moment-to-moment reality of the play. Let's give some clues for this search. First, how might one draw an analogy between Terayama's "inner hell" and some other artist's concept of it done in a different medium? Hieronymus Bosch's view of Hell in his triptych *The Garden of Earthly Delights* comes to mind immediately. This Dutch painter of the sixteenth century painted a nightmare vision of man's fall from grace in this and many other paintings. The panel "Hell" shows the damned in their final agony, grouped around the giant figure of an idiot on whose hat the devils dance. Both are set against a background of burning ramparts. There is an overall pattern to this panel, but there is also a series of smaller scenes, separate and yet part of the whole. The overall effect of the triptych is cumulative. Not only the subject matter but also the organizing principles of this masterpiece might shed light on how to approach Terayama's play.

You might also research new forms of musical composition. For example, there have been fascinating experiments with randomness in composition and performance. There are scores which are written literally in a circle and place different instruments in changing combinations. Before you record your sound or create it with your actors, listen to compositions by such modern composers as Krzysztof Penderecki (*The Entombment of Christ* is one example) and learn about "live" vocal effects which are unusual and highly theatrical. Certainly, it would be possible to mix filmed sequences with action or use projections. But would this beg the question? You probably already have the mechanical and nonhuman represented in lighting and, perhaps, in sound.

Some food for thought: If you were a fifth century Athenian, how would you react to a reading of the first act of *Death of a Salesman?* If you were part of a medieval crowd in front of the cathedral, watching a pageant, what would it mean to you if you saw a performance of Albee's *The American Dream*, done in one of the mansion structures on the edge of the town square? And as a modern theatre-goer, what if your ticket to the Majestic bought you a seat to watch an eleventh century Byzantine church service? These would not be shocks in terms of technical matters but would be surprises in terms of human content and values. This type of experimentation for your production of *Directions to Servants* could serve you better than more lights, more sound, nudity, or other forms of *razzmatazz*. Shows that loudly announce how strange they are or brag about their technical advances don't necessarily touch, entertain, or even amaze most audiences. It's interesting to me that even successful science fiction, which has license to explore any world or time, usually describes human personality and conflict in terms that are current or age-old. This shouldn't surprise us. I think it was the English author G. K. Chesterton who suggested that on a dark night with the wind rattling the bare branches above us and the street lamp throwing shadows across our path, we are most frightened, not when the shadow has the shape of something unknown, but when it resembles something human.

Figure 9-1. Detail from the "Hell" panel of Hieronymus Bosch's *Garden of Earthly Delights.* (Prado, Madrid.)

Directions to Servants (Nuhikun)

SHUJI TERAYAMA

(Translated by Tony Rayns and Shigenobu Nishiguch)

DIALOGUE AND SUMMARY OF ACTION *

1. The Saint-Master Machine

A man sits in a chair in the middle of the room. He is, as yet, no-one: he is naked, and has no body-hair. He looks forward expressionlessly. The Saint-Master Machine slowly lowers a wig on to his shaved head. Then another part of the Machine supplies him with a moustache . . . and then glasses, teeth and a hand. Now a Master, he stands up on his chair. He puts on a gown, but then realises that he has no shoes.

MASTER: Is anyone there? Bring shoes!

(*Doors open, and all the servants of the mansion enter: manservants, maids, housemaids, grooms, cooks, tenant farmers, nannies and others. Some of them are holding shoes in one hand; others are holding shoes up in the air. They all approach the Master, who is seated on his chair, and address him in unison.*)

SERVANTS: Your shoes, sir!

2. Eclipse of the Moon

On the night of the Eclipse of the Moon, a man visits the Servants' quarters. He carries a pair of shoes, which were probably left by his Master. He is searching for his Master, but his only clue to his identity is that he may be someone whose feet fit this size of shoe.

(*This man is in the habit of dozing off anywhere, at any time, even when he is talking to someone. He probably lost his Master while he was asleep. But he isn't sure where reality faded and dream began.*)

3. Coronation of the Dog

*Used by permission of Shuji Terayama.

4. A Dog's Plastic Surgery

(a) A dwarf Servant appears, and lays a red carpet on the stairs. Then a man in evening dress but with bare feet enters, descends the stairs and sits in the Master's chair. We will call him Coubeau. Seven tenants are standing in a line behind him. Coubeau yawns grandly. His tenants follow suit, but once their mouths are open, he orders them to freeze. Coubeau inspects each mouth, like a Master checking his rice-fields.

(b) Coubeau produces a large bone and tosses it away. One tenant goes to fetch it: he starts growling, drops to all fours, and turns into a dog. He returns to his Master with the bone between his teeth. Coubeau pats his dog's head. The other tenants applaud. This process is repeated, and each tenant in turn becomes a dog. The eighth time he throws the bone, there are no tenants left to retrieve it, and so Coubeau himself does so. The other man-dogs fight for possession of his chair while he is away from it. But Coubeau finally reclaims it: he is the most ferocious of them all.

5. Whip

In the mansion whose Master is absent, the Servants are taking turns to play at being "Master." This evening Dahlia, who has the role of Mistress, is torturing a man: he stole the shoes that are supposed to fit the Master, and tried to alter their size to his own.

DAHLIA: Come on, admit it! You've licked the vinegar bottle, haven't you?

SERVANT: Yes, madam, I have. I have licked the vinegar bottle.

DAHLIA: And what did the bottle contain apart from vinegar?

SERVANT: . . . . . .

DAHLIA: Come on, tell me what it was.

SERVANT: I don't know, madam, because my eyes were closed.

DAHLIA: You must be lying? *(She strikes him.)*

SERVANT: Ow! Yes, I lied!

DAHLIA: There was a tiny man inside too, wasn't there?

SERVANT: Yes, there was a tiny man inside.

DAHLIA: That tiny man had hair-clippers in his hand. He has a compulsion to cut hair; when he sees someone's head, he can't resist cutting off all their hair.

SERVANT: Yes, yes!

DAHLIA: I'll forgive you, because you're honest . . . *(Suddenly her voice turns cold.)* But why did you try to steal the clock from the study? Wrapped up in a blue furoshiki cloth?

SERVANT: . . . . . .

DAHLIA: Tell me! Why did you try to make off with it? *(She strikes him again.)*

SERVANT: Aah! Ouch!

DAHLIA: You were after a clock that had stopped!

SERVANT: Yes, I was after a clock that had stopped.

DAHLIA: You were told to fetch a clock that would be right twice a day.

SERVANT: Yes, I was told to.

DAHLIA: By whom?

SERVANT: . . . . . .

DAHLIA: By whom? *(She strikes him again.)*

SERVANT: I'll tell you, I'll tell you. By the Master in the attic.

DAHLIA: The Master in the attic? *(Her face registers doubt, then sweetness again.)* It's not possible. *(Suddenly cold.)* My husband died two years ago, when he fell from a horse.
Well, we'll finish there for today. I have to go out now.

SERVANT: Please—please don't stop . . . Just a little more . . .

DAHLIA: Like this? *(She strikes him.)*

SERVANT: Aah! Ouch!

DAHLIA: You! You're my sputum! *(Strikes him again.)*

SERVANT: Ouch! Aah! Ow!

DAHLIA: You! You eavesdropped on the chinless man's joke-box! *(Strikes his buttocks.)*

SERVANT: Ouch! Aah!

DAHLIA: You drowned the ungrammatical cat! *(Strikes again.)*

SERVANT: Aah! Ouch!

DAHLIA: You tied the fire extinguisher to the model duck! *(Strikes again.)*

SERVANT: Aah! Ow! Ouch!

DAHLIA: You're a full moon at the keyhole! You're a peeping tom with trachoma! *(Strikes again.)*

SERVANT: Ouch! Aah!

DAHLIA *(suddenly sweet)*: I forgive you, because you're honest.

6. The Singing Cupboard

A cupboard starts singing as soon as a Servant edges it open to pilfer some food. The cupboard has several unusual panels; each panel conceals a face, which sings. When the panel is closed, the voice stops. It appears to be an ordinary cupboard, but it is actually like a magic puzzle: it is impossible to close all the panels at once. The cook and the kitchen-help open the panels at random.

VOICE 1: Well, another fly! Another fly drowned in the soup!

VOICE 2: A plate of cheese for the chinless man!

VOICE 3: The woman who did a midnight flit is flying on a pot!

VOICE 4: Don't put the meat back on the plate once it's been in your mouth!

VOICE 5: Gosh, you live in a shoe!

VOICE 6: Yes, Master. I was born hairy!

VOICE 7: I want to smack your bottom with a violin until it almost breaks.

VOICE 8: . . . . . .

VOICE 9: Madam, your horse is ready!

VOICE 10: The man who entered the raffle was my father.

VOICE 11: Heavens, this mansion has no toilet!

VOICE 12: Shut up! You'll give away the lie in the letter.

VOICE 13: Disappeared, disappeared, the Master has disappeared!

VOICE 14: If you look in a mirror, you'll see how ugly you are.

VOICE 15: The man hiding in the sideboard!

VOICE 16: A new bed! Spit in it.

(More words are repeated in a chorus. These have no meaning as such; they are purely symbolic.)

Manservant. Cleaner. Maid. Butler, Milk-maid. Chauffeur. Laundry-woman. Valet. Gatekeeper. Junior maid. Shoe-maid. Kitchen-help. Groom. Coachman. Nursemaid. Tenant farmer. Nanny. Forester. Cook.

7. The Bottle of Vinegar

Dahlia's time as Mistress is running out, but she is reluctant to relinquish the role.

DAHLIA *(claps her hands)*: Are you there? *(A maid rushes in.)* I wanted a manservant.

MAID: Sorry, but all the manservants are out.

DAHLIA: So that's why you came?

MAID: Yes, madam.

DAHLIA: Well, I must say that you're very ugly indeed.

MAID: . . . .

DAHLIA: The stud-master who looks after the red horse told me that you're responsible for breaking all the mirrors in the house.

MAID: I'm very sorry, Madam.

DAHLIA: You can't rid yourself of your ugliness just by breaking all the mirrors. If you think you can, you'll have to break the mirrors in the eyes of all the manservants! *(She laughs loudly.)* Well, now, I'm going off to the ball. Lock all the doors before you go to bed.

(DAHLIA *puts on her fur coat with a flourish, revealing that it has been hanging on a human coatrack, which comprises two manservants.* DAHLIA *turns and shouts at them.*)

DAHLIA: Bet on zero at roulette 99 times!

(*The manservants squirm and shake convulsively.*)

Spit into somebody's soup!

(*They cover their eyes.*)

Type out the word "obedient" 100 times!

(*They spreadeagle themselves against the wall.*)

Drown the mice in the lavatory bowl!

(*They cover their ears.*)

Swim in the pool while the Master is out!

(*They stick out their tongues.*)

Count the number of times you yawn!

(*They lie on the floor and arch their backs.*)

Write the name of your sweetheart in the candlegrease on the kitchen ceiling!

(*They search for something on the kitchen floor.*)

Try to wipe your arse in 77 different ways!

(*They lick their lips.*)

Break your Master's best doll, and pretend it was an accident!

(*They laugh loudly.*)

Sew up one eye of the portrait of the Lady's niece with red cotton!

(*They cannot open the door.*)

Go out on the white horse — to betray them!

(*They idle.*)

Ask Opel where the exit is!

(*They hide quickly.*)

Hide the dead butterfly in the kitchen cupboard!

(*They jab their fingers at a guest.*)

Write out 100 letters about 100 milk-maids carrying 100 milk-churns for 100 days!

(*They go through the motions of applying lipstick.*)

Servants never answer back!

(*They bow deeply.*)

DAHLIA: (DAHLIA *looks around at the maid. Her voice changes.*) Well, have you heard the story about the Master in the attic waking up?

MAID: Yes, I've heard.

DAHLIA: Do you think we're in danger? Do you think our plot might be discovered?

MAID *(looks around, and replies very casually):* It's all right. I've put two big locks on the door. The pig's-trotter soup is boiling away in the kitchen as if nothing has happened.

(They nod at each other in complicity.)

DAHLIA: Now then, how many minutes can I go on playing Mistress?

MAID *(pulls out a watch on a long, gold chain)*: Just over ten more minutes, Dahlia.

DAHLIA: Just over ten minutes? *(Suddenly alters her bearing.)* Those clothes don't suit you! Don't you have anything else to wear?

MAID: What are you on about now, Dahlia?

DAHLIA: Don't call me Dahlia! You must say "Madam." Madam! I've put up with your ugly face for a long time, but now I'm really fed up with it. You have bad breath, and your language is appalling. You spit whenever you speak. Your nails are dirty, and you don't keep them trimmed. On top of that, you're a bad cook. Why don't you try to improve yourself for me? If you don't, I'll sack you, just as I sacked your sister.

MAID: Yes, Madam.

8. The Maid Cinderella

Dahlia sits in the Mistress' chair, singing, clearly very self-satisfied. Midnight comes, and her time in the role is up. Other manservants and maids appear, and take away her "robes of office." Who will be the new Mistress? Will it be the little nursemaid, or the kitchen-help?

Dahlia cries in the dark. Another woman's voice calls for someone to come and be her mirror.

9. Manual of Etiquette for Young Man

The gatekeeper, wearing the shoes whose size he altered, lectures all the rest of mansion's staff on etiquette. Suddenly a tenant rushes in and accuses the gatekeeper of having "false" shoes; he himself has the real pair that are supposed to fit the Master. Who switched the shoes, and when?

10. The Sleeping Man

The man, who was robbed of the Master's shoes while he was asleep, wanders about the mansion, looking for the missing shoes. He opens a drawer, and countless pairs of shoes pour out. He wonders which pair is his Master's.

11. Who Killed Cock Robin?

The man who tried to pilfer a little food from the cupboard is tortured by the voice of an unseen Master. The voice comes from a tape recorder, and so no-one can be sure whether it is really the Master's voice or not. Five maids watch as the Manservant submits.

MAID 1: In this mansion . . .

MAID 2: . . . the absent Master sometimes gets difficult. Someone is sharpening the sickle in the potting shed.

MAID 4: An egg is hanging inside the head.

MAID 5: The church bell: Ding Dong!

MAID 1: Poison on the plate.

MAID 2: The feet are in shackles.

MAID 3: Sew up the eyelids with red cotton.

MAID 4: Follow the manservant called Smoke . . .

MAID 5: . . . when you go to the potting shed at midnight.

MAID 1: Look, look, I'm pregnant!

MAID 2: Something funny . . .

MAID 3: . . . about that voice.

MAID 4: Tiptoe, tiptoe, not a sound.

MAID 5: When I arrived, that was all there was!

MAID 1: Chinese masseur, and . . .

MAID 2: coloured pencils, and . . .

MAID 3: the voice of strange machines.

(When one of the maids has disconnected the tape recorder, the voice of the HEAD MAID *is heard singing in the distance.)*

HEAD MAID:Who killed Cock Robin?
　　　　　The Servant in his counting-house, counting out his money,
　　　　　The maid in the parlour, eating bread and honey.
　　　　　Who killed Cock Robin?

12. The Bandages

When the bandages are removed from his body, the Master is revealed as a dwarf. The manservants and maids play with the bandages: they want a Master, so that they can torment him, but no-one is ready to take on the role. There is no dialogue. "It's a misfortune to have a house without a Master, but it's worse that a house should want a Master."

13. Eavesdropping; The Rice Gobblers

A political analogy: everyone who has to eat rice is a servant. Manservants and maids eat rice with tears running down their cheeks.

(DAHLIA *is heard crying.*)

SERVANT 1: Are you going to shut up, you noisy so-and-so?

SERVANT 2 *(he is nearly deaf, and questions* SERVANT 3*)*: What did he just say?

SERVANT 3: It's a nice voice—let her go on crying.

SERVANT 2: Yes, a really nice voice. I love the sound of a woman crying better than anything.

SERVANT 1: You're lucky—I think you'll probably get to play Mistress again tomorrow.

(DAHLIA *goes on crying.*)

SERVANT 1: Look, I never get lucky . . . I've never had the chance . . . Mind you, it's hard work acting as a Master.

SERVANT 2: What?

SERVANT 3: Hard work!

SERVANT 2: Couldn't agree more: talking on your own is hard.

SERVANT 1: The problem is Yonay's past.

SERVANT 3: He's got that maid pregnant again.

SERVANT 2: Mountain fires are really nice!

SERVANT 1: He'll be talking in dog-language before long.

SERVANT 3: He frightened the old woman with a sickle.

SERVANT 2: I'll make both of you wash my feet!

SERVANT 1: When I become Master, I'll have myself photographed every day.

(*A new* SERVANT *has been quietly eating rice near them; he joins in the conversation.*)

NEW SERVANT: If I stay here long enough, will I get a chance to play the Master too?

SERVANT 2: There was a nice mirror in the public bath-house, too.

SERVANT 1: The woman who drowned and died was your Mum! *(He laughs.)*

NEW SERVANT: If my turn comes, *(he looks round at* DAHLIA*)* I'll be kind to you . . .

(DAHLIA *begins to cry again.* SERVANT 1 *suddenly holds his nose;* SERVANTS 2 AND 3 *follow suit. The maid* NELLY *is passing by with a pot full of the* MASTER'S *shit.*)

SERVANT 1: It smells particularly bad today.

SERVANT 3: He must have had diarrhoea this last day or two.

SERVANT 1: And he doesn't get any exercise.

SERVANT 3: And he doesn't eat a balanced diet.

SERVANT 1: No, he eats nothing but rich food.

SERVANT 2: What?

SERVANT 3: Eats rich food, doesn't he?

SERVANT 2 *(he looks into his bowl, assuming that* SERVANT 2 *is talking about him)*: What?

SERVANT 1 *(he stands up)*: Let's move. We can't eat in a place as smelly as this.

(He walks off with his rice-bowl and chopsticks. SERVANTS 2 *and* 3 *follow. The* NEW SERVANT *hesitates, then turns to* DAHLIA.*)*

NEW SERVANT: May I talk to you?

DAHLIA *(She looks at him)*: . . . .

NEW SERVANT: Well, this is my 31st line of dialogue. What was in that chamber-pot that somebody carried through just now?

DAHLIA: It was shit. Or, if you want it put more politely, excrement.

NEW SERVANT: Whose?

DAHLIA: That person's.

NEW SERVANT: Who?

DAHLIA: Forget it. He's a recluse—he hates visitors.

NEW SERVANT: I'm not a visitor. I've been away for ten years, and I've just returned.

DAHLIA: Many people have come back here, but nobody has been able to see him.

NEW SERVANT: Now I understand? It's all clear to me. You can't see him, but he's hiding somewhere and watching everything. 35th line! He must be the Master of this mansion. Am I right?

DAHLIA: No! I am in charge of this mansion.

NEW SERVANT: I understand how you feel. But let's examine the situation objectively rather than subjectively.

DAHLIA: I'm in charge of this mansion, just me.

14. The Horseshoed Maid Opera

The maid Dahlia's time as Mistress has expired, but she refuses to stop living the role. As a result, she has been punished: she has a horseshoe on the sole of her foot. The experience pushes her into madness. She wanders about the mansion, half undressed, singing that she is the Mistress.

DAHLIA: Toothbrush! Toothbrush! Don't you know where I am? Dahlia, who left the mansion as Mistress, don't you know where she is?

I am my own Mistress!

I'm wrongly cast as a kitchen-help or a maid.

Look, that laundrywoman has left all that mess behind. Did she go out to have fun at the funeral? The plates are broken, the rooms are dirty, it's all terrible . . .

(She looks at her watch.) Oh, already! The guests will be here any minute. This will be the first ball we've held here, but I can't hear a sound from the kitchen. Are they ready? *(She claps her hands.)* No answer!

(The new SERVANT *is there, watching her.)*

Where are the maids? Is anybody there? *(She claps her hands.)* Anybody?

NEW SERVANT: There's one maid there.

DAHLIA: Where?

NEW SERVANT: You!

DAHLIA *(she tries to smile, but her face freezes.)* A very funny joke. Opel! How many lines have you spoken now?

NEW SERVANT: Counting the detective's lines, it's up to 67. But the 52nd was missing, though. Remember, I'm really a detective looking for the Master.

DAHLIA: No, you're just a new Servant. And I am the Mistress of this house.

NEW SERVANT: We were both acting roles, but that scene is over. In this scene, you're a maid who always lies, and I'm a detective.

DAHLIA: Well then, tell me where that man has gone—the sleeping man called Opel who was so kind to me.

NEW SERVANT: He was erased from the script. He was just a linking character.

DAHLIA *(she points at the toothbrush)*: But the toothbrush is here! Opel gave me this. If you stare at it, you see a dream of a time when there was no time.

NEW SERVANT: Look, it's already my 62nd line, and I have to wrap the whole thing up by the time I reach the hundredth.

DAHLIA: I don't understand what you're talking about, but if it has anything to do with tonight's party, would you care to show me your invitation?

NEW SERVANT *(he looks sheepish)*: What?

DAHLIA: The guests will be here soon, and I can't have any strange people hanging around upsetting them.

NEW SERVANT: Screw this! *(He jumps on* DAHLIA, *and pulls up her skirt. She tries to struggle free, in vain. There is a horseshoe on her foot. The new* SERVANT *sneers.)* Look, a horseshoe! It's the best way of dealing with women who are always wandering off into dreams. Would you like to neigh like a horse?

DAHLIA *(with as much dignity as she can muster)*: Leave me, let me alone!

NEW SERVANT: It's too late to go on. Or should I put a bridle on you?

DAHLIA: Opel, Opel, help me!

NEW SERVANT: There's no such person. The organic AC lightbulb stopped shedding blue light when its fuse blew! All of you, come along now, The horseshoed maid Dahlia is going to sing a kitchen-opera. Sing! Sing to us!

DAHLIA: Toothbrush! Toothbrush! Don't you know where I am? Dahlia, who left the mansion as Mistress, don't you know where she is?

Anybody there? Call the groom and tell him to get my horse ready.

Look, the fly is back again. How many times have I told her not to spill soup on the kitchen floor?

Are you still not ready? The candle will go out if you don't bring another one quickly.

You're wiping your mouth on the table cloth again. How many times do I have to tell you?

No cats! There'll be hair all over the the bed!

(She lights a candle.)

I am Dahlia, who spins like the wind-vane on the roof, the silver cockerel with a tiny man clinging to its head. The Mistress of this mansion.

This place is my mansion: all of it, all of it is mine.

A dead maid plays the flute,
There's a birthmark on the moon.

An old woman in a black cowl
Licks secretly at the Jam.
This place is my mansion: all of it, all of it is mine.

A blind child digs a hole,
And the smith makes a dark star.

The little nursemaid is dreaming
Of tying up the bottle with red string.

This place is my mansion: all of it, all of it is mine.

The lost key is in the forest,
And the pony is loose in the forest too.

It will be spring soon;
The Servant will ask to leave.

This place is my mansion: all of it, all of it is mine.

I'm not going to give any of it up! Nobody will touch it!

(By now, she is shouting. All the others move to grab her and tie her up with rope. She tries to struggle free.)

This place . . . this place is my mansion: all of it, all of it is mine.

15. *"You Are Nothing But the Present"*

Why, oh why? More than ten servants sit around a table, each with a pair of shoes, each claiming to be the Master. Which pair is the authentic one? Was there ever a pair that really belonged to the Master?

1: This is the 364th year.

2: Only one left.

3: In the whole year, only one evening when the moon comes out.

4: How's the milk coming?

5: Fine, fine . . . this is the third pail already.
(Giggles in a funny voice.) Last night, when I left the front door open, someone delivered a bag . . .

6: Someone wanted to wash the rice.

7: Catch all the cats, and shave off all their hair, one by one.

8: That's the sound of an eyebath running, coming from the manservant's room.

9: Now that the clothes have been washed in the basin.

10: The brat who was hidden by the maid is swimming in it.

11: At the time of the seven weeds of autumn . . .

12: . . . I heard that the poor nursemaid had got pregnant again.

13: Dog Brand safety band for mothers!

14: Kintaro Brand gumdrops!

15: In every house, Masters made of rice!

16: Well, well, the chief household's midwife,

17: and the second family's kitchen maid,

18: and the tenant who was adopted,

19: and the son-in-law's manservant . . .

20: . . . All of them are made of rice.

21: 100 Servants made of rice . . .

22: . . . are constantly searching for their Master with their left eyes . . .

23: . . . while their right eyes are fixed on the red mountain fire on the back of their references.

       *

1: Shall we hold another raffle?

2: "When a Servant is turned off, all his faults must be told, although most of them were never known by his Master or Lady . . ."

3: ". . . and all mischiefs done by others, charge to him—and instance them in full detail."

4: Well, shall we hold another raffle?

5: "If you are a sightly fellow, whenever you whisper to your Mistress at table, run your nose full in her cheek."

6: "If your breath be good, breathe full in her face; this is known to have had very good consequences in some families."

7: "And never come till you have been called three or four times."

8: Indeed. "For none but dogs will come at the first whistle."

9: Shall we hold a raffle again?

10: What raffle?

11: Raffle to decide who plays Master!

12: After all, if there isn't a Master, there's no pleasure in playing a Servant.

13: Yes, the game is no fun if there isn't any Master, even if we have to take turns to play the part.

14: "Take all Trademen's parts against your Master. . ."

15: ". . . and when you are sent to buy anything, never offer to cheapen it, but generously pay the full demand."

16: "This is highly to your Master's honour . . . and may be some shillings in your pocket."

17: Someone is missing here.

18: Right, the Master is missing.

19: But each of us has already had a turn as Master.

20: That's not true. I didn't get a turn.

21: Neither did I. I wanted to have a servant play a dog and lick my toes.
    (One girls stands up like a zombie.)

22: No, it isn't the Master who's missing. It's someone from outside.

23: From outside?

24: Yes. For example, the Servant Opel, who came here on the evening of the eclipse of the moon. He was carrying one toothbrush.

25: Well, that was my role.

26: That's right.

27: I wanted to play this mysterious visitor, who had only 100 lines and then disappeared.

28: I wasn't Opel. Did you know that? I was just a sleeping man, a Servant. Don't look at me like that!

29: No, you were Opel.

30: We need Opel.

31: Yes, too true. Without Opel, we can form a bond of friendship!

32: Stop it! Stay away from me! Don't do anything: *(the speaker retreats.)* It wasn't planned like that! Don't force me to play Opel!

33: But this mansion of Servants and Maids can be revived by the absence of Opel—just one visitor!

16. Anybody Can Be a Master

17. The Eve

18. Shoot the Southern Cross

19. Absence

These four scenes which include improvisations, demolish the storyline that has developed thus far. The world that has been dominated by the absence of a Master suddenly splits open, to reveal an inner hell.

(*The* MASTER's *bedroom.* SERVANTS *are trying on clothes.*)

SERVANT: Stupid! That's mine! Give it to me! It doesn't suit you. Look, even this bit is frilly.

(*Laughs.*) That's what education does for you!

(*Rips off the frills.*)

MANSERVANT (*wearing female stockings and garters*): Does it suit me? (*He poses effeminately.*)

MAID (*wearing a fur coat*): Can anybody be my mirror?

MAID (*shouting*): Horse! Where is my horse!

MANSERVANT: Let's disappear.

* *

(*In the final scene, the actors improvise words as they strike matches. The following phrases are examples of the kind of thing they say.*)

1: Write in the candle-grease on the ceiling: "This is Hell—jump here!"

2: Even the floor boards of the Master's bedroom have ricefields underneath, if you take them up!

3: A wolf in the sky, a Servant on the ground, and a disastrous fire raging in the grate!

4: Sharpen the knife-blade, the better to cut the Master's throat.

5: Break the plates! Rock the earth! Spring is coming!

6: "Wash the glasses in your piss, to save the Master's salt."

7: You need no ideal for a revolution—all you need is a match!

8: The crows are cackling as the Servants dig a grave. It's your turn to die next!

 9: If you want meat for supper, how about my body?

10: Straw in the potting shed—run away 1,000 miles!
I become my own horse!

11: There's a whirlwind on the horizon—and gales of laughter in the maid's room.

12: I cut open my eyelid with a meat-knife, and saw a red bird flying.

13: This is how to spit! Look, this is the maid's wedding.

14: Mind the lamp when the cat is leaping. I lust after the Master.

15: Look, the blossoms are falling like snow! Clear the way!

The End

Part Three

OTHER CONCERNS

Honoré Daumier. *A Literary Discussion in the Second Balcony.* (From the collection of the Zurich House of Arts.)

10

Reviewing a Play

In the course of this text we have emphasized the importance of research on the period of the play, type of theatre, audience, and playwright if one is going to direct, act, or design a show. These research criteria also apply to the people who review the production, but it is not always possible for them to be as thorough. In the commercial theatre, new shows are usually reviewed without any prior knowledge. Why this tradition has grown up is incomprehensible to this writer, just as it is amazing that I have only seen one or two professional reviewers change their minds in print about a production they had written about earlier. What it suggests is that over the years an adversary relationship has grown up between theatre artists and newspaper and magazine reviewers. Producers refuse to give critics scripts of new shows, and the reviewers themselves seem to be searching for ways to be witty and, often, savage. We may laugh at such reviews, but we have to admit that they rarely add much light and certainly little sweetness to the ongoing question of what is good theatre.

Criticism, on the other hand, is practiced by academics and specialists who have their work published in obscure periodicals and occasional volumes. Very often the dialogue in these publications is between contributors, not between the critics and the practicing artists. This circumstance has lasted for a considerable period of time, and there have been attempts made to correct it. One is the notion of having a resident dramaturg, or critic, working with a production company. This was the case with the Hamburg Theatre and the poet Lessing, but the experiment failed. There must be some way to marry these two constituencies, especially if they are both concerned with good theatre, just as practicing artists must learn how to balance their own artistic and critical faculties.

Dramatic criticism is a fascinating study. A number of the world's greatest thinkers have tried their hand at it: Aristotle, Hegel, and Santayana are but three. Plato is one of the few great thinkers of all time to show a marked aversion to drama. The body of criticism that has emerged is based upon analysis of plays and notions of how to improve them aesthetically, how to make them work as a moral or political force, or how they can be used as a revelation of society and man to show their respective attitudes, strengths, and follies.

The newspaper reviewer may know something of this, but rarely states a preference. Instead, newspaper criticism seems to be *visceral*. The reviewer tells us what he *feels*. Some have explained that they attempt to be an ideal audience person, that is, they watch both the play and the audience. If the audience likes something they don't, then they adjust their impressions. A few reviewers in every generation have come from the ranks of directors and producers. Walter Kerr produced and directed plays at Washington's Catholic University for years and his wife was a successful playwright. Consequently, what he says is read avidly by players and producers. A few reviewers over the years have achieved a sort of fame for their consistency, standards and humanity. They have generally tried to play philosopher on an everyday level, discovering certain truths about art and people that they modestly incorporate into their writings, no matter how pressing the deadline. The last generation in America was blessed by the presence of a number of these critics who indeed did bring some sweetness and light to reviewing and by so doing were at least partially responsible for the greatness of that period in theatre: Stark Young, James Mason Brown, and Brooks Atkinson immediately come to mind. They do consummate juggling acts in their reviews by remaining on the level of the everyday playgoer and yet connecting with some of the prevailing notions of criticism. Usually, as well, it is very clear to the readers that they love theatre.

What can a student who is learning about theatre do when asked to write a review? If there is world enough and time, one should read the play and as much about its background as possible. There is rarely this much time, however, so the student reviewer is usually seated in the theatre seeing a play for the first time. Probably in this circumstance the following methodology is the best compromise:

1. Don't take notes during the performance. If there is a program, it will give you the necessary information on characters and their names, the place, the time, and the author. Immerse yourself in the play.

2. The more you know about an art form the less you can accept it strictly on an emotional basis. The experience of seeing a play when you know the rudiments of acting, directing, and designing has been described as a series of blinks. We find ourselves absorbed and staring and then we blink and we're back to the critical posture of evaluating how something was done. This staring and blinking goes on throughout a play. It happens to all of us; you don't need to hide it.

3. What were your honest reactions to the play? I suppose that if one respects the effort actors and others put into any play, it is difficult to dismiss even the worst production "out of hand." Professionals who are not doing their best, however, should probably not be suffered gladly. The story is told of Noel Coward's being so incensed with Marlon Brando's behavior in the first act of *A Streetcar Named Desire* that he went backstage and gave the young actor a piece of his mind about the professional's responsibility to his audience.

4. When the play is over, collect your thoughts. Avoid the loud voice in the lobby or the student reviewer who has the *line* on the production. One of the crucial considerations in developing your own appreciation is learning how to sort out what you did and didn't like and finding a fair way to express it. Remember that the greatest art collectors are not simply rich people with enough cash to make mistakes. The great collectors take time to develop their taste. If the only thing you have to squander is time, use it to develop your taste.

5. When the dust has settled in a day or two, write the review. A review is not a recitation of the plot. Write it for someone who has also seen the production and will not be offended if you let slip the fact that "the butler did it." What is important in your review is (a) the evidence that you have thought about what the director/actors/designer/playwright were striving for. You may or may not agree with how they did it or feel that they succeeded, but you understand the process; (b) you are aware of the many facets of the production. You do not naively believe that the actors were wearing their own clothing or that the lights were hung in the same way that they were for the preceding production; (c) you can single out and comment on the major artistic achievements of the production, because you know what is required and because you have tried many of these arts yourself and have respect for people who can do them well; (d) you can react to the overall theme or message of the production. It has provoked thought.

These are simply guidelines, but the major points in writing a review are the need to react to the range of skills involved in a production, the theme and meaning of the production, and the evening you have spent in the theatre. By the way, if the producers were also careful to make your stay in their facility pleasant, then they are true professionals and deserve praise for this as well.

Appendix: A List of Plays for Reading and Study

Classical Greek and Roman Plays

Aeschylus: *Prometheus Bound; Agamemnon; Choephori; Eumenides;* and *Seven Against Thebes.*

Aristophanes: *The Clouds; The Birds; The Frogs;* and *Lysistrata.*

Euripides: *Alcestis; Medea; Hippolytus; The Trojan Women;* and *Iphigenia in Aulis.*

Menander: *The Dyskolos* and *Arbitration.*

Plautus: *The Menaechmi; The Braggart Warrior; Captives;* and *Crock of Gold.*

Seneca: *Medea* and *Thyestes.*

Sophocles: *Antigone; Oedipus Rex; Electra;* and *Oedipus at Colonus.*

Terence: *Phormio; The Brothers;* and *The Eunuch.*

The Middle Ages

Anonymous: *Abraham and Isaac; Second Shepherd's Play; Castle of Perseverance; Maitre Pierre Patelin; Everyman; Adam; Death of Pilate;* and *Coventry Nativity Play.*

England: 1550–1660

Beaumont, Francis and John Fletcher: *The Knight of the Burning Pestle* and *The Maid's Tragedy.*

Chapman, George: *Bussy d'Ambois.*

Dekker, Thomas: *The Shoemaker's Holiday.*

Ford, John: *'Tis Pity She's a Whore.*

Gascoigne, George: *The Supposes.*

Greene, Robert: *The Honorable History of Friar Bacon and Friar Bungay.*

Heywood, John: *The Four P's.*

Heywood, Thomas: *A Woman Killed with Kindness.*

Jonson, Ben: *Volpone; The Alchemist; Every Man in His Humour;* and *Epicoene.*

Kyd, Thomas: *The Spanish Tragedy.*

Lyly, John: *Endymion* and *Alexander and Campaspe.*

Marlowe, Christopher: *Tamburlaine; The Tragical History of Doctor Faustus;* and *Edward II.*

Marston, John: *The Malcontent.*

Massinger, Philip: *A New Way to Pay Old Debts.*

Middleton, Thomas: *A Trick to Catch the Old One.*

Middleton, Thomas and William Rowley: *The Changeling.*

Peele, George: *The Arraignment of Paris.*

Preston, Thomas: *Cambyses King of Persia.*

Sackville, Thomas and Thomas Norton: *Gorboduc.*

Shakespeare, William: Read the complete canon of plays.

Stevenson, William: *Gammer Gurton's Needle.*

Tourneur, Cyril: *The Revenger's Tragedy.*

Udall, Nicholas: *Ralph Roister Doister.*
Webster, John: *The White Devil* and *The Duchess of Malfi.*
Wilkins, George: *A Yorkshire Tragedy.*

Spanish and French: 1500–1700

Calderón de la Barca, Pedro: *Life Is a Dream* and *The Physician of his own Honor.*
Corneille, Pierre: *The Cid; Cinna;* and *Polyeucte.*
Lope de Vega: *Fuente Ovejuna; The Gardener's Dog;* and *The King the Greatest Alcalde.*
Molière: *The Affected Young Ladies; The School for Wives; The School for Husbands; The Misanthrope; The Physician in Spite of Himself; The Miser; Don Juan; Tartuffe; The Bourgeois Gentleman;* and *The Imaginary Invalid.*
Racine, Jean: *Andromaque; Phèdre; Athalie; Iphigénie; Bérénice;* and *Britannicus.*
Tirso de Molina: *The Deceiver of Seville and the Stone Guest.*

England: Restoration and Eighteenth Century

Congreve, William: *Love for Love* and *The Way of the World.*
Dryden, John: *All for Love.*
Etherege, George: *The Man of Mode.*
Farquhar, George: *The Beaux' Stratagem* and *The Recruiting Officer.*
Fielding, Henry: *Tom Thumb (The Tragedy of Tragedies).*
Gay, John: *The Beggar's Opera.*
Goldsmith, Oliver: *She Stoops to Conquer.*
Lillo, George: *The London Merchant.*
Otway, Thomas: *Venice Preserved.*
Sheridan, Richard: *The Rivals* and *The School for Scandal.*
Steele, Richard: *The Conscious Lovers.*
Wycherley, William: *The Country Wife* and *The Plain Dealer.*

Continental Europe: Eighteenth Century

Beaumarchais, Pierre-Augustin: *The Barber of Seville* and *The Marriage of Figaro.*
Goethe, Johann Wolfgang von: *Goetz von Berlichigen; Faust (Part I); Egmont.*
Goldoni, Carlo: *The Mistress of the Inn* and *The Fan.*
Gozzi, Carlo: *Love of the Three Oranges.*
Grillparzer, Franz: *Sappho; The Golden Fleece;* and *The Jewess of Toledo.*
Kleist, Heinrich von: *The Prince of Homburg.*
Lessing, Gotthold: *Nathan the Wise; Miss Sara Sampson; Minna von Barnhelm; Emilia Galotti.*
Schiller, Friedrich von: *Mary Stuart; William Tell; Don Carlos; Wallenstein;* and *The Maid of Orleans.*

England and the Continent: Nineteenth Century Prior to Ibsen

Büchner, Georg: *Danton's Death* and *Woyzeck.*
Dumas, Alexandre, *fils*: *La Dame aux Camélias (The Lady of the Camellias* or *Camille)* and *Le Demi-Monde.*
Gogol, Nikolai: *The Inspector General.*
Hebbel, Friedrich: *Maria Magdalena.*
Hugo, Victor: *Hernani.*
Kotzebue, August: *The Stranger.*
Ostrovsky, Alexander: *The Storm.*
Pushkin, Alexander: *Boris Godunov.*
Sardou, Victorien: *A Scrap of Paper.*
Scribe, Eugène: *A Glass of Water.*
Turgenev, Ivan: *A Month in the Country.*

The Modern Theatre: Europe

Andreyev, Leonid: *He Who Gets Slapped.*
Anouilh, Jean: *Thieves' Carnival; Antigone;* and *Waltz of the Toreadors.*
Apollinaire, Guillaume: *The Breasts of Tiresias.*
Beckett, Samuel: *Waiting for Godot* and *Endgame.*
Becque, Henry: *The Vultures.*
Betti, Ugo: *Queen and the Rebels.*
Brecht, Bertolt: *The Threepenny Opera; Mother Courage; The Good Woman of Setzuan;* and *Galileo.*
Brieux, Eugène: *False Gods.*
Camus, Albert: *Caligula.*
Čapek, Karel: *The Insect Play* and *R.U.R.*
Chekhov, Anton: *The Sea Gull; Uncle Vanya; Three Sisters;* and *The Cherry Orchard.*
Claudel, Paul: *The Tidings Brought to Mary.*
Cocteau, Jean: *The Infernal Machine.*
Dürrenmatt, Friedrich: *The Visit* and *The Physicists.*
Frisch, Max: *The Firebugs.*
Genet, Jean: *The Maids; The Blacks;* and *The Balcony.*
Ghelderode, Michel de: *Escurial.*
Giraudoux, Jean: *Tiger at the Gates* and *The Madwoman of Chaillot.*
Gorky, Maxim: *The Lower Depths.*
Hauptmann, Gerhart: *The Weavers.*
Ibsen, Henrik: *Brand; Peer Gynt; A Doll's House; Ghosts; Enemy of the People; The Wild Duck; Hedda Gabler; The Master Builder;* and *When We Dead Awaken.*
Ionesco, Eugène: *The Bald Soprano; The Chairs;* and *Rhinoceros.*
Jarry, Alfred: *Ubu Roi.*
Kaiser, Georg: *From Morn to Midnight.*
Lorca, Garcia: *Blood Wedding; Yerma;* and *The House of Bernarda Alba.*

Maeterlinck, Maurice: *Pelleas and Melisande* and *The Intruder*.

Molnar, Ferenc: *Liliom*.

Pirandello, Luigi: *Six Characters in Search of an Author* and *Henry IV*.

Rostand, Edmond: *Cyrano de Bergerac*.

Sartre, Jean-Paul: *The Flies; No Exit;* and *The Respectful Prostitute*.

Schnitzler, Arthur: *La Ronde* and *Anatol*.

Strindberg, August: *The Father; Miss Julie; The Dream Play;* and *Dance of Death*.

Toller, Ernst: *Man and the Masses*.

Tolstoy, Leo: *The Power of Darkness*.

Wedekind, Frank: *Spring's Awakening*.

Weiss, Peter: *The Persecution and Assassination of Jean-Paul Marat, As Performed by the Inmates of the Asylum of Charenton under the Direction of the Marquis de Sade (Marat/Sade)*.

The Modern Theatre: England and Ireland

Arden, John: *Live Like Pigs*.

Auden, W. H., and Christopher Isherwood: *The Ascent of F6*.

Barrie, James: *The Admirable Crichton*.

Behan, Brendan: *The Quare Fellow*.

Coward, Noel: *Private Lives* and *Blithe Spirit*.

Eliot, T. S.: *Murder in the Cathedral* and *The Cocktail Party*.

Fry, Christopher: *The Lady's Not for Burning*.

Galsworthy, John: *Strife*.

Gilbert, William S., and Arthur Sullivan: *The Mikado; H.M.S. Pinafore;* and *The Pirates of Penzance*.

Maugham, Somerset: *The Circle*.

O'Casey, Sean: *Juno and the Paycock* and *The Plough and the Stars*.

Osborne, John: *Look Back in Anger* and *Luther*.

Pinero, Arthur: *The Second Mrs. Tanqueray*.

Pinter, Harold: *The Caretaker* and *The Homecoming*.

Shaw, George Bernard: *Candida; Caesar and Cleopatra; Heartbreak House; Man and Superman; Major Barbara; Pygmalion;* and *Saint Joan*.

Synge, John M.: *Riders to the Sea* and *The Playboy of the Western World*.

Wesker, Arnold: *Roots* and *Chips with Everything*.

Wilde, Oscar: *Lady Windermere's Fan* and *The Importance of Being Earnest*.

Yeats, William B.: *Purgatory* and *At the Hawk's Well*.

The American Theatre: From the Beginnings to 1900

Aiken, George: *Uncle Tom's Cabin*.

Boker, George: *Francesca da Rimini*.

Boucicault, Dion: *The Octoroon*.

Dunlap, William: *André.*
Godfrey, Thomas: *The Prince of Parthia.*
Jefferson, Joseph: *Rip Van Winkle.*
Mowatt, Anna: *Fashion.*
Tyler, Royall: *The Contrast.*

The American Theatre: 1900 to the Present

Abbott, George, and John Holm: *Three Men on a Horse.*
Albee, Edward: *Zoo Story; The American Dream;* and *Who's Afraid of Virginia Woolf.*
Anderson, Maxwell: *Elizabeth the Queen* and *Winterset.*
Barry, Philip: *The Philadelphia Story.*
Belasco, David: *The Girl of the Golden West.*
Connelly, John, and George Kaufman: *Beggar on Horseback.*
Fitch, Clyde: *The Girl with the Green Eyes.*
Gibson, William: *The Miracle Worker* and *Two for the Seesaw.*
Gilroy, Frank D.: *The Subject Was Roses.*
Gordone, Charles: *No Place to Be Somebody.*
Green, Paul: *In Abraham's Bosom.*
Hellman, Lillian: *The Little Foxes.*
Howard, Sidney: *They Knew What They Wanted.*
Inge, William: *Come Back, Little Sheba* and *Picnic.*
Jones, LeRoi (Imamu Amiri Baraka): *Dutchman.*
Kaufman, George, and Moss Hart: *You Can't Take It with You.*
Kaufman, George, and Morrie Ryskind: *Of Thee I Sing.*
Kelly, George: *The Show-Off.*
Kopit, Arthur: *Indians.*
Lawson, John: *Processional.*
Lindsay, Howard, and Russel Crouse: *Life with Father.*
MacKaye, Percy: *The Scarecrow.*
MacLeish, Archibald: *J.B.*
Miller, Arthur: *All My Sons; Death of a Salesman; The Crucible;* and *A View from the Bridge.*
Moody, William: *The Great Divide.*
Odets, Clifford: *Waiting for Lefty* and *Awake and Sing.*
O'Neill, Eugene: *The Emperor Jones; The Hairy Ape; Desire Under the Elms; The Great God Brown; Strange Interlude; Mourning Becomes Electra; Ah, Wilderness!; The Iceman Cometh;* and *Long Day's Journey Into Night.*
Rice, Elmer: *Street Scene.*
Rodgers, Richard, and Oscar Hammerstein: *Oklahoma.*
Saroyan, William: *My Heart's in the Highlands* and *The Time of Your Life.*
Sherwood, Robert: *The Petrified Forest.*
van Itallie, Jean-Claude: *America Hurrah.*

Wilder, Thornton: *Our Town* and *The Skin of Our Teeth*.

Williams, Tennessee: *The Glass Menagerie; A Streetcar Named Desire; Camino Real;* and *Cat on a Hot Tin Roof*.

Wilson, Lanford: *The Hot L Baltimore*.

Zindel, Paul: *The Effect of Gamma Rays on Man-in-the-Moon Marigolds*.

Glossary of Technical Terms

ACT: (1) A principal division of a play. (2) To perform, to enact a role in performance.

ACT CURTAIN: American term for a curtain behind the asbestos curtain, and behind the grand drape, if there is one. Raised or drawn to reveal an act or scene. English: ACT DROP, FRONT CURTAIN, HOUSE CURTAIN.

ACT DROP: Act curtain.

ACTING EDITION: Usually the authorized edition of a play which reflects the form a play took, and costume plot, and ground plan for an approved performance of a play.

ACTOR-PROOF: Said of a play which is so well written that even poor actors can manage a credible performance.

ACTORS' EQUITY ASSOCIATION: The professional guild or union of actors in America.

ADJUSTABLE PROSCENIUM: A proscenium which can be adapted and adjusted to a number of configurations.

AD LIB (AD-LIB): To add lines or business not in a script, or to invent the same for an improvisation.

AESTHETIC DISTANCE: Maintaining a sense of distance between performers and audience. For example, the fourth-wall convention does this. The actors never react to the presence of the audience. Prohibitions against moving out into the audience follow this notion, and theatricalist notions of "playing to the audience" are the reverse.

AFFECTIVE MEMORY: Stanislavski's notion of the actor using personal memories to help create the reality of a character.

ALLEGORY: In theatre a drama which connects symbolic, personified, or metaphoric characters in a narrative structure.

AMATEUR: Usually it means someone who "pretends" to know a craft or art. However, it has another meaning which should be resurrected: a person who loves doing something.

ANAGNORISIS: A Greek term used in *The Poetics* which means a "recognition," usually of relatives, which leads to a climax or the ending of a play.

ANTA: American National Theatre and Academy founded in 1935 to encourage the "best in theatre, both professional and nonprofessional."

APPRENTICE: In America it usually means someone who works for nothing in the theatre while learning their craft. In Shakespeare's time it meant a young man learning the craft (usually playing female and young male roles), who would then become a journeyman or guildsman at the end of his training.

APRON: Forestage measured from the plaster-line (the upstage side of the proscenium).

ARENA: A theatre arrangement without a proscenium in which the seats surround or partially surround the stage.

ASIDE: A stage convention in which a character speaks out to the audience and makes a comment about other characters, while they pretend not to hear.

AVANT GARDE (AVANT-GARDE): We would say vanguard. It means those who are trying new approaches and forms in an art.

BILL: A playbill or poster, sometimes a program.

BIT: (1) A small role. (2) A small portion of dialogue or business, often humorous.

BLACK OUT (BLACKOUT, BLACK-OUT): (1) To suddenly darken a stage. (2) A kind of variety skit which ends with a blackout.

BLOCK: To work out the movements of the actors for a production.

BOARD: (1) in the plural, the stage. As in "walk the boards": to act. (2) A dimmer board or switchboard.

BOOK: (1) To engage a performance. (2) A script or manuscript. (3) The libretto or text for a musical. (4) Two flats hinged together.

BORDER: (1) A strip of cloth hung from a batten above the stage, usually flown in. Used to represent part of a scene: for example, clouds, tree limbs, etc., which continue the scene represented on the wings and backdrop.

BREAK A LEG: A good luck comment exchanged by actors.

BREAKAWAY: Said of scenery, properties, and costumes that are made to come apart and then be reassembled for the next performance.

BACKFLAP: A type of hinge used to join flats because it can be turned back on itself.

CALL: (1) A notice to actors. (2) A curtain call or bow.

CATHARSIS: Term used by Aristotle to describe the "cleansing" of the emotions at the end of a well-constructed tragedy.

CENTER: A stage position, as in center stage. Other parts of a stage are stage right, stage left; upstage and downstage. The nine sections of a stage are: downstage right, center right, upstage right, etc.

CENTER LINE: A dividing line from upstage to downstage in any theatre used to locate stage positions, often in conjunction with the plaster line.

CLOWN WHITE: A make-up material used by performers (usually zinc oxide).

CONSTRUCTIVISM: A scenic technique which stresses structure rather than realistic representation of buildings, rooms, etc.

COSTUME PLOT: A list of the characters of a play showing the costumes to be worn for a production, by scene and act.

COUNTERWEIGHT SYSTEM: A mechanical system for flying scenery, most often from the stage floor, which balances the weight of the scene with metal counterweights.

DARK: A term used to describe a theatre that is not performing on a given night.

DIMMER: Any electrical or mechanical device used to regulate the intensity of a lighting unit.

DOWN CENTER, DOWN LEFT, DOWN RIGHT, etc.: See CENTER.

DRAMATIS PERSONAE: The characters in a play. Used in published versions of older plays in place of the term cast list.

DUTCHMAN: A strip of cloth used to conceal a joint or crack in a flat.

ENSEMBLE: (1) Another name for a company. (2) A company that emphasizes the group rather than "stars" in assigning of roles and the type of playing done on stage.

EPIC THEATRE: A term used by Brecht and Piscator for theatre which would instruct instead of entertain and would break illusion rather than allow audience involvement at all times.

FRENCH SCENE: A scene division marked by the entrance or exit of a major character.

GOBO: A cutout pattern placed in front of an instrument in order to throw patterns on surfaces.

GREEN ROOM: A room reserved for actors to rest, study, and wait for cues.

GRIDIRON (GRID): A framework of beams over the stage used for suspending scenery and lights.

GRIP: A stagehand.

GROUND PLAN: A floor plan of the stage for a show.

GROUND ROW: A long, low set piece used to represent a wall, hedge, etc.

HOLD: In acting, a pause made by an actor to allow for an audience's laughter or applause.

HOUSE: (1) An audience. (2) The permanent management of a theatre which is hired out to companies.

INGENUE: An actress who plays young women or girls; a description of the role itself.

IN THE ROUND (THEATRE IN THE ROUND): Arena staging with seating on all sides.

LAMP: A light source, as in gas light or incandescent light.

LEFT, LEFT CENTER, UP LEFT, etc.: See CENTER.

LEG: A vertical strip of cloth hung from a border, simulating a tree trunk or column, for example. Also, a piece of masking or curtain.

LIBRETTO: The book for a musical comedy, opera.

LIGHT PLOT: A diagram showing positions of instruments for a show with specifications of types of instruments, circuitry, etc. Used by electricians to "hang" lights for a show.

MASQUE: Renaissance spectacle for the wealthy involving music, dance, scenery, and drama.

MISE EN SCENE: All of the elements which comprise the stage picture: scenery, lighting, and actors.

OBJECTIVE: An actor's goal within a unit or a scene.

OFF BROADWAY: An term for theatres not in the area of Broadway. Usually professional theatre. Now the term OFF OFF BROADWAY is heard and suggests theatres not only farther away but often not in New York at all.

PACE: A term much misused by reviewers. It is not literally the speed of a performance but a measure of both the overall shape and cohesion of a performance and the audience's involvement in it.

PARALLEL: A hinged trestle which, when unfolded and with a lid placed on it, becomes a stage platform.

PATCH PANEL: A system for providing connections between stage circuits and dimmers.

PERIPETEIA, PERIPETY: A dramatic reversal. From Aristotle's *The Poetics*.

PINRAIL: The rail holding belaying pins to which fly lines are tied.

PIPE BATTEN (PIPE): A length of pipe from which lights and scenery can be suspended. Standard unit in the counterweight system.

PLAY DOCTOR: Someone employed to fix a play with problems.

PRACTICABLE, PRACTICAL: Said of a scenic unit or property which can be used for what it appears to be. For example, a practical door works as a door and is not just decorative.

PRESENTATIONAL: Theatrical, obvious. A style of theatre which does not pretend to be real.

PROMPT BOOK: A copy of the script developed during and for rehearsals which has important directions for actors, music and lighting cues, etc. Used by the Stage Manager during performances.

RAKE: Usually the slope of a stage from downstage "up" to upstage, but also any floor angle on stage.

REPERTORY (REP): (1) A group of plays which a company performs in alternating sequence during a season. (2) Sometimes interchangeable with the term STOCK, though this may also mean a company which does plays one after another in a season and not in an alternating sequence. (3) Roles which an actor has in mind and ready for performance.

REVIEW: (1) A published comment in a newspaper or magazine on a production. (2) A production made up of skits and songs. Often topical.

REVUE: Another spelling for (2) above.

RIGHT, RIGHT CENTER, etc.: See CENTER.

ROYALTY: A payment made to an author for the performance or reproduction of a play, etc.

RUN: (1) The period of time a production plays at a theatre. (2) To operate a switchboard, follow spot, etc., during a show.

SCENARIO: A detailed synopsis of a dramatic production. Also, in commedia dell'arte, a plot and character outline used as a basis for improvisation.

SCRIM: A drop or partial drop made of lightweight, open-weave fabric which is painted so that it will appear solid when lit from the front but will disappear when objects are lit behind it and front light is taken off it.

SHIFT: To change the setting for a show during a performance.

SHOWCASE: A production in which amateurs or beginning professionals often pay or work for nothing in order to demonstrate their talents to producers and critics.

SHUBERT ALLEY: An actual alley between 44th and 45th Streets in Manhattan which is the heart of "Broadway," just west of Times Square.

SIDE: One way of reproducing the roles of a play: the character's speeches are listed with brief cue lines for the entire part. The number of "sides" or sheets is one way of evaluating the size and importance of a role.

SKETCH: A playlet or scene.

SLAPSTICK: Broad comedy, but literally two paddles attached to one another so as to make a loud slapping noise when striking something or someone.

SLEEPER: A surprise success.

SLICE OF LIFE: Another name for naturalistic plays of the nineteenth century. Translated from French *tranche de vie*.

SOCK AND BUSKIN: Comedy and tragedy. Literally the sock worn as a headpiece by Renaissance comics and the leg wrappings used by early Greek tragedians.

SOLILOQUY: A speech, a monologue that reveals to the audience a character's inmost thoughts. Cf. Elizabethan drama. The usual convention is that the truth is always said.

SPACE STAGE: A stage that uses little if any scenery and in which scenes are played in lighted areas while the rest of the stage is dark and neutral.

SPECIAL: In lighting, an instrument which is used for an unusual and infrequent assignment.

SPIKE: A mark made on stage to indicate the location of scenery, furniture, and reference points. Also used as a verb.

SPILL: In lighting, unintended light from instruments which extends beyond the planned area.

SPINE: The through line of a play. Sometimes also a play's essential meaning and dramatic thrust.

STAGE BRACE: A piece of wood or metal which is used to hold up a flat by being attached to it and going diagonally to the floor where it is weighted or screwed down.

STAR SYSTEM: Descriptive of those periods in theatre history when well-known actors are used as the principal draw. The opposite of ensemble.

STRIKE: Either to remove the scenery of a given scene or play and store it for the next performance, or the dismantling, storing, and removal of scenery at the end of a run.

SUPERNUMERARY (SUPER): An extra, a walk-on.

SWITCHBOARD: A control panel for all of the electrical equipment used on the stage and, perhaps, in the house.

TABLEAU (-X): The stage picture presented intentionally by motionless and silent actors. For instance, in a "frozen moment" at the end of a play.

TEASER: A short horizontal curtain or flat used to mask and to frame the top of the inner stage opening. See TORMENTOR.

THEATRE IN THE ROUND: See IN THE ROUND.

THEATRICALISM: A style of production which emphasizes the artifice of theatre. Opposed to realism or naturalism.

THESPIAN: Someone involved in theatre. Adapted from the name (Thespis) of an early Greek dramatist and producer.

THROW AWAY: To deliberately lighten or undersell an important speech or piece of business.

TORMENTOR: One of a pair of narrow curtains or flats just behind the proscenium and teaser used to further limit the stage space. Part of an inner proscenium.

TRAGIC FLAW (HAMARTIA): A term taken from Aristotle to describe the so-called "tragic flaw" of a hero.

TRAVELER: (1) A draw curtain. (2) A means to suspend and move a performer across the stage in a simulated flight.

TRIM: (1) To adjust scenery so that it is at the proper height. Place scenery in its proper position. (2) Decorative woodwork. (3) Small pieces of furniture and stage dressing used to complete the scene.

TURKEY: A show which fails. Two of many guesses at its origin: (1) Because it was put together without real care. (2) Because it competed with Thanksgiving, a traditional family, stay-at-home holiday. Hence, a show that doesn't draw an audience.

TYPE: A name used to describe particular kinds of actors and the roles that they play.

UNDERSTUDY: To learn the role of another actor, usually a lead, as insurance against their illness.

UNIT SETTING: A stage setting which uses a number of scenic units which can be rearranged for different scenes. Some units may stay in place for a number of scenes or the entire play.

UPSTAGE: See CENTER.

VAUDEVILLE: An entertainment consisting of skits, songs, special acts, and dances.

WALK-ON: A small part, an extra.

WARN: To alert technicians and actors of a coming cue.

WEST END: The major theatre district in London. By extension, London's entire theatre district.

WING IT: To perform without having the lines firmly in mind and rely on improvisation or the prompter.

OTHER CONCERNS

Index

A